CITIZENSHIP AND DEMOCRACY IN A GLOBAL ERA

Citizenship and Democracy in a Global Era

edited by

Andrew Vandenberg

CITIZENSHIP AND DEMOCRACY IN A GLOBAL ERA

St. Martin's Press, Scholarly and Reference Division, 175 Fifth Avenue, New York, N.Y. 10010

First published in the United States of America in 2000

This book is printed on paper suitable for recycling and made from fully managed and sustained forest sources.

Printed in China

ISBN 0–312–23364–7 (cloth)
ISBN 0–312–23365–5 (paperback)

Library of Congress Cataloging-in-Publication Data
Citizenship and democracy in a global era / edited by Andrew Vandenberg.
p. cm.
Includes bibliographical references and index.
ISBN 0–312–23364–7 (cloth) – ISBN 0–312–23365–5 (pbk.)
1. Citizenship. 2. Democracy. I. Vandenberg, Andrew, 1960-

JF801 .C566 2000
320.9–dc21

00-021170

to Lisa, Elin, Anders and Britta

CONTENTS

PREFACE

The relationship between citizenship and democracy is not nearly so well established as it is commonly assumed to be within contemporary liberalism. In the past three decades the rise of international economic liberalism and debate about the decline of national sovereignty has prompted much more interest in issues of citizenship. The collapse of communist states, the apartheid regime in South Africa and Soerharto's regime in Indonesia has at the same time prompted renewed interest in issues of democracy and the achievement of stability and prosperity.

This book attempts to counteract the effects of a tendency for sociologists to study citizenship and for political scientists to study democracy. Sociologists tend to look at divisions due to class, gender, race and ethnicity and to focus on issues of cohesion, belonging and exclusion. Political scientists tend to look at institutions and organisations and focus on issues of power, violence, order and sovereignty. Obviously, many of these issues overlap, but not often in the same book. Part I of this book pursues one way to upset this disciplinary apartheid between sociology and political science. The chapters of Part I contribute to general debates about community and the individual, modernity and post-modernity and the nation-state in a global era, which are widely addressed throughout the humanities and social sciences. A second way, taken up in Part II, is to undertake case studies of how citizenship or democracy, or both, have developed in particular countries. The particularity of experience in one country compared to others introduces important qualifications to disciplinary generalisations about social cohesion or division, and political stability or instability. The case studies look at cohesive and fractious societies, as well as old, stable regimes and new, unstable regimes. Several of them do study either citizenship or democracy, but taken together they offer cross-disciplinary lessons. A third way, undertaken in Part III, is to turn to developments wider than any one nation-state. Here, one chapter analyses how poorly the liberal rhetoric of a New World Order after the collapse of communism applies to experience in the long prosperous dictatorships of East and South-East Asia. Another chapter discusses the contradictory prospects of positive and negative developments that the Internet and multimedia capitalism pose for citizenship and democracy.

Since citizenship, democracy and national sovereignty are closely inter-related in both practice and theory, it makes sense to study them in a cross-disciplinary way. This book offers useful lessons both for students of sociology and politics and students of the multidisciplinary study of public policy, nationalism and globalism, as well as cross-disciplinary debates about individual and community, norms and realities, and modernity and postmodernity.

At the beginning of each chapter except the first one, I have added an editor's abstract that points out broad similarities with other chapters and presents a brief summary of the chapter's argument. In the body of each chapter, I have occasionally used square brackets to insert more specific cross-references to other chapters.

ANDREW VANDENBERG

Deakin University
http://arts.deakin.edu.au/cchr

NOTES ON THE CONTRIBUTORS

Greg Barton teaches religious studies at Deakin University, and is associated with the Centre for Citizenship and Human Rights at Deakin University.

Scott Burchill teaches international relations at Deakin University and is associated with the Centre for Citizenship and Human Rights at Deakin University.

Anne Coleman is a PhD student in the Politics Department, Faculty of Humanities, Macquarie University.

Jennifer Curtin teaches politics at the University of Canberra.

Alastair Davidson is the Inaugural Professor of Citizenship Studies at Swinburne University of Technology.

David Dorward teaches African history and women's studies at La Trobe University and is Director of the African Research Institute there.

Katrina Gorjanicyn teaches social policy in the School of Social Science and Planning at the Royal Melbourne Institute of Technology University.

Linda Hancock is a visiting Senior Researcher in public policy at Melbourne University.

Winton Higgins is a Senior Research Fellow in the Politics Department, Faculty of Humanities, Macquarie University.

Barry Hindess is Professor of Political Science in the Research School of Social Sciences at the Australian National University.

Robert van Krieken teaches sociology in the Department of Sociology and Social Work, Sydney University.

Vera Mackie is Foundation Professor of Japanese Studies at Curtin University.

Vince Marotta is a PhD student in sociology at La Trobe University.

Michael Muetzelfeldt teaches politics at Deakin University and is Director of the Centre for Citizenship and Human Rights.

Bryan Turner is Professor of Sociology at Cambridge University and editor of *Citizenship Studies*.

Andrew Vandenberg teaches politics at Deakin University and is associated with the Centre for Citizenship and Human Rights at Deakin University.

Derek Verrall teaches politics at the University of Tasmania.

Anna Yeatman is Professor of Sociology at Macquarie University.

PART 1
ISSUES OF CITIZENSHIP
AND DEMOCRACY IN A
GLOBAL ERA

1 CONTESTING CITIZENSHIP AND DEMOCRACY IN A GLOBAL ERA*

Andrew Vandenberg

The collapse of communist regimes in the 1990s, worries about the consequences of a renewed global capitalism, and arguments about the end of a modern era of nation-states have all provoked new rounds of controversy about what citizenship and democracy mean. And this is so because they are what W. B. Gallie (1964: 157–91) called 'essentially contested concepts'. Along with concepts such as 'art', 'Christianity' (Gallie 1964), 'politics', 'interests', 'freedom' (Connolly 1983), 'power' (Cox, Furlong and Page 1985: 26–30) and 'modernity' (Turner 1990b), 'democracy' and 'citizenship' clearly qualify to be considered not just controversial but *essentially* controversial. To put contestedness at the core or essence of concepts such as citizenship and democracy is a post-liberal rather than liberal argument. It is an argument that hopes to promote open-ended debate and subvert long-standing processes of exclusion and secrecy in government. Citizenship and democracy have been central to modern concepts of mass society and the nation-state, respectively. In the changing circumstances of a global era, societies and states, stable and unstable alike, face questions of cohesion, order and sovereignty. Before looking at contemporary controversies about liberal and post-liberal concepts of citizenship and democracy (Beiner 1998), we need to detail how essentially contested concepts differ from other concepts.

* An initial version of part of the argument here appeared in 'Politics of Democracy and Citizenship', pp. 3–10 in Vandenberg (1996). Thanks go to Robyn Clifford and Catherine Gray for reading and commenting on this chapter.

History and the essential contestedness of citizenship and democracy

In his article, which was first published in 1956, Gallie (1964) carefully considered seven aspects of essentially contested concepts and Connolly (1983: 22–35) has usefully revisited Gallie's argument in the light of more recent literary theory. These considerations can be summarised in three points. First, essentially contested concepts are *ascriptive*, which is to say they characterise important things in ways that describe 'what is', and at one and the same time also appraise 'what is' by comparing it against 'what ought to be'. Like the proverbial scrambled eggs, this mix of description and appraisal defies unscrambling into analytic and synthetic propositions. The mix also precludes empirical testing of the truth of any ascription, and this contributes to the usage of contested concepts in a reflexive way. Users accept that their usage differs from others' contrary but reasonable usage. In the twentieth century, a contrast between usage of 'citizenship' and 'democracy' in the peoples' republics of communist countries and in the liberal democracies of capitalist countries provides the most obvious example. In communist countries, the influence of Lenin's pamphlet *The State and Revolution* saw 'democracy' retain its Athenian connotations of direct participation in a 'politics of activity' (Polan 1984: 3), while 'citizen' retained its French revolutionary connotations of 'comrade'. In Western capitalist countries, 'citizen' came to be a type of consumer, in a market place of ideas, who watched from a distance as 'democracy' became procedures for operating an apparatus to select and elect leaders. These illustrations show that, behind the ideological contest between peoples' republics and liberal constitutions, there is another contest over what democracy and citizenship meant in the past and can mean now.

Second, essentially contested concepts are *internally complex* and *open* to divergent interpretations about which of the defining characteristics are the most important in particular circumstances. They can also be called 'cluster concepts' because they have several defining characteristics that are pretty much concepts in their own right (Connolly 1983: 19). Citizenship requires a sense of belonging, solidarity or 'social glue' (Turner 1996), some autonomy of thought and action (Held 1996), some element of equality in a 'realm of rights' that are universal among its members (Okun 1975), and some regime of common obligations. Similarly, various proponents of democracy emphasise one or other of its defining characteristics. For some, democracy rests primarily on wide participation in the making of important decisions (Pateman 1970; Macpherson 1977; Barber 1984). For others, democracy requires means of governing the internal consequences of external developments (Held 1987; Hindess 1991). And for yet others, it is the rule of law that is central to democracy (Bobbio 1987; Davidson, Chapter 7 below). The number of these defining characteristics of citizenship and of democracy make them internally complex and leave them open to differing interpretations.

Third, essentially contested concepts have developed from an original *exemplar*, which remains exemplary despite disagreement about how it is exemplary. In our case, fifth century BC Athens, from the time of Solon to the time of Pericles, provides the exemplary conceptions of citizenship and democracy (Sabine 1961; Wolin 1960; Finley 1964; Kitto 1986; Farrar 1992; Hornblower 1992; Lloyd 1992). The republican period of Roman history might also be considered part of the exemplar. It fashioned concepts of universal citizenship and the rule of law that might be applicable for any human society (Sabine 1961; Petit 1997, 1998). These concepts played a particularly important role for Machiavelli, his Elizabethan English followers and the American revolutionaries, but I follow Wolin's (1960) argument that the rise of Alexander the Great and then Roman republicanism followed the collapse of the Greek *polis* and its particular sense of active citizenship and direct democracy. This makes Roman history part of the history of contesting citizenship and democracy rather than their exemplar-forming origins. However, I want to emphasise that this position is a matter of interpretation, which is to say it is contestable. There is nothing absolute or beyond debate about what the origins of citizenship and democracy are.

From the collapse of democracy in Ancient Greece, almost all thinkers and political elites in Rome and later Western Europe followed the anti-democratic philosophies of Plato and Aristotle. They thought that to institute a sovereign assembly of direct democracy among morally, culturally and politically equal citizens would see the rule of law degrade into rule of the rabble, guaranteeing economic decline and cultural degradation. The republican traditions of Ancient Rome added to aspects of Athenian citizenship and democracy but the Roman emperors abandoned them. Subsequently, the Vikings invented their own egalitarian assemblies while the Italian Renaissance cities, the Swiss canton and medieval England all kept the

Athenian tradition alive, but introduced no major conceptual amend-
ments (Dahl 1998: 7–25). After the English Civil War and the rise of
social contract theory in the second half of the seventeenth century,
and particularly after the American and French revolutions a century
later, citizenship and democracy underwent significant reconception.
Military innovations revived interest in the freedom and autonomy of
the republican citizen-soldier and the rise of market economies promoted challenges to the aristocratic rule of a few, in favour of the more
democratic rule of law. Such reconceptions coincided with the rise of
mercantile capitalism in first Italy and later Holland and England
(Ehnmark 1986). It also coincided with European 'discovery' and
imperial conquest of other parts of the world. [Chapter 4 below takes
up this point].

By the second half of the twentieth century citizenship and democracy had become a grand narrative about cohesion within mass society
[Turner discusses this point in his Chapter 2] and a grand narrative
about representation and misrepresentation within the modern state
[Hindess discusses this point in his Chapter 3]. But citizenship and
democracy each underwent a long journey from the English Civil War
to the Second World War before they had attained the status of grand
narrative deployed by all nation-states, irrespective of ideology. That
journey saw successive liberals, from Madison and Bentham, to J. S.
Mill and later T. H. Marshall, face difficult issues of order and cohesion in large states. They grappled with the ancient Roman problem
of how to reconcile civilisation and prosperity in states that have large
populations and extensive territories with the Greek sense of citizenship and democracy in a small and immediate political community. In
the middle of the twentieth century, another significant development
took place when liberals effectively turned the tables on their socialist critics. After the First World War, universal suffrage became a defining feature of citizenship in a liberal democracy. Subsequently, in
the Great Depression of the 1930s, mass democracy threatened
populist or socialist attacks on capitalism. But after the Second World
War and the defeat of Fascism, liberals celebrated democracy as a
pre-condition for law and order and market capitalism. Now it was
taken to support rather than threaten civilisation and prosperity
(Therborn 1977; Hodgson 1984; Vandenberg 1996a). That switch in
the ideological charge, from negative to positive, which liberals put
on 'democracy' involved abandoning what Michael Sandel (1996)

calls the 'political economy of citizenship' in favour of a 'procedural republic'.

In the 1950s and 1960s, Robert Dahl (1957) became an internationally prominent theorist of the new liberal argument about democracy. In his widely read book, *Power: A Radical View*, Stephen Lukes (1972) criticised Dahl's one-dimensional view, contrasting it against reformers' two-dimensional and radicals' three-dimensional view of how power operates in a capitalist democracy (Clegg 1989). Dahl (1985) never espoused Marxism but, in the 1970s and 1980s, he joined the radical critics of liberal pluralism. He emphasised the paradoxical role of organisations in pluralist democracy and the corrosive effects of industrial capitalism on the background social cohesion necessary for democracy. More recently, Dahl underscored how short the experiment in liberal citizenship and democracy had been when he registered 'an arresting thought: if we accept universal adult suffrage as a requirement of democracy, there would be some persons in practically every democratic country who would be older than their democratic system of government' (Dahl 1998: 3). The same arresting point can be noted by comparing Fukuyama's (1992: 49–50) and Therborn's (1977: 11) quite different lists of which countries became democratic when. Using an ideas-oriented and Hegelian concept of how rights of citizenship interact with the formal institutions of democracy, Francis Fukuyama lists the USA and Switzerland as becoming democratic in the 1790s. Using a practice-oriented and Marxist concept of citizenship rights and liberal democracy, Göran Therborn (1977) argues that the USA and Switzerland did not become liberal democracies until the 1970s. They excluded large numbers of black people and women, respectively, from the rights of citizenship. This contrast between Fukuyama's liberalism and Therborn's socialism demonstrates that the sudden switch in liberal thought during the 1940s required major modifications to the concepts of citizenship and democracy. It also illustrates how ideology and politics, theory and practice, interact in complex ways over time.

Liberalism and essential contestedness

C. B. Macpherson (1977) and David Held (1987) have argued that between about 1800 and 1950 successive models of liberal democracy culminated in the current conventional wisdom about liberal democracy. Joseph Schumpeter (1976: 250–73) first formulated that wisdom in 1943. His realism about human nature, economics and politics posed a powerful metaphor between parliamentary politics and a market in ideas, election campaigns and advertising campaigns, parties and corporations, leaders and entrepreneurs, citizens and customers. Macpherson (1977: 77–92) argued that this market equilibrium model was a poor description (the so-called political market is highly oligopolistic) but most effective as a justification of the prevailing systems of actual government. The market model had become such a powerful metaphor that most people had forgotten that it was a metaphor, model or theory. Other critics of liberalism have focused on the shortcomings of Schumpeter's dismissal of idealism (Pateman 1970; [see also Hindess's Chapter 3]), or focused on the philosophy of John Rawls (1972). Comparable developments took place in a post-war reconception of citizenship, best advanced by T. H. Marshall whose ideas have been revisited by other thinkers since the mid-1980s.

Marshall (1964) advanced a sociological theory about how the welfare state could counteract the class divisions sown by capitalism. He based it on a historical evolution in the UK of legal, political and social rights of citizenship, which instituted a successively wider scope for a minimum of societal cohesion. When welfare states came under sustained criticism in the 1970s and 1980s, Turner (1986) and Mann (1987) were among the first to revisit Marshall's theory. They addressed its shortcomings and proposed modified concepts of citizenship to deal with the different histories of liberalism in various countries and with the contemporary issues of gender, aborigines and settlers, multiculturalism and diasporas, and many refugees or other immigrants seeking citizenship in the rich and stable countries of the world (Turner 1990a, 1993, 1996). Subsequently, an extensive literature about how citizenship might counteract a wide range of social divisions has emerged (Mouffe 1990; Young 1990; Andrews 1991; Beiner 1992; Kymlicka 1995, 1998). Yet it is the definitions from the 1940s and 1950s, best formulated by Schumpeter and Marshall, that remain conventional wisdom.

Economists such as Keynes and Beveridge assumed that full employment would be a crucial feature of achieving stable states, societies and economies in the West after the Second World War (Cutler, Williams and Williams 1986). Forty years later, the collapse of both high employment and the communist alternative to poorly operating capitalist labour markets therefore amounts to a significant change in the ideological circumstances of what citizenship and democracy mean in practice. But as Fukuyama has put it:

> What is emerging victorious . . . is not so much liberal practice, as the liberal *idea*. That is to say, for a very large part of the world, there is no ideology with pretensions to universality that is in a position to challenge liberal democracy, and no universal principle of legitimacy other than the sovereignty of the people. (1992: 45)

Fukuyama is quite right: no ideology is in a position to challenge liberalism *as an ideology*. However, the challenges that radical groups and thinkers do mount against liberalism do not criticise the gap between liberal practice and ideology, which Fukuyama freely admits and accurately notes. Contemporary critics of liberalism focus instead on the 'politics of truth' (Barrett 1991), sweeping generalisations, totalising ideas, aspirations to universalism, essential origins (Clegg 1989), pre-political foundations (Barber 1984), and supposedly 'unencumbered' selves (Sandel 1982, 1998).

Criticism of liberal ideologies of the abstract individual has become a central aspect of what is known as communitarianism. According to several prominent versions of this argument, the members of a political community cannot be considered abstract individuals, free to pursue any objectives they wish. People grow up in a specific culture, gender, race and social position, which intrinsically forms their view of the world and the objectives they pursue. Arguments between liberals and communitarians (Mulhall and Swift 1992) have largely displaced older theoretical debates between liberals and Marxists in Europe, and between liberals and conservatives in North America. In this context, putting forward contestedness as a 'foundation' for concepts of citizenship and democracy that have an 'essential origin' in Ancient Athens poses some complicated issues about ideology and philosophy. I have already addressed some of those issues, arguing that essentially contested concepts have historical depth and definitional complexity beyond whatever ideological charge they acquire in twentieth-century contests. But concepts can also be philosophically contested and the distinction between philosophically and essentially contested concepts differs from the distinction between ideologically and essentially contested concepts.

Philosophy and essential contestedness

In the striking first paragraph of a chapter subtitled 'Philosophy Against Practice' in his book *The Conquest of Politics*, Benjamin Barber makes good use of his pet dog to introduce his argument. He argues that there is a 'profound and provoking kinship' between political theory and the politics of democracy (1988: 21). Such kinship must find a common and conversational language that both informs and explains the imperatives of common conduct that addresses common concerns. However:

> Thinking about politics creates a unique dilemma, for it seems inevitably to lead to thinking about thinking; and the more we think about thinking, the less we think about politics. Human thought has a natural tendency to narcissism, and narcissism disposes it to reflexivity. Like the uncomprehending pet spaniel who stares curiously at his master's pointing finger rather than the direction in which the gesture is intended to move him, we humans are often led to dwell introspectively on the processes of our own consciousness rather than gaze outward at the myriad objects that are its presumed targets . . . In much of what we have chosen to call political philosophy in the liberal postwar era, philosophy has flourished while politics has wilted. (Barber 1988: 3)

Later in that book, Barber argued that John Rawls's (1972) widely read and debated *Theory of Justice* was 'an attempt to ground political justice in indestructible philosophical bedrock'. It constituted 'the most impressive, one might even say noble, chapter in the postwar history of liberal philosophy's attempt to conquer politics' (Barber 1988: 56). Rawls had ignored Wittgenstein's 'complex doubts' about the capacity of language to represent anything at all and aspired 'to endow muddy, *much-contested* politics with the clarity of a rational consensus rooted in political theory' (Barber 1988: 77; italics added here). That phrase 'much contested' is different from *essential* contestedness because: 'All liberal theories seem finally to reduce to premises that are "essentially contestable" – rooted in irreducible, pretheoretical grounds about which there is no agreement and can be no argument' (Barber 1984: 44). In this final part of the chapter, I want to take up Barber's call to appreciate the 'profound and provoking kinship' between philosophy and politics, but I will rely upon rather than reject essential contestedness as a support for that argument.

One way of looking at how philosophy and politics, theory and practice, can be mutually reinforcing is to look at an instructive debate between Richard Rorty and Michael Sandel. Sandel's views on philosophy, politics and Rawls are similar to Barber's, while Rorty takes an unusual tack. In complete rejection of Fukuyama's approach – philosophical celebration of liberal ideology and worries about the shortcomings of liberal practice – Rorty dismisses the traditional concerns of philosophy altogether. They are irrelevant to politics and a 'liberalism without foundations' (Mulhall and Swift 1992: 232–49). What is interesting about Rorty is that he takes Wittgenstein seriously and yet supports Rawls's liberalism. Before discussing Rorty and then the exchanges between Rorty and Sandel, a very brief reminder of the basics of Rawls's philosophical liberalism is in order.[1]

In 1972, Rawls put forward a theory of justice as fairness that starts with an intuitive link between fairness and ignorance. A child dividing a cake will be careful to make each piece the same size, if he or she is to have the last piece. Similarly, were people not to know who they were going to be or where they would be placed in a future society, then they would be careful to design fair principles to regulate that society. To model this intuition, Rawls put forward a hypothetical 'original position' in place of Locke, Rousseau and Kant's hypothetical state of nature populated by rational men seeking a social contract to draw up a civil society. In this original position, individuals are ignorant about their natural endowments and their position in society. They are also ignorant of any ideas about how they might want to lead their lives in worthwhile ways (ideas commonly summed up as 'conceptions of the good'). The ignorance of natural endowments and social position leads to suppositions of distributional fairness (fair shares of the cake). More importantly, both for Rawls and many of his followers and critics, individuals in the original position who are ignorant of their conceptions of the good would be concerned to protect people's right in the future society to make up their own mind, and to change their mind, about what their objectives in life are, and then pursue those objectives as they like. This priority of a right for people to lead life the way they want to over any particular way of life is summed up as a priority of right over the good. It is a way of modelling a supposition of religious and cultural tolerance that is appropriate for a diverse, multicultural and democratic society.

In his defence of Rawls, Rorty (1991: 183, fn. 21) admits that initially he read *A Theory of Justice* as resting on pre-political assumptions about human nature and society which served to legitimise liberal society. He had agreed with Sandel's (1982: 19) view that Rawls's theory rested on an untenable metaphysical claim that 'what is most essential to our personhood is not the ends we choose but our capacity to choose them. And this capacity is located in a self which must be prior to the ends it chooses.' When Rawls later clarified that his arguments were meant to be a political theory rather than a philosophical theory, Rorty changed his mind. Now he endorses Rawls's pragmatic bracketing of a wide range of philosophical issues because 'as a practical political matter no general moral conception can provide the basis for a public conception of justice in a modern democratic society' (cited by Rorty 1991: 179). A workable, public conception of justice needs to start from not the aspirations to general truths found in philosophy or religion but instead 'such settled convictions as the belief in religious toleration and the rejection of slavery' (cited by Rorty 1991: 180). Against Sandel's (1982) critique of Rawls, Rorty (1991: 189) now counters that 'Rawls is not interested in conditions for the identity of the self, but only in conditions for citizenship in a liberal society.' But are there any such 'settled convictions'?

In his book, *Democracy's Discontent, America in Search of a Public Philosophy*, Sandel (1996) undertakes a historical study to flesh out his philosophical critique of the 'procedural liberalism' in Schumpeter's realist model of democracy and Rawls's model of tolerant citizenship. An upshot of that study is that the premises of contemporary liberalism, so well identified by Rawls in 1972, entailed a rejection during the 1940s, roughly, of an older American public philosophy. From the founding fathers of the American Revolution through to President F. D. Roosevelt, all public figures (regardless of ideological or other differences) took part in a project to form citizens' political and moral sensibilities of how to lead a worthwhile life. Paralleling Macpherson and Held's studies of successive models of liberal democracy, Sandel surveys first what he calls the formative project or the political economy of citizenship and then the midtwentieth century switch to a supposedly tolerant value neutrality. This new public philosophy pre-supposed an abstract individual, an unencumbered self, which would enjoy a priority of right over the good. His substantive study includes chapters about morally contentious developments in the courts on free speech and pornography, family law, homosexuality and abortion, and developments in wider political arenas about wages, small business and national retail chains, and welfare.

Rorty first defended Rawls against Sandel's critique in an essay 'The priority of democracy over philosophy', and repeated his arguments there in his contribution to a recent collection of essays (Allen and Regan 1998) about Sandel's *Democracy's Discontent*. In a reply to his critics, Sandel responds to Rorty and makes two main points. One is that Rorty, and Rawls, are mistaken in thinking that there are 'settled convictions' such as religious tolerance and the end to slavery upon which to build consensus about a minimal public philosophy. As he puts it, 'To invoke the tradition of American liberty is to invoke a contest not a consensus' (Sandel 1998: 322). In response to another defender and follower of Rawls, Sandel makes a similar point that 'Kymlicka (1998) attributes the failures of liberal egalitarian politics in the United States to endemic features of its political culture ... But these cultural ideals are not pre-political sociological facts that public philosophies cannot address.' Sandel's other main point against Rorty's unusual approach to philosophy *vis-à-vis* liberalism, politics, sociology and history is that he exaggerates a choice between pre-political, cultural, philosophical or metaphysical foundations and everyday, pragmatic and workable principles for minimalist liberalism and a good society. This is much the same sort of argument as Barber's in favour of the kinship between philosophy and politics.

Sandel argues that practice and theory are mutually constitutive. He agrees with Beiner's (1998) comments that theory can claim to interpret the practice of liberalism or it can claim to explain how philosophers' statements have caused a shift in practice, and points out that his argument in *Democracy's Discontent* is interpretative rather than causal. Procedural liberalism has since the Second World War increasingly defined the concepts of public politics, setting the terms of argument between conservatives and liberals. This has crowded out older republican concepts of self-government and the citizenry's autonomy, which set the terms of argument between republicans and democrats. But Sandel offers instructive clarification of his oblique explanatory comments on the cause of the rise of procedural liberalism:

> Broadly stated, the rise of the procedural republic might be explained as follows: the advent of a national, and now global economy complicated the republican project of subjecting economic power to democratic authority. Meanwhile, the emerging consumer society held out an alternative, privatized vision of freedom less demanding than the republican vision of freedom as self-rule. The great waves of immigration and the growing diversity of the nation

rendered the formative project more difficult, and so heightened the appeal of a public philosophy that professed neutrality towards the ends its citizens espoused. (Sandel 1998: 320)

In America, the early twentieth-century republicans failed to defend local businesses, as a source of citizen autonomy in local government, against nationwide chain retailers. Today, contemporary republicanism at the level of nation-states appears to have an even slimmer prospect of resisting the anti-democratic and anti-republican implications of global capitalism. Barber (1995) argues that where consumerism from the 1950s to 1970s offered people attractive cars and household white goods that had direct links to national manufacturing and the possibility of full employment, consumerism in the 1980s and 1990s has become a free-floating 'McWorld'. Today, fast food, computers, films and rock music are much less closely linked to any particular national economy. This suggests that, contrary to Rorty, the meaning of citizenship and democracy will remain contested not just at a surface level but right through to its core. Their historical depth and definitional complexity defies attempts at any authoritative or final definition, whether it is advanced by scholars of classical Greece or Rome, by historians, sociologists, political theorists or by philosophers.

Barber is right to reject the view that contest can be at the core of a concept *if* that implies debate about the meaning of essentially contested concepts should be written off as pointless. Perhaps the descriptor 'essential' is misleading but I think Connolly is right. Regarding some concepts as essentially contested fits well with Wittgenstein's views on language, and that goes well with Barber and Sandel's campaigns for a common language to describe and understand common concerns, rather than Rorty's campaign against philosophy.

Conclusions

Against the various attempts of philosophy and ideology, liberalism in particular, to take moral, religious, philosophical or theoretical debates out of the arenas of political contest, this chapter has argued that the meanings of citizenship and democracy have long been and will continue to be contested. It is precisely because they have been contested for so long that they will continue to be contested. Another reason is that their definitional complexity provides an endless supply of fuel for debate and contest. Barber warns that this can all too easily lead people to give up contesting what such concepts mean, and this is a serious warning that should be heeded. At the same time, it is most important to insist on their contestability no matter what. Such an insistence is useful against the predominance of economic liberalism in a global era. When nation-states, local government and all other arenas where citizens might gather to formulate and address their common concerns are under a cloud, and when the experiment with representative democracy combined with universal suffrage and social citizenship has been only brief, then any argument that can penetrate the certitudes of liberalism is important. To regard citizenship and democracy as essentially contested can therefore help different people to maintain the several diverse values that they use citizenship and democracy to express.

Note

1   The next paragraph follows Mulhall and Swift's (1992: 3–9) attempt to sum-
marise Rawls and steer around the various areas of contention among Rawls's
followers and critics.

References

Allen, Anita and Regan, Milton (eds) (1998) *Debating Democracy's Discontent,
Essays on American Politics, Law, and Public Philosophy*, Oxford: Oxford Uni-
versity Press.
Andrews, Geoff (ed.) (1991) *Citizenship*, London: Lawrence & Wishart.
Barber, Benjamin (1984) *Strong Democracy, Participatory Politics for a New Age*,
Berkeley, CA: University of California Press.
——(1988) *The Conquest of Politics, Liberal Philosophy in Democratic Times*,
Princeton, NJ: Princeton University Press.
——(1995) *Jihad vs. McWorld*, New York: Times Books.
Barrett, Michèle (1991) *The Politics of Truth, From Marx to Foucault*, Cambridge:
Polity Press.
Beiner, Ronald (ed.) (1992) *Theorising Citizenship*, New York: State University of
New York.
——(1998) 'Introduction: the Quest for a Post-Liberal Public Philosophy', in Allen
and Regan (1998).
Bobbio, Norberto (1987) *The Future of Democracy: A Defence of the Rules of the
Game*, ed. and trans. by R. Griffin, Cambridge: Polity Press.

Clegg, Stewart (1989) *Frameworks of Power,* London: Sage.

Connolly, William (1983) *The Terms of Political Discourse,* 2nd edn Princeton, NJ: Princeton University Press.

Cox, Andrew, Furlong, Paul and Page, Edward (1985) *Power in Capitalist Societies: Theory, Explanations, and Cases,* Brighton: Wheatsheaf Books/Harvester Press.

Cutler, T., Williams, J. and Williams, K. (1986) *Keynes, Beveridge and Beyond,* London: Routledge & Kegan Paul.

Dahl, Robert (1957) 'The Concept of Power', *Behavioural Science,* no. 2: 201–5.

—— (1985) *A Preface to Economic Democracy,* Cambridge: Polity Press.

—— (1998) *On Democracy,* New Haven, CT, and London: Yale University Press.

Dunn, John (ed.) (1992) *Democracy: The Unfinished Journey, 508 BC to AD 1993,* Oxford: Oxford University Press.

Farrar, Cynthia (1992) 'Ancient Greek Political Theory as a Response to Democracy', in Dunn (1992).

Finley, M.I. (1964) *The Ancient Greeks,* Harmondsworth: Penguin.

Fukuyama, Francis (1992) *The End of History and the Last Man,* New York: Free Press.

Gallie, W.B. (1964) 'Essentially contested concepts', reprinted from *Proceedings of the Aristotelian Society* vol. 56 (1956): 167–98, in W.B. Gallie, *Philosophy and the Historical Understanding,* London: Chatto & Windus.

Held, David (1987) *Models of Democracy,* Cambridge: Polity Press.

Hindess, Barry (1991) 'Imaginary presuppositions of democracy', *Economy and Society* vol. 20, no. 2: 173–95.

Hodgson, Geoff (1984) *The Democratic Economy,* Harmondsworth: Penguin.

Hornblower, Simon (1992) 'Creation and Development of Democratic Institutions in Ancient Greece', in Dunn (1992).

Kitto, H.D.F. (1986) *The Greeks,* Harmondsworth: Penguin.

Kymlicka, Will (1995) *Multicultural Citizenship,* Oxford: Clarendon Press.

—— (1998) 'Liberal Egalitarianism and Civic Republicanism: Friends or Enemies?', in Allen and Regan (1998).

Lloyd, G.E.R. (1992) 'Democracy, Philosophy, and Science in Ancient Greece', in Dunn (1992).

Lukes, Stephen (1972) *Power: A Radical View,* London: Macmillan.

Macpherson, C.B. (1977) *The Life and Times of Liberal Democracy,* Oxford: Oxford University Press.

Mann, Michael (1987) 'Ruling class strategies and citizenship', *Sociology,* vol. 21: 339–54.

Marshall, T.H. (1964) *Class, Citizenship and Social Development,* Chicago: University of Chicago Press.

Mouffe, Chantal (ed.) (1990) *Dimensions of Radical Democracy – Pluralism, Citizenship, Community,* London: Verso.

Mulhall, Stephen and Swift, Adam (1992) *Liberals and Communitarians,* Oxford: Oxford University Press.

Okun, Arthur (1975) *Equality and Efficiency, The Big Trade-Off,* Washington DC: Brookings Institute.

Pateman, Carole (1970) *Participation and Democratic Theory,* Cambridge: Cambridge University Press.

Petit, Philip (1997) *Republicanism, A Theory of Freedom and Government*, Oxford: Clarendon Press.

—— (1998) 'Reworking Sandel's Republicanism', in Allen and Regan (1998).

Polan, A.J. (1984) *Lenin and the End of Politics*, London: Methuen.

Rawls, John (1972) *A Theory of Justice*, Oxford: Oxford University Press.

Rorty, Richard (1991) *Objectivity, Relativism, and Truth*, Cambridge: Cambridge University Press.

—— (1998) 'A Defence of Minimalist Liberalism', in Allen and Regan (1998).

Sabine, George H. (1961) *A History of Political Theory*, 3rd edn, London: Harrap.

Sandel, Michael (1982) *Liberalism and the Limits of Justice*, Cambridge: Cambridge University Press.

—— (1996) *Democracy's Discontent, America in Search of a Public Philosophy*, Cambridge MA: Belknap Press/Harvard University Press.

—— (1998) 'Reply to Critics', in Allen and Regan (1998).

Schumpeter, Joseph (1976) *Capitalism, Socialism and Democracy*, London: Allen and Unwin.

Therborn , Göran (1977) 'The rule of capital and the rise of democracy', *New Left Review,* no. 103 (May–June): 3–42.

Turner, Bryan S. (1986) *Citizenship and Capitalism, The Debate over Reformism*, London: Allen and Unwin.

—— (1990a) 'Outline of a Theory of Citizenship', in Mouffe (1990).

—— (1990b) 'Periodisation and Politics in the Postmodern', in B.S. Turner (ed.), *Theories of Modernity and Postmodernity*, London: Sage.

—— (1993) 'Contemporary Problems in the Theory of Citizenship', in B.S. Turner, *Citizenship and Social Theory*, London: Sage.

—— (1996) 'An introduction to contemporary citizenship theory', in Vandenberg (1996b).

Vandenberg, Andrew (1996a) 'Politics of Democracy and Citizenship' in Vandenberg (1996b).

—— (1996b) *Politics of Democracy and Citizenship, Study Guide*, Deakin University, Geelong, Australia.

Wolin, Sheldon (1960) *Politics and Vision: Continuity and Innovation in Western Political Thought*, Boston, MA: Little, Brown.

Young, Iris Marion (1990) *Justice and the Politics of Difference*, Princeton, NJ: Princeton University Press.

2 LIBERAL CITIZENSHIP AND COSMOPOLITAN VIRTUE

Bryan S. Turner

In this chapter, Bryan Turner uses arguments by Barber and Rorty, which featured in the previous chapter, to develop an argument about cosmopolitanism as a virtue. Further to his earlier work on typologies of the historical emergence of modern citizenship (particularly Turner 1986, 1990a), he develops an argument based on a dual dichotomy that pits Benjamin Barber's contrast between thick and thin democracy against Marshall McLuhan's contrast between hot and cool loyalty to a community. Cosmopolitan virtue is a possibly good outcome of the combination of thin democracy and cool loyalty to a nation. A cosmopolitan citizenly virtue within something like Richard Rorty's postmodern liberalism is perhaps the only viable strategy against worrying developments towards tribalism, political parochialism and global consumerism.

Introduction: defining terms

In this chapter on the transformation of modern politics, I want to consider an ancient problem of cultural diversity and political power. The word 'ancient' is used advisedly, because it was the fear of diversity in ancient Greece that was the condition that produced political theory in the first instance (Saxonhouse 1992). Although this problem of cultural diversity within the framework of the city-state has a long history in political thought, there are some new ingredients within the contemporary context. The essence of these new circumstances is the globalization of economic and cultural relationships and, second, the postmodernization of cultural phenomena. In reality, these are the same issues because the postmodernization of culture is closely related to the development of hybridization, and hybridity is a function of cultural globalism. The question then is: how can one be a citizenship in such a context of staggering diversity? How can citizens be committed to some political community (the city or the state) when fragmentation makes the possibility of solidarity unlikely? Generally speaking, the response to this circumstance has been somewhat apologetic and typically nostalgic. The point of my chapter is to celebrate diversity and to do so through the development of a notion of cosmopolitan virtue. In turn, this virtue is a component of the republican tradition, and here again the ancients and the moderns cannot be kept apart. It was the Stoics who, in response to the anxieties of diversity, created the notions of cosmopolitanism and universal order as a suitable ethic for the imperial city (Wolin 1961). In order to conduct this debate, however, I need to start by defining some terms.

It is important to distinguish between the notion of postmodernity and postmodern theory (Turner 1990b). By the former, I mean a social condition of advanced societies in which cultural and social relations are transformed by new modes and methods of communication and information storage, especially by electronic means of delivery. Postmodern society is the product of the transformations of communication systems as described initially by theorists like Marshall McLuhan (1964). By postmodern theory, I mean a way of theorising society in which the principal mode or style of theoretical analysis is ironic, employing textual devices which signify the constructed and malleable forms of reality representation, and which indicates a certain distance from the object of analysis or signification. In short, postmodern theories question grand narratives (Lyotard 1984) or, in the words of Richard Rorty, the ironist is somebody who profoundly doubts the authority of any final vocabulary about reality (Rorty 1989). Since democracy can be regarded as the grand narrative of the modern state, postmodern theory would appear to be incompatible with much coventional political philosophy. Postmodern theory, with its sensitivity to simulation, metaphor and artificiality, describes or attempts to describe the condition of postmodernity. Postmodern theory is thus an effect of and response to a social world which is increasingly complex and differentiated, and to a culture which is increasingly reflexive and sceptical about its own sources of authority. Questions about the status and role of authors in postmodernity are invariably questions about authorisation and authority. Who has authority to speak in a context of competing cultures? In this chapter, I attempt to describe the emergence of a mode of political identity in a global postmodern society and to describe these social changes within the paradigm of an ironic theory of social relations, but my purpose is to go beyond description in order to prescribe a response to the erosion of nationalistic citizenship.

Although he was not particularly interested in the question of political identity, T. H. Marshall's analysis of citizenship still provides a useful route into the discussion of political identity and contemporary citizenship (Marshall 1964). Marshall's silence on this issue is, however, instructive, because it points to a period in British history in which, at least in public debate, the problem of identity politics had not fully emerged. Marshall's argument is well known. He claimed that citizenship evolved through three stages of legal, political and social rights from around the middle of the seventeenth century to the creation of the welfare state in the middle of the twentieth century. This evolution of citizenship has to be seen against the background of the emergence of antagonistic urban social classes in the context of industrial capitalism. The growth of capitalist markets was accompanied by the emergence of class-based urban communities characterised by a high level of class consciousness and class conflict. Traditional sources of solidarity and legitimacy in rural communities, which had been partly held together by Christian rituals and beliefs, were challenged by the class-based ideologies of the working-class movement, namely by socialist ideas of working-class co-operation. Old status relations were being replaced by the solidarities of class. 'Class', which in traditional political economy was an impersonal association of individuals with the same relationship to economic relations of ownership, began to assume characteristics normally associated with community or *gemeinschaft* (Holton and Turner 1986).

The growth of the welfare state in Great Britain between 1850 and 1950 was seen by Marshall to be a reformist response to the divisive and conflictual nature of class society. However, Marshall's (1981: 123–36) later work on the concept of a 'hyphenated society' was more relevant to the contemporary discussion of democracy and citizenship. This concept referred to the structural contradiction between democracy and capitalism in such notions as 'democratic-capitalist society', or 'welfare capitalism'. In short, contemporary capitalist societies contained within them a tension or contradiction between, on the one hand, the possibility of political emancipation through the democratisation of the polity, and on the other hand, the reduction of the inequalities and deprivations of a class-based system through state provision of welfare benefits. Welfare entitlement was a safety device that constrained the negative consequences of an unregulated capitalist economy. Competitive capitalism thus historically gave way through these structural changes either to various forms of monopoly capitalism or to post-industrialism. The connections with Daniel Bell's work were explicitly recognised by Marshall (1981: 125).

Citizenship took different forms depending on the historical circumstances of its formation (Mann 1987). It is possible to distinguish between active and passive forms of citizenship, which arise from variations in the relationship between the subject and the state. Thus, radical social movements expand citizenship rights through a process of political conflict, while the more passive forms of citizenship are the effect of the political strategies of the dominant political elite (Turner 1990a). In England, there has been a tradition of passive citizenship, which followed the 'Glorious Rebellion' and political settlement of 1688, and which was enshrined in John Locke's justification of constitutional social contract theory in *Two Treatises of Government* in 1690. The absence of a genuinely revolutionary working-class confrontation in Britain in the eighteenth and nineteenth centuries contributed further to this history of 'gradualism'. It has often been argued, following the Halevy thesis, that the Methodist Revolution was, as it were, a substitute for a socialist revolution and that Methodism created the conditions for social mobility of individuals out of the working class, but at the same time the inherent political conservatism of Wesleyan theology spawned an ideology of acceptance (Halevy 1962). The English citizen evolved as a 'subject' of the monarchy which remained largely unchallenged in political terms, at least from outside the monarchy itself. The nature of citizenship in different European societies varies according to the specific history of its class formation, the impact of warfare and the peculiar features of its political history. It is this specificity of the historical constitution of class relationships which determines the peculiarities of the national combination of rights, obligations and immunities within citizenship (Janoski 1998).

Scarcity and solidarity

In more theoretical terms, citizenship has to be seen within the dynamic contrast between the economics of scarcity and the nature of loyalty and solidarity in human societies. All human societies are structured around the question of scarcity and solidarity. More specifically, they are structured around the relationship between allocative functions, which are concerned with the distribution of scarce resources, and integrative functions, which are concerned with the nature and production of commitment and loyalty in human social systems. This method of analysing society gave rise, for example, to Talcott Parsons's four-fold paradigm to analyse the allocative and integrative functions of social systems in the now famous AGIL scheme (Parsons 1951). Within the allocative functions of the social system, political processes are concerned with the identification and establishment of social goals, while economic systems are concerned with the distribution and production of scarce resources. The integrative functions are concerned with the nature of identity formation through socialisation and training, and the creation of motivation and commitment to social systems. Social sciences can be categorised around these poles, which address the political economy of scarcity and the sociology of maintaining social order against a background of struggle over resources.

This formulation represents the response of classical sociology to the so-called 'Hobbesian problem of social order'. For sociology, the notion of a social contract in Hobbes and Locke provides no satisfactory account of either the creation or the continuity of society. This is so for the simple reason that seventeenth-century contractualism was a political theory of the state. There has to be a 'non-contractual element' to the contract which is provided by common values, shared purposes, integrating rituals and a pattern of identification with existing social arrangements. Civil society has to be built up around these social elements, which ultimately give the polity some social foundation of legitimacy. Now citizenship is primarily about the allocative and integrative questions in social systems, because citizenship is a set of institutions, which are related to the possibility of an egalitarian distribution of resources; but, at the same time, citizenship produces and sustains various forms of commitment to the social order.

National citizenship: rights and obligations

We may define citizenship as an ensemble of rights and obligations that determine an individual's access to social and economic
resources. In historical terms, citizenship creates a juridic identity that
determines an individual's status within the political community. In
fact citizenship is itself one of the most important resources which a
society ascribes to an individual as a legal personality. Finally, this
juridic identity is part of a civil society organised around a set of values
which we may broadly define as 'civic virtue' (Turner 1997). My argument is that the historic rise of modern citizenship in the nineteenth
and twentieth centuries was primarily associated with the growth of
nation-states and nationalism, which became the principal political
ideology of nation-state building.[1] To be precise, modern citizenship
dates from the Treaty of Westphalia in 1648, which launched the
modern system of nation-states as the principal actors within the
world system. National identity and citizenship identity became fused
in the late nineteenth century around the growth of nation-states characterised by the dominant ideology of nationalism. In many societies,
this juridic identity was given strong racist characteristics in the creation of such notions as 'the British people' or 'the German folk'. The
growth of national citizenship was associated with Occidentalism (as
an adjunct of Orientalism), creating strong notions of Otherness as
the boundary between the inside and outside world. National citizenship became crucial to the building of loyalties and commitments
around the nation-state.

Citizenship in this framework can be seen as: (1) an inclusionary
principle for the distribution and allocation of entitlements, and
(2) an exclusionary basis for building solidarity and maintaining
identity. In this sense, national citizenship is constructed around
institutionalised racism because it excludes outsiders from access to
entitlements characteristically on the basis of a racial or national
identity. The creation of the nation-state based upon citizenship
involved various levels and degrees of 'ethnic cleansing' because the
exclusionary principle of citizenship was structured around a juridic
and racial identity. As nation-states were challenged from within by
class division and from without by warfare and imperial struggle,
there was the requirement for a strong basis of loyalty in the national
community.

Following these arguments, we can analyse citizenship as a system for the allocation of entitlements and immunities within a political community. These entitlements are themselves organised around three principles, namely reproduction, production and destruction. People can achieve entitlements by the formation of households and families, which become the sites for the reproduction of society through the birth and upbringing of children. These services to the state via the family provide entitlements to both men and women as parents and as reproducers of the nation-state (Yuval-Davis 1997). These entitlements become the basis for family security systems, various forms of support to mothers and health, and educational provision for children. Questions of justice as a result become closely tied to principles of cross-generational responsibilities for the management and conservation of environment and society (Barry 1977). Second, entitlements can be achieved through the production of goods and services, namely through work. This has been the most significant basis for the provision of superannuation and pension rights, but these entitlements also include rights to safety at work, insurance schemes relating to health and employment and various provisions for retirement. It is for this reason obvious that the entitlements of men have been more significant than entitlements for women in societies where values relating to work form the core of the value system as a whole. Finally, service to the state through warfare generates a third range of entitlements for the soldier-citizen. War-time service typically leads to various pension rights, health provisions, housing and other entitlements for returning servicemen.[2] Here again the entitlements of men dominate over entitlements for women, who may be able to claim rights indirectly as war widows. These three routes to entitlement (family, work and war) also generate particular types of identity such as the soldier-citizen, the working citizen and the parent-citizen.

The erosion of entitlement

In contemporary society, these routes to citizenship entitlement are becoming weaker and less reliable as guarantees or conditions for resource allocation. For example, in the advanced industrial societies warfare has become, in the post-war period at least, far less common and therefore the soldier-citizen has become less significant as an identity and as a mode for distributing entitlement. In general terms, compulsory service has become less common in the industrial capitalist West and military activities have become a profession for an elite rather than a requirement of all able-bodied men. We can also argue that in many circumstances the use of mercenary soldiers is a way of 'outsourcing' the need for military service to minority communities such as the 'hill tribes' of India and South-East Asia. As warfare becomes more technical, so the employment of mass troops becomes less important, thereby closing off a traditional avenue for the working class into welfare provision. The traditional tie between the militia and the citizenry has been broken. Second, following the work of Ulrich Beck and Elizabeth Gernsheim-Beck (1990), there has been a significant erosion of the classical nuclear family as a social location of reproduction. Levels of reproduction have declined with an increase in life-expectancy, the mass availability of contraceptive methods and changing value systems. The classical S-shaped demographic revolution means that the advanced industrial societies are characterised by a rapid process of ageing and by either declining or stationary populations. Many European societies now depend heavily on migration as a method of reproducing the nation-state in demographic terms. Hence one can expect that there will be an erosion of family-based rights and entitlements relating to reproduction. At the very least, the notion that there is a crisis in the family as an institution of modern societies will continue to grow in intensity. Many states in the industrial societies have withdrawn from direct welfare provisions for the family in the wake of fiscal rationalism and depend increasingly on third-sector provision. These forms of privatisation also weaken the overt link between parenthood and citizenship.

Finally, with the transition of the economy from Fordism to post-Fordism, there has been a profound restructuring of the occupational system due to growth in the service sector, decline in industrial manufacturing, and an increase in the number of jobs relating to communication and the leisure industries. My picture of the economy is influenced by the work of Robert Reich (1991) in his *The Work of Nations*, which predicts a significant growth in the importance of symbolic analysts: the managers and controllers of information and knowledge systems. To some extent Reich's view of the economy follows the earlier work of Daniel Bell (1974) and his now famous discussion of the post-industrial society in which he emphasised the importance of knowledge and the university system as crucial components of economic production. However, I remain pessimistic about the long-term problems associated with structural unemployment and under-employment, and with the decline of large-scale manufacturing industries. It is difficult to see how young workers in the twenty-first century will find sufficient employment to provide entitlements within the welfare state. The indications are that work will become increasingly scarce, typically short-term and casual, and normally unpredictable. For many, the absence of work threatens the traditional access to superannuation benefits and other retirement schemes. This economic scenario is a recipe for significant industrial and social unrest in which struggles will be frequently based on generational rather than class conflicts. Paradoxically, 'the death of class' may also parallel the death of citizenship (Lee and Turner 1996). Class conflict was a motor of interest formation in which the social rights of citizenship expanded, because the state was forced to respond to industrial unrest. The erosion of class loyalties and identities signals the decline of a mass labour market.

While the traditional labour markets of the capitalist West have contracted, there has been a cultural and ethnic diversification of labour through migration in the world economy. The consequences of the globalisation and postmodernisation of society are an erosion of national loyalties and identities based upon a traditional racial homogeneity. The growth of a global labour market has increased the number of migrant workers in the industrialised modern societies, bringing a consequent growth in the heterogeneity of those economies. Alongside this growing ethnic diversity and multiculturalism, there is a weakening of the sovereignty of the nation-state as the state is drawn into global political relations.

These developments are clearly uneven, and globalisation is typically followed or accompanied by powerful forces of localisation as communities attempt to protect themselves from global cultures. These global changes raise questions about the stability and integration of citizenship identities based upon traditional modes of loyalty and commitment. I have already noted an erosion of entitlements within the traditional system of the welfare state and citizenship entitlements. The twenty-first century will be characterised by a growing scarcity of work (hence a decline in the traditional route into citizenship entitlement) and a corresponding decline of loyalty and solidarity within the nation-state. How can the state secure the loyalty of younger generations who are under-employed or unemployed, who will never serve in a national army, and who may not form families either out of personal sexual preference or financial incapacity to support children? They are citizens only in a superficial and formal sense; in fact we may give them the title of 'quasi-citizens'. We can anticipate that the loyalties of these marginalised groups may be 'artificially' sustained by creating in them a fear of outsiders and foreigners who are 'stealing' their jobs, their homes and their girlfriends. Their alienation may eventuate paradoxically in an increased patriotic loyalty that targets strangers as the cause of their misery. Nationalist and fascist revivals in the former regions of East Germany and racial unrest in France are indications of these fears. The traditional mixture of youth unemployment, racial antagonism and political alienation is providing a fertile basis for xenophobic politics in contemporary Europe.

The postmodernisation of identity

We can think of these two dimensions (loyalty to the state and solidarity in society) in terms of a dual dichotomy defined on one dimension by the notion of hot/cool loyalty (following the work of Marshall McLuhan) and on the other dimension by thick/thin solidarity which indicates the depth and strength of the forms of inclusion.[3] This dual dichotomy forms a four-fold property space that enables us to develop an ironic theory of loyalty and solidarity in modern society. Thick solidarities very well describe the type of social involvement of, for example, the Arunta tribe in Emile Durkheim's (1954) analysis of mechanical solidarity in *The Elementary Forms of the Religious Life*. The Arunta world involved the closed communities of a quasi-nomadic life of hunter-gatherer tribalism. Their social relations were largely permanent, emotional and solid, and their belief systems were not regularly challenged. By contrast, modern societies are organised around the market place of anonymous strangers, where these strangers are mobile and disconnected. The distinction between hot/cool loyalties is taken from McLuhan's analysis of modern communication: for example, the telephone offers a unidimensional communication with high definition. It is a cool medium, where the tribal mode of communication of tradition by oral and ritualistic means is hot. This distinction in McLuhan's theory of the media is redeployed in this chapter to talk about modes of loyalty in the modern state.

Now postmodern or cosmopolitan citizenship will be characterised by cool loyalties and thin patterns of solidarity. Indeed, we could argue that the characteristic mode or orientation of the cosmopolitan citizen would in fact be one of disloyalty and ironic distance. An ironist always holds her views about the social worlds in doubt, because they are always subject to revision and reformulation.[4] Her picture of society is always provisional and she is sceptical about grand narratives, because her own 'final vocabulary' is always open to further inspection and correction. Her ironic views of the world are always 'for the time being'.

These postmodern cool loyalties will be characteristic of the global elite of symbolic analysts who are geographically and socially mobile, finding employment in different global corporations in different parts of the world. The mobile symbolic analyst is quite likely to enjoy multiple citizenships, several economic identities and various status positions within a number of blended families. They have become reflexive citizens because their world is characterised by contingency, risk and mobility. The postmodern citizen is only moving on. By contrast, those sections of the population which are relatively immobile and located in traditional employment patterns (the working class, ethnic minorities and the under-classes) may continue in fact to have hot loyalties and thick patterns of solidarity. We may call these pure loyalists the 'ethnic patriots' of the nation-state. The third possibility would be characteristic of the liberal middle classes and professional groups who have relatively cool loyalties to the nation-state, but are involved in a dense network of voluntary associations and other institutional links within society and therefore have thick solidarity. Finally, there will be a group of reactive nationalists, probably drawn from the petty bourgeoisie, who will retain hot nationalist loyalties, but will be less involved socially in terms of their institutional linkages. In an ironic sense we could also characterise this four-fold property space in terms of the McDonaldisation of political commitments where, from the point of the view of the cosmopolitan symbolic analyst, modern political life would resemble a 'drive through democracy'. By contrast, the ethnic patriots resemble the neo-tribalism described by Michel Maffesoli (1996) as a subterranean *gemeinschaft* in contemporary societies. Their affective world will revolve around social spectacle, particularly the gladiatorial struggles between national football teams.

One can argue that the old loyalties of the national welfare state system as expressed through citizenship will be eroded and there will be, in Durkheim's terms, a loss of organic solidarity. Whereas the traditional nation-state encouraged hot loyalty and thick solidarity, the globalisation of the polity will produce an increase in a political style characterised by cosmopolitan coolness and indifference towards the claims of traditional patterns of solidarity. Reganonomics and Thatcherism encouraged economic individualism and political individualism whereby societies became more sharply divided during the retreat from the welfare state. Indeed Mrs Thatcher claimed that there is no such thing as society; there are only individuals and families. There are good reasons to believe that the traditional nuclear family is disappearing, leaving behind the 'sovereign individual' of Thatcherite capitalism (Abercrombie, Hill and Turner 1986). We can see this new pattern of cosmopolitan 'disloyalty' as a more exaggerated form of the economic individualism created in the 1980s as part of the revolution of economic rationalism leading to, from a traditional point of view, political disloyalty. There will be significant class differences in orientation to the state and loyalty to society. I have suggested that the remnants of the traditional manufacturing and working classes will be characterised by ethnic patriotism. As the workplace becomes global and ethnically differentiated, there will be increasing racial conflict between social groups competing for scarce resources within the economy. These new patterns of loyalty will be characterised by what Maffesoli has called neo-tribalism, but it will not be a cosy pattern of *gemeinschaftlich* solidarities.

Conclusion: cosmopolitan virtue

While these postmodern commitments and disloyalties have been described in a negative fashion so far, I conclude by arguing that they are perfectly functional in a world where the rigidities of the nation-state with its thick solidarities are collapsing in the face of globalised economies. Cosmopolitanism within this Rortian world can be justified morally, because hot loyalties and thick solidarities are more likely to be points of conflict and violence in postmodern, ethnically diverse labour markets. Indifference and distance may be useful personal strategies in a risk society where ambiguity and uncertainty reign. In a more fluid world, the ironic citizen needs to learn how to move on, how to adjust and to adapt to a world of cultural contingency. Because historically we have learned to respect the virtues of loyalty and duty, we find it difficult to embrace the suggestion that the next century will not be able to afford strong nationalist commitment in a global community. Hybridity and diversity will have all but obscured the stable world of nineteenth-century nationalism. It was the political environment of loyalty to the state and trust in the leadership which contributed to twentieth-century authoritarianism on both the left and the right. The ironic citizen of the next century may be less likely to give her undivided support to whatever government happens to be in power. We need an ideology of membership therefore which will celebrate the uncertainty of belonging where our 'final vocabularies' are never final.

It is interesting finally to connect this discussion of movement with the origins of social contract theory in the late sixteenth century. In the little known work of Simon Stevin, a native of Bruges who was born in 1548 and who wrote on the life of the citizen (*Het Burgherlick Leven*) in 1590, there is an interesting idea. Before becoming the citizen of a particular place, individuals have a right to travel in order to study the civil societies and constitutions of different lands (Romein-Verschoor 1955). Before giving his loyalty to a particular state and entering into a social contract, the citizen had to be well informed about his options; travel and mobility were thus essential pre-conditions for loyalty and commitment. This view of peripatetic citizenship was a consequence of Stevin's own experiences of political uncertainty and conflict in the 'low countries' of that time. There is, however, an important lesson for us in this early version of contractarianism that psychological and political distance may be necessary conditions for any subsequent and conditional identity with the polity. Uncertain loyalties and contingent identities may become virtues of a postmodern society.

Notes

1   In *Citizenship: Critical Concepts* (Turner and Hamilton 1994), I argued that the concept of citizenship was primarily a modern political notion, namely a concept of political relations which dated from the French and industrial revolutions. It charts the history of the growth of bourgeois civil society: that is, a public space of opinion formation in relation to democratic institutions. Any

use of the concept with respect to Athens or Greece is misleading, because the very existence of the modern concept indicates the decline of slavery and feudalism. I do not wish to depart radically from that view, except to note here that the Treaty of Westphalia recognised a necessary pre-condition for such a development, namely the creation of an international system of nation-states.

2   There is an important, but somewhat neglected argument, that warfare is a fundamental force in the modern creation of national citizenship. Richard M. Titmuss (1963) argued that war had contributed significantly to the creation of social security schemes. The theme was taken up by Marshall and further elaborated as a cause, along with migration and social movements, of the expansion of social rights in *Citizenship and Capitalism* (Turner 1986). Perhaps the point to stress, however, is that warfare also creates a cultural identity in which the individual fortunes of servicemen and women are tied to the self-image of the nation-state as a historical actor.

3   This model of solidarity was first presented as a public lecture to celebrate the 50th anniversary of the Department of Sociology at Lund in a symposium on 'Sociology Facing the 21st Century'. The paper was published as a research report (Isenberg 1998).

4   This use of gendered terminology is consciously employed here to reflect Rorty's use of 'her' in describing the attitudes of the modern ironist (Rorty 1989).

References

Abercrombie, N. Hill, S. and Turner, B.S. (1986) *Sovereign Individuals of Capitalism*, London: Allen & Unwin.

Barry, B.M. (1977) 'Justice between Generations', in P.M.S. Hacker and J. Raz (eds), *Law, Morality and Society, Essays in Honour of H.L.A. Hart*, Oxford: Clarendon Press: 268–84.

Beck, U. and Gernsheim-Beck, E. (1990) *Das ganz normale Chaos der Liebe*, Frankfurt: Suhrkamp.

Bell, D. (1974) *The Coming of Post-Industrial Society*, New York: Basic Books.

Durkheim, E. (1954) *The Elementary Forms of the Religious Life*, London: Allen & Unwin.

Eyerman, R. and Turner, B.S. (forthcoming) 'Outline of a theory of generations', *European Journal of Social Theory*.

Halevy, E. (1962) *A History of the English People in the Nineteenth Century*, 2nd edn, London: Benn, 2 volumes.

Holton, Robert J. and Turner, Bryan S. (1986) *Talcott Parsons on Economy and Society*. London and New York: Routledge & Kegan Paul.

Isenberg, B. (ed.) (1998) *Sociology and Social Transformation*, Lund University, Research Report.

Janoski, T. (1998) *Citizenship and Civil Society. A Framework of Rights and Obligations in Liberal, Traditional and Democratic Regimes*, Cambridge: Cambridge University Press.

Lee, D. and Turner, B.S. (eds) (1996) *Conflicts about Class. Debating Inequality in late Industrialism*, London and New York: Longman.

Lyotard, J.-F. (1984) *The Postmodern Condition. A Report on Knowledge*, Manchester: University of Manchester Press.

Maffesoli, M. (1996) *The Time of the Tribes. The Decline of Individualism in Mass Society*, London: Sage.

Mann, M. (1987) 'Ruling class strategies and citizenship', *Sociology*, vol. 21: 339–54.

Marshall, T.H. (1964) *Class, Citizenship and Social Development*, Chicago: University of Chicago Press.

——(1981) *The Right to Welfare and Other Essays*, London: Heinemann Educational Books.

McLuhan, M. (1964) *Understanding the Media. The Extension of Man*, Toronto: McGraw-Hill.

Parsons, T. (1951) *The Social System*, London: Routledge & Kegan Paul.

Reich, R. (1991) *The Work of Nations. Preparing Ourselves for 21st Century Capitalism*, New York: Random House.

Romein-Verschoor, A. (1955) *Civic Life by Simon Stevin*, Amsterdam: Swets & Zeitlinger.

Rorty, R. (1989) *Contingency, Irony, and Solidarity*, Cambridge: Cambridge University Press.

Saxonhouse, A.W. (1992) *Fear of Diversity. The Birth of Political Science in Ancient Greek Thought*, Chicago and London: University of Chicago Press.

Titmuss, R.M. (1963) *Essays on 'the Welfare State'*, London: Unwin University Books.

Turner, B.S. (1986) *Citizenship and Capitalism. The Debate over Reformism*, London: Allen & Unwin.

——(1990a) 'Outline of a theory of citizenship', *Sociology*, vol. 24, no. 2: 189–217.

——(ed.) (1990b) *Theories of Modernity and Postmodernity*, London: Sage.

——(1997) 'Citizenship studies: a general theory', *Citizenship Studies*, vol. 1, no. 1: 5–18.

Turner, Bryan S. and Hamilton, Peter (eds) (1994) *Citizenship: Critical Concepts*, London and New York: Routledge.

Wolin, S.S. (1960) *Politics and Vision. Continuity and Innovation in Western Political Thought*, London: George Allen & Unwin.

Yuval-Davis, N. (1997) *Gender and Nation*, London: Sage.

3 REPRESENTATIVE GOVERNMENT AND PARTICIPATORY DEMOCRACY*

Barry Hindess

In this chapter Barry Hindess avoids any search for viable or sound norms about the virtuous citizen in a global era. Instead he focuses on the modern co-existence of two opposed understandings of democracy: as involving, on the one hand, the direct participation of the people themselves in governmental decision making and, on the other, the rigorous separation of the people from their government through a system of representative government. While the second is now the more influential, the first persists as a basis for radical political critique. Both are concerned with the possible corruptions of government resulting from sectional interests – whether among the people or within the ranks of professional politicians and public servants – but, not surprisingly, they have very different views about the most important dangers and how they might be combated.

In eighteenth-century Europe and North America, 'democracy' was usually understood to mean, in something like the sense it had for the Greeks of classical antiquity, government by the people themselves;

---

*This paper makes use of arguments developed at greater length in my Repre-sentation ingrafted upon democracy', *Democratization*, vol. 7, no. 1, Spring 2000.

not by their representatives and certainly not by a collection of state agencies that pretended to act in their name. Thus, in its early years the USA was often regarded not as a democracy but rather as a kind of republic. It was a state governed by its citizens but it was far too big to be a democracy and its government was actually in the hands of elected representatives, not the people themselves. Indeed James Madison, writing in 1788, insists that what most distinguished America's governments from those of earlier republics was not their democratic character but rather the reverse, 'the total exclusion of the people, in their collective form, from any share' in their government (Madison, Hamilton and Jay 1987 [1788] no. 63).

Nevertheless, the term 'democracy' was soon used to describe such a system of representative government (Wood 1992). In *The Rights of Man*, for example, Tom Paine reserves the term 'pure democracy' for government by the people themselves, but he also celebrates the American system in which 'representation [was] ingrafted upon Democracy' (Paine 1989: 170) to produce a combined form of government, which was even better than pure democracy alone. While this understanding of democracy as a form of representative government has since come to dominate both popular and academic usage, it has co-existed with the earlier meaning of the term. As a result, we now find two conflicting images of democracy. It is seen, on the one hand, as involving open public debate and the direct participation of the people themselves in governmental decision-making and, on the other, as combining the separation of the people from their government with a necessary minimum of popular participation. While, in the second half of the twentieth century, the second image is clearly the more influential, the first still has considerable appeal. The tension between them is part of what is at issue in debates around the 'realist' theory of democracy, which I consider below.

A further consequence of the emergence of representative government is the appearance of a distinction, which would have made little sense to the Greeks of the classical period, between the political life of the people on the one hand and their government on the other. More precisely, modern forms of representative government involve the separation of at least three levels of political activity: the political activity of the people themselves, that of elected representatives and professional politicians, and the work of the administrative machinery of the state. The last of these has expanded enormously since the first appearance of representative government in the late eighteenth century. To appreciate the significance of these developments for contemporary understandings of democracy it is necessary to consider modern conceptions of government, representation and the relations between *the* government and other agencies involved in the governing of conduct. We begin with the idea of government.

Government

In political analysis the term 'government' is usually understood as referring to 'the supreme authority in states' (Aristotle 1988, III, 1279a 27). However, it is not difficult to identify other usages. For example, Aristotle also refers to 'the government of a wife and children and of a household' (Aristotle 1988, III, 1278b 37–8). This is a form of rule which he distinguishes both from the government of a state and from the rule of a slave by his master. In yet another usage the term refers to a rule over oneself. What these various usages have in common is a perception of government as what has been called 'the conduct of conduct',[1] that is, the regulation of the manner in which individuals manage their own behaviour. Government, in this sense, refers to the activity of regulating the conduct of oneself or of others (for example, of a household, a community or a state).

This more general sense of government, as the conduct of conduct, is important here for a number of reasons. First, while democratic governments regulate the conduct of their citizens by means of laws and other imperative commands, the behaviour of their populations is also governed in a variety of other ways. The significance of this point is easily overlooked. Indeed, the conventional understanding of government as supreme authority suggests that government should be seen as emanating from a single centre of control, albeit one which may itself be divided: for example, between executive, legislature and judiciary, between central and local government, or between the states of a federal system and the federal commonwealth itself. In fact, of course, government of the state and of the population which the state claims to rule is not restricted to the work of *the* government and its agencies.

The second point, and one which will particularly concern us in later parts of this chapter, is that the state can no longer be identified, as it was by Aristotle, simply with 'a body of citizens sufficing for the purposes of life' (Aristotle 1988, III, 1275b 21–2). On the contrary, the modern democratic state also includes substantial administrative apparatuses and a stratum of professional politicians, many of whom will be elected representatives of the people. Consequently, government of the state is a matter of regulating the conduct of a variety of public and private organisations and of elected representatives and other professional politicians, in addition to that of members of the population at large.

However, there is another aspect of Aristotle's understanding of government which should also be noted here since it continues to play a fundamental part in modern discussions of the government of a state. This concerns the idea of the *telos* or purpose of government, which Aristotle describes as differing according to the kind of rule that is in question. Thus the government of a household is 'exercised in the first instance for the good of the governed' while that of a slave is 'exercised primarily with a view to the interest of the master, but accidentally considers the slave, since, if the slave perishes, the rule of the master perishes with him' (Aristotle 1988, III, 1275b 39, 34–7) Here a true form of government is one which operates according to its own proper purpose or *telos*. In the case of the state, Aristotle maintains, the only true forms of government are those 'which have a regard to the common interest', the others being 'defective or perverted' (Aristotle 1988, II, 1279a 17–21).

The idea that the government of a state has its own distinctive *telos* has played a major role in the development of modern forms of government. Michel Foucault refers us to the work of anti-Machiavellian writers in the early modern period who aimed to combat what they understood to be Machiavelli's 'conception of the art of government which . . . took the sole interest of the prince as its object and principle of rationality' (Foucault 1991: 89). In its place, 'they attempted to articulate a kind of rationality which was intrinsic to the art of government, without subordinating it to the problematic of the prince and his relationship to the principality of which he is lord and master' (Foucault 1991: 89). What is at stake here, Foucault suggests, is the idea that the government of a state has its own autonomous rationality, an idea which he also contrasts to the view that the government of a state should be subordinated to religious or other external principles of legitimacy.

This view of the government of a state has significant consequences for the manner in which members of the underlying population are themselves regarded as objects of government. By identifying the relevant sense of autonomy in contrast to both the problematic of the prince and the idea of an order laid down by God, Foucault counter-poses it also to the most influential Western rationalisations of the subjection of large numbers of human individuals to the rule of a small number of others. As a result, the claim that the state has its own intrinsic rationality should be seen as undermining any suggestion that members of the population ruled by the state are naturally or essen-tially in a condition of subjection. The idea of an autonomous rationality of government suggests, in other words, that the popula-tion consists of free individuals, not of subjects. On this view, a true form of government would be one that rules a population of free persons, and a government which failed to respect their freedom would have to be seen as partial and therefore distorted.

This is not to say that the self-consciously anti-Machiavellian writers invoked by Foucault were supporters of popular govern-ment. On the contrary, they were commonly defenders of absolutism, arguing that the principal task of the ruler and his ministers was pre-cisely to promote the welfare of the community. My aim in introduc-ing the idea of an autonomous rationality of government at this point is rather to suggest that modern ideas of representative government have emerged within the framework of a broader view of government as having its own proper purpose or rationality, distinct from the per-sonal interests of the ruler or rulers, a view which was shared by advo-cates of (some form of) popular rule as much as by those who focused rather on the maintenance of order and the defence of individual liberty. Thus those who promoted the idea of government by the people were often far from advocating that the wishes of the major-ity should always prevail. It is for this reason, for example, that Rousseau takes care in *The Social Contract* to distinguish between the idea of the general will, which defines the proper concerns of the state, and that of the will of all, which is simply what the citizens might happen to agree upon. Or again, in his contributions to the debates over the design of the American constitution, James Madison presents himself as a 'friend of popular government'. But he nevertheless insists on the importance of protecting 'the permanent and aggregate interests of the community' from the 'dangerous vice' of faction, which he understands as, 'a number of citizens, *whether amounting to a majority or minority of the whole*, who are united and actuated by some common impulse of passion, or of interest, adverse to the rights of other citizens, or to the permanent and aggregate interests of the community' (Madison, Hamilton and Jay 1987 [1788] no. 10; emphasis added).

This modern view of the *telos* or purpose of government differs from that of Aristotle not so much in terms of its general content – the promotion of the common interest or some equivalent – but rather because of the need to consider that content in relation to the three-way separation noted earlier between the citizens, their representatives and the administrative apparatuses of the state. The effect of these divisions is to multiply the potential sources of governmental corruption: that is, of the diversion of the government of a state from its own proper purposes. In the modern world it seems that governments may be corrupted, like those of the Greeks, by the misguided political activities of the people, but they may also be corrupted by the political activities of the people's representatives and the conduct of public servants. This point brings us to the debates between the 'realist' theory of democracy and its radical democratic opponents.

Realists and radical democrats

The 'realist' theory of democracy is commonly associated with Joseph Schumpeter's *Capitalism, Socialism and Democracy*, first published in 1943, and with perhaps the most influential school of post-war American political science.[2] It can be briefly characterised as the view that the term 'democracy' should be seen as referring to the systems of government now in place in the major Western societies rather than to an abstract ideal against which those systems could be measured and perhaps found wanting. What makes these systems 'democratic' on this view is that they each represent a viable form of popular government, one that it is appointed by and ultimately answerable to the people themselves. What makes them viable is the fact that the participation of the people in their own government is nevertheless severely limited, in part by the practical impossibility of direct democracy in the government of large populations and in part by the ignorance and political apathy of the majority. The latter point in particular leads many 'realists' to insist that the restriction of popular participation is in fact a good thing, and that any attempt to expand participation much beyond its present limits would be detrimental to good government.

In the realist account of democracy, popular participation is regarded on the one hand as necessary and on the other as potentially so destructive that it must be kept strictly within bounds. Thus, one of the most important reasons why modern representative democracy is thought to be viable is that, for an overwhelming majority of the population, participation is limited to elections while, for the active minority, it is channelled through a range of competing parties, movements and pressure groups. As the image of channelling suggests, these latter are seen both as transmitting and as controlling popular pressure on government. Furthermore, in addition to these constraints on the effect of popular participation in government, there are in place a variety of other institutions (the judiciary, public service bureaucracies, the professions), which serve both to promote the common interest and to give the system some degree of stability.

In fact, while the self-conscious promotion of a 'realist' theory of democracy is largely a phenomenon of the mid- to late-twentieth century, the major elements of that theory have a much longer history. In the early years of this century, for example, Roberto Michels and Max Weber argued that mass democracy involved mass parties, and that these were inescapably hierarchical and bureaucratic organisations. To the extent that popular participation was channelled through these organisations and through competition between them, it resulted in only a limited degree of popular control over government. Or again, in contrast to what he thought of as democracy, Madison argued that representative government was a form of popular rule which had among its many advantages the fact that it kept the people out of any direct part in their government. It promised the advantages of popular government while avoiding the worst effects of popular participation.

This reference to the supposed dangers of popular participation brings us to the democratic critics of the 'realist' camp who tend not so much to reject representative democracy as to argue that it is not sufficiently democratic. Perhaps the most substantial issues in dispute here relate to the practicability and the risks of popular participation in government. The latter concern, which has been a feature of Western political thought from its beginnings in classical antiquity (Roberts 1994), focuses on the supposed apathy, ignorance and narrowly self-interested character of the relatively poor and uneducated majority: how could anyone seriously propose that significant areas of government be placed directly in the hands of such people?

Advocates of increased participation respond by insisting that the character of an individual is not immutable. In particular, the weaknesses attributed by realism to the poor, the ignorant and the uneducated can be transformed by the experience of participation in government. In his *Considerations on Representative Government*, John Stuart Mill argues that promotion of 'the virtue and intelligence of the people themselves' (Mill 1977 [1865]: 390) is among the most important tasks of government. He goes on to argue that a polity in which the people participate in their own government 'promotes a better and higher form of national character, than any other polity whatsoever' (Mill 1977 [1865]: 404). Through participation in public life the citizen:

> is called upon, while so engaged, to weigh interests not his own; to be guided, in case of conflicting claims, by another rule than his private partialities; to apply, at every turn, principles and maxims which have for their reason of existence the common good: and he usually finds himself associated with him in the same work minds more familiarized than his own with these ideas and operations, whose study it will be to supply reasons to his understanding and stimulation to his feeling for the general interest. (Mill 1977 [1865]: 412)

Such participation will be practicable, in MIll's view, only if the people have already achieved a considerable degree of civilisation or 'improvement'. But, when it can be implemented, participation in the conduct of public affairs serves both to discipline and to educate the citizens, thereby adding to the general level of improvement. For these reasons, Mill concludes, 'participation should everywhere be as great as the general degree of improvement of the community will allow' (Mill 1977 [1865]: 412). Carole Pateman advances a powerful contemporary version of this case in her *Participation and Democratic Theory*.

In fact, the argument that the risks to good government of properly organised popular participation are substantially less than the 'realist' case suggests, also serves to introduce a number of different points. First, to say that participation in decision-making develops the character of the participants themselves is to say that it functions as a powerful means of regulating their behaviour (Minson, 1993). Those who chair meetings, for example, are required to put at least some of their own convictions to one side in order to allow the alternative viewpoints represented in the meeting to be considered, otherwise they will be seen as abusing the power of the chair. Or again, the need for a quorum imposes a minimal discipline of attendance on members of a committee, while actual participation in its deliberations often requires a considerable degree of self-restraint, an ability and a willingness to conceal one's own views and a capacity to deal peacefully with periods of boredom and intense frustration.

It might be suggested that such requirements relate to the conduct of meetings in general and that, with minor variations, they apply to a wide range of contexts of participation. But there are often more specific requirements that determine the extent to which one will be able to participate at all. In many of England's North American colonies, where religious sectarianism played a major part in community life, the requirements of participation were often remarkably exclusive.[3] An obvious example in contemporary Western societies concerns the standards of dress and personal comportment which are thought to be appropriate in meetings of national and local government organisations, major political parties and in many other areas of public life. Iris Young notes that 'the norms of deliberation are culturally specific and often operate as forms of power that silence or devalue the speech of some people' (Young 1996: 123). What Mill and Pateman present as the educative aspects of participation can also be seen as favouring the interests of the 'better-educated white middle class' (Young 1996: 124).

I noted above that, while it is often understood as relating to the exercise of supreme authority, the term 'government' also has the broader meaning of the 'conduct of conduct'. We can now see that the promotion of participation is itself a form of government, imposing a variety of significant constraints on the behaviour of those concerned and requiring them to develop appropriate habits of self-control. Those who participate in making *decisions* which govern their lives invariably find themselves governed in ways they have not decided upon, and sometimes in ways that many recent advocates of increased participation would find oppressive. Participation appears to provide individuals with the opportunity to control their government, but it does so by subjecting their behaviour to control in other ways. Contemporary advocates of greater participation tend to emphasise the virtues of the former. Liberals and many 'realists', on the other hand, worry about the implications of the latter.

Finally, before turning to the question of the practicability of a more participatory democratic regime in the modern world, there is a further component of the anti-realist case to be considered. Both the arguments of Mill and Pateman concerning the educative qualities of political participation and my more general comments about its governmental character assume that there is more to participation than voting on particular decisions: it also involves participation in discussion and debate. Up to this point I have focused on the supposed impact of participation on the participants themselves, but open discussion and debate can also be seen as having an independent value of their own. Thus, while acknowledging that the promotion of widespread popular participation in government may not be realistic in the modern world, Jürgen Habermas nevertheless emphasises 'the original meaning of democracy in terms of the institutionalization of a public use of reason jointly exercised by autonomous citizens' (Habermas 1996: 23). This stress on the public use of reason is the core of the argument for 'deliberative democracy'.[4] The point to be noted here is that it represents an aspect of the anti-realist critique which does not depend on the quantitative involvement of the citizens in decision-making. What is at issue, rather, is the public character of political deliberation which is seen by its advocates as promoting the virtues of accountability, impartiality and rationality in political decision-making.

Many of the 'realist' reservations concerning the practicability of participation and public deliberation relate to the long-standing Western concerns about the supposed apathy, ignorance and other dubious characteristics of the majority which we have just considered. However, as the self-conscious adoption of the 'realist' label suggests, there is also a more general point at issue here. This concerns the view that the democratic proposals of those who are not of the 'realist' persuasion are quite simply unrealistic, a condition which is seen as resulting either from their carelessness and ignorance or, perhaps more seriously, from their romantic and utopian inclinations.

In fact, while realist theorists despair of the utopianism of those who advocate participatory and deliberative democracy, most of the latter maintain that their proposals for an expansion of democracy through popular involvement and openness in decision-making are entirely realistic. I have already referred, for example, to Pateman's influential *Participation and Democratic Theory*, first published in 1970. Pateman uses the case of industrial democracy, and the particular example of workers' self-management in Yugoslavia, to illustrate the practicability of extensive participation in the management of industry and also, more generally, to establish 'the validity . . . of the notion of a participatory society' (Pateman 1970: 108).

While the example of the former Yugoslavia seems rather less compelling in the 1990s than it may have been when her book first appeared, Pateman's discussion illustrates the general participatory strategy of using a variety of examples and other considerations to show that, contrary to the claims of the 'realist' theory, substantially greater involvement of people in decisions affecting their lives is both desirable and achievable in the societies of the modern West. Similarly, advocates of deliberative democracy maintain that, even in the absence of such increased popular involvement, a more open system of public deliberation would significantly improve the quality of political decision-making. From these standpoints, the 'realist' opposition to the participatory and deliberative ideal must be seen, if not as reflecting an actual hostility to democracy, properly understood, then at least as representing 'a considerable failure of the political and sociological imagination' (Pateman 1970: 111).

Leaders and organisations

'Realists' and most of their democratic critics agree that organisations such as political parties and interest groups are essential to the operation of democracy on a large scale. Political parties usually consist of elected members of national parliaments and other such bodies, a party machine consisting of employees and elected officers, some of whom occupy leadership positions within the party, and other party members. In modern discussions of democracy this state of affairs has been seen as posing two related sets of issues, concerning first the relationship between leadership and democracy, and second, the more general role of parties and organisations.

We can begin the discussion of leadership by observing that, like the system of representation in which it develops, democratic leadership combines the particular involvement of the people in their government through periodic elections on the one hand with the rigorous separation of the people from their government on the other. Acceptance of the former represents a common ground shared by the 'realist' theorists of democracy and by most of their democratic critics. Contrasting perspectives on the latter define one of the most important lines of debate between them. On the one side are those who follow Madison in regarding the separation of the people from any direct part in their government as one of the principal virtues of the system of representation. Thus the classical text of contemporary 'realism', Joseph Schumpeter's *Capitalism, Socialism, and Democracy*, criticises what Schumpeter calls the 'classical' doctrine because of its insistence on the decision-making role of the people. It would be more realistic, he argues, to say that what the people do is vote. He therefore proposes to define democracy simply as: 'that institutional arrangement for arriving at political decisions in which individuals acquire the power to decide by means of a competitive struggle for the people's vote' (Schumpeter 1976: 269). On this 'realist' account, then, it is the free and open competition for election to positions of leadership that most distinguishes democracy from other political systems, not the direct involvement of the people in their government.

On the other side are those who see democratic leadership, like representation itself, as an unfortunate necessity at best. In *The Social Contract,* Rousseau maintains that the will cannot be represented: 'it is either the same, or other; there is no intermediate possibility' (Rousseau 1968, book III, c16: 267). Whether we regard representation as a matter of desires, interests or something more complex (Pitkin 1967), the fact remains that the representative is not the person or persons represented, and in the difference between them lies the prospect of misrepresentation and even perhaps of betrayal. Many radical groups have attempted to minimise the difference between elected representative and represented through rigorous regimes of accountability or by insisting, like the German Greens, that representatives should be allowed to serve only for a strictly limited period.

The problem of the difference between representative and represented is more acute in the case of leader and follower. The leader must provide others with reasons for following, and that point alone is sufficient to ensure that the leader's concerns are not those of any individual follower. Nevertheless, the fact of difference between leader and follower provides ample scope for distrust of one by the other, tending in the extreme to the view that the essence of leadership is to betray. It was not uncommon for the Athenian democracy to punish those who had earlier been elected as leaders. However, there is a fundamental difference in this respect between the situation of modern democratic leaders and that of their classical predecessors. Unlike the leaders who were often cast aside by Athenian citizens,

their modern democratic successors are sustained by party and sometimes also by state machines. Thus modern leaders have greater scope
to pursue objectives which are not those of their followers while, for
the same reason, the followers have a much reduced capacity to bring
errant leaders to heel. This, indeed, is the import of Roberto Michels's
'Iron Law of Oligarchy': 'It is organisation which gives rise both to the
domination of the elected over the electors, of the mandatories over
the mandators, of the delegates over the delegators. Who says organisation, says oligarchy' (Michels 1962: 365). Democracy on a large
scale requires organisation and organisation makes democracy impossible: 'The democratic currents of history resemble successive waves.
They break ever on the same shoal. They are ever renewed. . . . It is
probable that this cruel game will continue without end' (Michels
1962: 371).

It would not be appropriate here either to endorse Michels's
pessimistic conclusion or to dispute it. The difference between
leaders and followers will sometimes be celebrated and sometimes
condemned, and a switch from one perception to the other may be
triggered by a variety of circumstances. My point, then, is not that
one perception is correct and the other false, but rather that the co-
existence of these contrasting perceptions of leadership and the persistent tension between them are precisely what we should expect to
observe whenever, in Paine's words, representation is 'ingrafted upon
Democracy' (1989: 170); whenever, that is, the people are said to rule
but without being able to rule directly.

Closely related points could be made about the more general role
of parties and other organisations: on the one hand, organisations are
necessary for the operation of democracy on a large scale while, on
the other, they are not always to be trusted. The first claim can be
pressed in a number of ways. It would be difficult, for example, for the
election of representatives to be contested on the scale of large
national populations without organised political parties of some kind.
Or again, the idea of a representative assembly acting on behalf of the
people would seem to imply that citizens should be free to organise
to make their views known to representatives, and indeed to each
other. A case for freedom of the press and other kinds of publishing
could be made on related grounds. Even the limited degree of participation required by the 'realist' theory of democracy depends on
the presence of organisations that provide citizens with the conditions
of effective participation.

Such arguments identify an essential role for parties, interest groups and other organisations in the operation of democratic government on a large scale. But, as with leaders, it is not clear that they can always be trusted to perform that role. In *Dilemmas of Pluralist Democracy*, for example, Robert Dahl notes that parties and other voluntary membership organisations 'are not mere relay stations that receive and send signals from their members about their interests. Organizations amplify the signals and generate new ones. Often they sharpen particularistic demands at the expense of broader needs' (Dahl 1982: 44). We might add that parties do not simply pick up and transmit the views of their members, perhaps with some modification. The need to secure membership and voting support does impose real constraints, but these constraints are far from being the only significant determinants of the behaviour of such organisations. The need to secure financial support (as distinct from individual membership) continues to promote other forms of influence on political activity in all Western democracies, most flagrantly, perhaps, in Japan and the USA.

Dahl goes on to argue that the dependence on organisations is largely responsible for four significant defects of contemporary Western democracies: the maintenance of significant political inequalities, the deformation of civic consciousness, the distortion of public debate, and the alienation of the people from final control over the agenda of government.

Here too, my point is neither to praise parties and other organisations nor to condemn them. They can be seen both as serving democracy and as distorting it, and a strong case can usually be made for each of these perceptions. The invocation of such conflicting views is part of the culture of representative democracy.

Government and bureaucracy

There is one further aspect of the role of organisations in representative democracy that should be considered before we conclude this chapter. My discussion so far has focused on what might be called the representational functions of organisations such as parties, social movements and interest groups, newspapers and radio and television stations. To leave the matter there would be to suggest that people are separated from their government primarily by the fact of representation: that representative democracy is essentially a matter of the people electing representatives, of representatives forming a government, and of the government issuing laws and other instructions which the people normally obey on the grounds that they have, albeit at some considerable remove, issued those instructions to themselves.

What is missing from such an account is a second major sense in which modern representative democracies separate the people from their government. In addition to a stratum of professional politicians, the modern democratic state also includes substantial administrative apparatuses. On the 'realist' account of democracy, in which the role of the people is restricted to the appointment of leaders, the most important issues here concern the relationship between politicians and these other governmental agencies. Max Weber's political writings place considerable stress on the tension between the politician and the bureaucrat in modern systems of government. The politician, in his view, regards bureaucracy as both an indispensable instrument of government and an independent (and sometimes insubordinate) centre of power.[5] In fact there is a more general tension here within modern governmental thought, since similar problems arise from state reliance on professions and corporations as instruments of government. Thus the politician's desire to make use of (and therefore to preserve) the organisational capacities of bureaucratic organisations, professions and corporations may well co-exist with a desire to undermine their status as independent centres of governmental control. This latter motivation provides much of the impetus for recent neo-liberal attempts to extend market arrangements into areas of public life that had previously been organised in other ways: for the privatisation of public instrumentalities or the introduction of competition and quasi-market regimes where privatisation is not regarded as expedient, for attempts to bring competition and market regulation into fields otherwise regulated by professional controls (law, medicine, academia), and for the promotion of generic managerial skills in place of bureaucratic specialisation within hitherto distinct public sector agencies.

What should be noted here is that this 'realist' perspective on relations between politicians and other agencies has been questioned on two distinct and (in many respects) opposed grounds. On the one hand, advocates of greater popular participation see the administrative apparatuses of the state as prime targets for democratisation. Thus David Held (1986) has argued for a 'double democratisation', encompassing the major organisations of both civil society and the state while Hirst (1993) advocates the devolution of many of the administrative functions of the state to self-governing associations of citizens.

On the other hand, public choice theorists have focused on two ways in which the proper conduct of government might be subverted by the institutions of representative government and its associated administrative apparatuses.[6] These are first, that government agencies which are supposed to promote the public interest might in fact be 'captured' by private interest groups, and second, that public servants and elected politicians alike will be tempted to use their control over administrative and other resources to promote their own private interests. Contrary to the participatory argument for greater popular involvement in administration, the first of these public choice concerns suggests that this would be a certain recipe for the capture by its clients of the agency concerned.

The second concern is closer to the participatory analysis in offering a critical perspective on the effects of the separation of the people from their government, but it does so without suggesting that popular participation itself might be seen as a solution. Taken together these elements of the public choice analysis suggest that the threat to good government should be addressed not by greater involvement of the people, but rather by minimising the scope for political corruption through the removal of issues from political control; in effect, by replacing government through state administration with government through market interaction.

Finally, I return to a point made at the end of my discussion of leadership and the representative functions of organisations. I suggested there that, rather than attempt to choose between the major competing accounts of these matters, we would do better to regard them as aspects of the culture of representative democracy. The same applies in the present case. In view of the contrasting understandings of democracy as involving either the direct or the indirect (and frankly rather distant) involvement of the people in their government, and the intimate connection of the second understanding with a powerful belief in the need to defend the true purpose of government from political interference by the people, we should not be surprised to find a range of distinct and sometimes incompatible perspectives on the democratic role of the administrative apparatuses of the state.

Notes

1   This usage derives from Michel Foucault's work on government. See Foucault (1988, 1991) and my discussion in Hindess (1995).
2   Sartori (1987) offers a forceful recent statement of the realist position. Pateman (1970) remains one the clearest 'democratic' critiques.
3   See, for example, Clark (1994), Shain (1994) and de Tocqueville (1994).
4   See Dryzek (1990); Fishkin (1991).
5   See especially 'The profession and vocation of politics' in Weber (1994).
6   See the short account of the public choice theory of the state in Dunleavy and O'Leary (1987).

References

Aristotle (1988) *The Politics*. Cambridge: Cambridge University Press.

Clark, J.C.D. (1994) *The Language of Liberty, 1660–1832: Political Discourse and Social Dynamics in the Anglo-American World*, Cambridge: Cambridge University Press.

Dahl, R.A. (1982) *Dilemmas of Pluralist Democracy*, New Haven, CT: Yale University Press.

Dryzek, J.S. (1990) *Discursive Democracy: Polities, Policy and Political Science*, Cambridge: Cambridge University Press.

Dunleavy, P. and O'Leary, B. (1987) *Theories of the State: The Politics of Liberal Democracy*, New York: Meredith Press.

Fishkin, J. (1991) *Deliberative Democracy*, New Haven, CT: Yale University Press.

Foucault, M. (1988) 'The ethic of care for the self as a practice of freedom', in J. Bernauer and D. Rasmussen (eds), *The Final Foucault*, Boston, MA: MIT Press: 1–20.

——(1991) 'Governmentality', in G. Burchell, C. Gordon and P. Miller (eds), *The Foucault Effect*, Chicago: University of Chicago Press: 87–104.

Habermas, J. (1996) 'Three Normative Models of Democracy', in S. Benhabib (ed.), *Democracy and Difference: Contesting the Boundaries of the Political*, Princeton, NJ: Princeton University Press: 21–31.

Held, D. (1986) *Models of Democracy*, Oxford: Polity.

Hindess, Barry (1991) 'Imaginary Presuppositions of Democracy', *Economy and Society*, vol. 20: 173–95.

Hindess, B. (1995) *Discourses of Power: From Hobbes to Foucault*, Oxford: Basil Blackwell.

Hirst, P. (1993) *Associative Democracy: New Forms of Social and Economic Governance*, Cambridge: Polity.

Madison, J., Hamilton, A. and Jay, J. (1987 [1788]) *The Federalist Papers*. Harmondsworth: Penguin.

Michels, R. (1962) *Political Parties: A Sociological Study of the Oligarchical Tendencies of Modern Parties*, New York: Collier Books.

Mill, J.S. (1977 [1865]) 'Considerations on Representative Government', in J.M. Robson (ed.), *Collected Works of John Stuart Mill*, Toronto: University of Toronto Press: 371–577.

Minson, J. (1993) *Questions of Conduct: Sexual Harassment, Citizenship, Government*, London: Macmillan.

Paine, T. (1989) *Thomas Paine: Political Writings*, Cambridge: Cambridge University Press.

Pateman, C. (1970) *Participation and Democratic Theory*, Cambridge: Cambridge University Press.

Pitkin, H.F. (1967) *The Concept of Representation*, Berkeley, CA, and London: University of California Press.

Roberts, J.T. (1994) *Athens on Trial: The Antidemocratic Tradition in Western Thought*, Princeton, NJ: Princeton University Press.

Rousseau, J.-J. (1968) *The Social Contract*, Harmondsworth: Penguin.

Sartori, G. (1987) *The Theory of Democracy Revisited*, Chatham, NJ: Chatham House.

Schumpeter, J. (1976) *Capitalism, Socialism and Democracy*, London: Allen & Unwin.

Shain, B.A. (1994) *The Myth of American Individualism: The Protestant Origins of American Political Thought*, Princeton, NJ: Princeton University Press.

Tocqueville, A. de (1994) *Democracy in America*, London: Fontana.

Weber, M. (1994) *Political Writings* (ed. Peter Lassman and Ronald Spiers), Cambridge: Cambridge University Press.

Wood, G.S. (1992) 'Democracy and the American Revolution', in J. Dunn (ed.), *Democracy. The Unfinished Journey: 508 BC to AD 1993*, Oxford: Oxford University Press: 91–106.

Young, I.M. (1996) 'Communication and the Other: beyond deliberative democracy', in S. Benhabib (ed.), *Democracy and Difference: Contesting the Boundaries of the Political*, Princeton, NJ: Princeton University Press: 120–35.

4 RACIAL AND CULTURAL DIVERSITY IN CONTEMPORARY CITIZENSHIP

Ann Coleman and Winton Higgins*

This chapter takes up communitarian, Foucauldian, and other critiques of liberal individualism but Coleman and Higgins set out to develop viable norms for some (provisional) form of socially or culturally embedded liberalism in a postmodern and global era. They argue that the liberal tradition of a social contract, stretching from John Locke to John Rawls, has promoted European imperialism in the past and a deceptive multicultural tolerance today. They draw on several contemporary critics of liberalism, including Tully, Clastres, Fanon, Said and Hall to support a harsh conclusion. The central problem of racism and intolerance is not how to prevent the Holocaust ever happening again; it is instead how to stop the long-standing ethnocide of disadvantaged cultures that is still proceeding today in the settler societies of Australia, New Zealand, Canada and the USA.

With few exceptions today's Western societies contain significant racial and cultural minorities. Equally striking is the inequality and

* We would like to thank Tony Nolan and Colin Tatz for the helpful comments and suggestions on an earlier draft of this chapter.

tension that typically exists between minorities on the one hand and the dominant groups and cultures in Western societies on the other. These blemishes challenge two of the fundamental assumptions underpinning Western nation-states: that citizenship is equal and inclusive, and that a nation consists of the bearers of a particular ethnicity or culture.

Three ideas have gained considerable acceptance in attempts to paper over the gap between the ideal of the unified nation and its fractured reality. First, citizenship as an ideal has been downgraded from the substantive participation in the political community that the nation-state represents, to mere formal and passive membership. For example, all Americans are said to be equal in enjoying the same 'rights' and being subject to the same laws, no matter how vastly unequal groups within this nation-state might be in all other respects (not least civic dignity, life chances and ability to influence the political process). Second, racial and ethnic conflict is presented as a timeless given of 'human nature' that enlightened education campaigns can ameliorate without reference to the specific historical wrongs which spawned them in each national history. Third, most Western societies now define themselves, in a presumed new age of 'globalisation', as 'multicultural'. All races and cultures within the nation are then supposed to be equal and equally included, and the nation-state itself culturally neutral.

Tolerance of difference, substantive equality and inclusiveness deserve their places as fundamental modern Western values. As aspirations they express the modern stage in the 'democratic revolution' that intensified with the French Revolution (Laclau and Mouffe 1985). The central problem we address here is whether the three ideas in the previous paragraph do these democratic aspirations justice. Do they adequately address the problems of racial and ethnic conflict, inequality and civic exclusion? Do they do so in ways that are likely to lead us towards ways of making citizenship substantively equal and inclusive in culturally diverse societies? Or do they actually obscure the specific historical and social sources of conflict, exclusion and subordination, and so lead us to ineffectual, purely cosmetic enhancements of modern citizenship? What better analytic strategies present themselves for conceiving of ways to make good the inter-ethnic shortfalls in modern Western citizenship?

We will first look at the historical origins of the modern West's ethnic conflicts and cultural diversity, which powerfully mould today's issues. Unlike more mainstream sociological treatments, we will analyse racism and ethnocentrism in a historical context from the specific point of view of modern ideals of citizenship and of *effective* membership of the political community that the nation-state stands for. For this purpose we need to focus on the predicament of indigenous peoples, which in important ways differs from that of migrant minorities.

In the second section we will look more closely at the objective mechanisms and subjective experience of exclusion and subordination on racial or ethnic grounds. In the third we will explore options in how to better conceive – and rise to the challenge of – equal and inclusive citizenship in culturally and racially diverse Western societies.

European 'civilisation' and monocultural expansion

Ethnic conflict between different tribes and nations does indeed extend back through recorded history. But less eye-catching peaceful contacts, settlements and institutionalised co-existences between groups have also been legion over this span of human affairs. In one of the most important recent contributions in this area, James Tully (1995: ch. 4, esp. 119–25) has isolated three 'ancient' conventions that gradually crystallised to facilitate inter-ethnic treaties, constitutions and a *modus vivendi*. First is the convention of mutual recognition of the various groups concerned and a willingness to listen to each other (*audi alteram partem*). Recognition encompasses what we today would call *sovereignty*, the right of self-government within and over a given homeland. The second convention requires the consent of all affected parties in whatever settlements and constitutional arrangements are arrived at (*quod omnes tangit ab omnibus comprobetur*). The third convention guarantees the survival and integrity of each group entering into the pact; none is to be assimilated or obliterated in any way. The principles of *recognition, consent* and *continuity* encapsulate these three crucial conventions.

The treaties and constitutional arrangements that emerged out of the application of these conventions during migrations and other contacts were untidy by ideal modern standards, as the most famous (the *Pax Romana* of the Roman Empire from Augustus) illustrates. Many tribes and nations could make up an over-arching political conglomeration and yet each could retain self-government, a distinct social system and sources of authority. There was no necessary one-to-one relationship between a territory and a single source of political authority, and all arrangements were typically subject to renegotiation as required by the principles of recognition and consent. In other words, no arrangement was ever final; the dialogue could recommence at any time.

At the dawn of European modernity political philosophers, and above all the founder of liberalism, John Locke (1632–1704), announced a quite antithetical approach to inter-ethnic contacts and constitutionalism, one that overturned the three conventions and flatly negated the principles of recognition, consent and continuity. Europe – and especially England – stood poised for a new period of massive imperial expansion into the Americas and Africa. As Tully (1995) argues, the new *modern constitutionalism* provided a convincing apology and compelling mission statement for imperial authorities in their typical practice of military incursion into the homelands of other peoples and the latters' extermination, subjugation, dispossession and assimilation.

Today's Western nation-states are living monuments to this modern constitutionalism, in the economic advantage they continue to reap from Europe's imperial expansion, in the perpetuation of the doctrine's basic premises in state policy, and in the intense ethnic and racial conflict (the dark side of the imperial inheritance) that troubles them. We must turn to this doctrine, its survival today and the practices it continues to inform, if we are to understand the specific nature of some of the most important ethnic conflicts, exclusions and inequalities that bedevil modern citizenship. Its analysis will take us much further than vague notions of a primordially intolerant human nature and of a brave new world of 'globalisation'.

The notion of contemporary 'multiculturalism' plays its own mischievous role in obscuring the contemporary patterns of ethnic conflict. It suggests that *all* inter-ethnic conflicts spring from the same source ('prejudice'), admit of the same solutions (acknowledgement and tolerance of cultural difference) and can be treated together. This approach obscures the drastic difference between the moral claims of indigenous peoples on the one hand and those of minority migrant cultures on the other. A broadbrush approach also blinds us to the uniquely aggressive nature of Western ethnocentrism, as we shall see.

Let us look briefly into the historical implications of modern con-stitutionalism, starting with Locke's cultural – and specifically agri-cultural – premises. Like most Western political theory, Locke's is intensely ethnocentric. We can assume that ethnocentrism (the belief in the superiority of the ways, culture or religion of one's own ethnic group over those of others) has accompanied ethnic conflict since time immemorial. But Locke's ethnocentrism had original features that would carry through into the main schools of Western political theory, into liberalism above all (Parekh 1994), up to and including our own time.

For Locke human cultures are not just variegated but *represent stages in human development*, and could be arranged on a scale from 'primitive' and 'brutish' (the indigenous cultures of prospective colonies and sources of slaves) at one end, to 'civilised' (that is, Euro-pean) at the other. Locke approvingly translates his French contem-porary Pierre Nicole thus:

> If one takes a general Survey of the World, one shall find the Bulk of Mankind buried in a Stupidity so gross, that if it does not wholly dispossess them of their Reason, yet it leaves them so little Use of it, that one cannot but wonder how the Soul can be depressed into so low a Degree of Brutality. What does a *Canibal, Iroquoi, Brasilian, Negro, Cafer, Groenlander, or Laplander* think on during his whole Life? The ordinary wants of the Body, and some dull ways of supplying them, Fishing and Hunting, Dancing, and Revenge on his Enemies, is the whole Compass of his Contemplations. (Quoted in Tully 1995: 89)

On this view Europeans are no mere aggressors: they represent the vanguard of human *progress* with a God-given mission to rescue the vast 'primitive' majority of humankind from its 'gross Stupidity'.

It is worth pausing here to observe the origins of modern European racism to which Locke contributed, not just in theory but also in prac-tice, in the latter part of the seventeenth century. As a government functionary concerned with the promotion of trade and as a share-holder in the Africa Company among other joint stock companies (Cranston 1957: 153–5, 399–406; Laslett 1988: 43), he promoted the slave trade and the cultivation of England's Caribbean and American colonies on the basis of slave labour. Today we regularly discern two types of racism based on cultural and biological differentiation respec-tively (for example, McConnochie, Hollinsworth and Pettman 1989: ch. 1). Locke's racism was unambiguously cultural. Only upbringing and education separate the 'brutish' Hotentot from 'a more *improved English*-Man', he opines (Locke 1975: 92).

Thereafter, however, the rise of natural science (botany, and then biology) provided a pseudo-scientific discourse in which to couch racist sentiments and imperial apologies. In 1770 – the year Captain Cook 'discovered' the east coast of Australia, at least 55 000 years after its inhabitants! – Locke's successor in liberal political philosophy, David Hume (1711–76), presents the new *biological racism*, which distinguishes itself from the former's cultural variety:

> I am apt to suspect the negroes, and in general all the other *species* . . . to be *naturally* inferior to the whites. There scarcely ever was a civilized nation of any other complexion than white, nor even any individual eminent either in action or speculation. No ingenious manufactures amongst them, no arts, no sciences . . . Not to mention our colonies, there are negro slaves dispersed all over Europe, of whom none ever discovered any symptoms of ingenuity. (Quoted in Tatz 1987: 40; emphasis added)

Ironically, neither the benefits of the finest British education nor racial superiority could save Hume from the breathtaking ignorance he reveals here of such well-known non-white civilisations as China, Persia, Egypt, Arabia, India, the Incas and the Mayas. More importantly, we should note the implicit claim that significant racial difference has a *biological* basis which determines cultural development and intellectual capacity.

The subsequent development of biological racism is now fairly familiar (see, for example, Tatz 1987: 40–4). In the nineteenth century some of the most 'advanced' white male minds found lifetime employment developing Hume's 'suspicion' into a scientistic hocus-pocus now known as 'scientific racism'. Elaborate correlations between variables such as cranial capacity, physiognomy, skin colour and hair type on the one hand and intelligence, criminality and sexual profligacy on the other predictably proved to the investigators' own satisfaction that European men like themselves were a superior species to all women and all non-Europeans. European men emerged as the exclusive bearers of Reason and therefore of civilisation and government, while the intellectual and moral handicaps of women and non-Europeans condemned them to either a deviant or childlike status in European male culture and institutions. Scientific racism and scientific sexism bubbled forth from one and the same test tube, one might say (see Lindkvist 1995: 13–14).

On these 'scientific' foundations extremely influential writers, above all Comte de Gobineau and Houston Stewart Chamberlain, erected theories of history in which natural racial inequality was the central variable. Among their other distinctions, they would become the direct progenitors of Nazism (Tatz 1987: 43–4). Partly through this discreditable association, and partly through later scientists' dismissal of the charlatanry of biological racism, the latter lost some of its grip on political elites and official ideology in Western countries. It lives on today at the level of popular prejudice, in pseudo-scientific backwaters (see, for instance, Hoberman 1997), and more significantly, as we shall see in the next section, in the subjective experience of racial subjugation and persecution.

The less familiar history of racism concerns its cultural dimension. In his classic essay on ethnocide, Pierre Clastres (1988: 53) points out that ethnocentrism is a standard component of all cultures, but Western culture is uniquely *ethnocidal*. It is so 'because it imagines itself and chooses to be *the* civilisation' with a God-given mission to suppress all cultural difference as bad by definition, and because Western societies have had powerful states capable of pursuing this mission.[1]

The ethnocidal impulse has moulded modern constitutional thought. Its European, male and imperial discourse continues, as Tully (1995) argues, to powerfully subvert social harmony and equal, inclusive citizenship in both European countries and in the colonial settler nations that their imperial expansion spawned: nations such as Canada, USA, Australia and New Zealand. Modern constitutional thought provided the moral alibi for European powers' bloody wars of conquest against non-Europeans, vast land grabs, and systematic attempts to obliterate indigenous cultures and peoples to make way for European 'civilisation'.

The father of modern constitutionalism and liberalism – the one who moulded them to the requirements of the imperial mission – was John Locke himself.[2] Prominent within Locke's living heritage today is his intellectual strategy to overturn the ancient principles of recognition, consent and continuity in inter-ethnic contacts. His strategy remains embedded in modern constitutionalism and liberal conceptions of citizenship in our own time.

Locke's contribution builds on his cultural racism and the ethnocidal conception that European 'civilisation' represents a vanguard culture with a mission to drag the rest of humanity along the path of Progress and so into European ways of life. His tale thus remains faithful to modernity's grand narrative, an epic that starts with 'the State of Nature' (represented by indigenous peoples) and terminates in Western European society based on private property and commerce (what early modern writers like Locke *mean* by 'civilisation').

The economic importance and moral claims of private property lay in its creating the social conditions and the incentive to 'improve' land and to exploit natural resources intensively.

> For I aske whether in the wild woods and *uncultivated wast* of America left to Nature, without any *improvement, tillage or husbandry*, a thousand acres will yield the needy and wretched inhabitants as many conveniences of life as ten acres of equally fertile land doe in Devonshire where they are well cultivated? (Locke 1988: 294; emphasis added)

'Improvement, tillage or husbandry' – European farming – thus becomes the sole basis of land rights and sovereignty. In Clastres' (1988: 57) analysis, it is precisely the West's 'system of economic production' that respects no territorial or moral boundaries to the exploitation of resources, and so propels an ethnocidal crusade against all peoples and cultures that stand in its way. Land not intensively exploited is thus 'vacant', *terra nullius*, and ought rightly to belong exclusively to whoever claims it for the purpose of cultivating it. This manoeuvre motivates land grabs on a basis that *withholds recognition of non-European land usage, rights and sovereignty* and *obviates the need for indigenous consent to European land grabs.*

Contempt for indigenous ways of life ('needy and wretched inhabitants' who indolently perpetuate 'uncultivated wast') provides the rhetorical cover for obliterating indigenous cultures, thus *overruling the principle of continuity in inter-ethnic contacts.* There is room for only one culture, and its enforcement leads to what Tully (1995: ch. 3) dubs 'the empire of uniformity'. Ethnocide spills over into genocide in Locke's advice about how to deal with indigenous resistance to Europeans' newfound 'property' and thus to 'civilisation' and law and order as such. Indigenous resisters declare 'War against all Mankind, and therefore may be destroyed as a *Lyon* or a *Tyger*, one of those wild Savage Beasts, with whom Men can have no Society nor Security' (Locke 1988: 274). As Tully (1995: 73) comments, '[t]his violent doctrine provided a major justification for the imperial wars against the Aboriginal peoples of North America'.

Locke's influence on the European takeover of North America –

a process that formed part of history's largest scale genocide, that in the Americas as a whole (Stannard 1992) – was strong, but his thought had not yet attained its later status as Moses and the Prophets of modern constitutionalism. By contrast we can appreciate the tragedy that later overtook the Australian Aborigines whose land the British 'discovered' in 1770 and 'settled' from 1788 when Locke's imperial liberalism had attained its epiphany and European racism was about to intensify in biological and scientific modes. The Australian case thus exemplifies the heritage of imperial liberalism.

Braced by the heady cocktail of this doctrine and scientific racism, the unholy alliance between colonial officialdom and feral white settlers slaughtered, poisoned, infected and starved Aborigines on a massive scale as it dispossessed them of an entire continent (Reynolds 1990) to make way for 'improvement, tillage and husbandry'. The post-colonial unholy alliance between state authorities and Christian churches interned many Aboriginal survivors in authoritarian settlements and missions where they were denied the most elementary civil rights, including the right to cultural continuity. The invaders' heirs cultivated the image of Aborigines as an archaic dying race to cover their hoped-for disappearance (Smith 1980), which would make way for the new ethnically and racially compact nation. Between 1910 and 1970 Australian governments authorised a new mechanism for promoting this self-fulfilling prophecy in the enforced removal of Aboriginal children from their families, though the practice itself pre-dates official blessing and continued after its withdrawal (the Human Rights and Equal Opportunities Commission, or HREOC, 1997: Part 2). Both morally and legally, this policy in itself constitutes an act of genocide (HREOC 1997: 270–5, Tatz 1999). Needless to say, the principles of recognition, consent and continuity were conspicuous by their absence in the making of the new nation.

The Australian case also exemplifies how this sort of history powerfully moulds the present arrangements and conflicts, and how perceptions of that history underpin contemporary power relations (see Tatz 1999). At the time of writing, a fierce debate is raging over the significance of the atrocities that go to the heart of Australia's emergence as a modern nation, and over whether it is best to induce an officially sanctioned amnesia about such matters in order to propagate a mythic history 'we can all take pride in'. Three centuries ago John Locke prescribed in advance how that history of a proud modern nation-state should be written.

> In summary, Locke's account covers over the real history of the interaction of European imperialism and American Aboriginal resistance. The invasion of America, usurpation of Aboriginal nations, theft of the continent, imposition of European economic and political systems, and the steadfast resistance of the Aboriginal peoples are replaced with the captivating picture of the inevitable and benign progress of modern constitutionalism. (Tully 1995: 78)

In the third section we will see how vital a shared history is to a common citizenship.

As Ross Poole (1996: 425–8) argues, Aborigines were morally and legally entitled to recognition of their sovereignty in 1788, and they are likewise entitled to it now (Thompson 1990: 313–29). In 1989, the High Court overthrew the *terra nullius* doctrine in the Mabo case, which is often hailed as a breakthrough in the recognition that Aborigines originally owned the continent. Yet the court heavily circumscribed the present effectiveness of the land rights so recognised and – true to its residual loyalty to modern constitutionalism – incoherently refused to acknowledge the Aborigines' sovereignty over the continent they are now supposed to have owned. This refusal reinforces the claim of the successors to the conquering imperial authorities, the Australian government, to sole sovereignty and thus to the right to unilaterally reduce or extinguish Aboriginal land rights.

At the time of writing the Australian Government is in the process of exercising its presumed exclusive sovereignty to extinguish much of what is left of 'native title', signally without negotiating with Aborigines. The government thus continues to follow the Lockean agenda of 'securing property' in the interests of white expropriation and exploitation of natural resources, and of systematically negating the principles of recognition, consent and continuity. The refusal to recognise Aboriginal sovereignty means that only a very small fraction of living Aborigines – those who can show continuous connection with particular areas – will enjoy any claim to compensation for the whole people's loss of the entire continent (Mansell 1992; Burgmann 1997; Marr 1998).

As with indigenous peoples of other stolen continents, historical dispossession and ethnocidal persecution mould the daily reality of the surviving Aboriginal population in Australia. On any index of social development, standard of living and quality of life they present a drastic contrast to the population as a whole (see Castles 1994: 411–16): they constitute a Third World enclave in a First World nation and are thus excluded from effective citizenship. In this way they now

attract a further dimension of systematic discrimination, marginalisation and vulnerability as a mere 'welfare problem'. Beckett (1989: esp.
120) has dubbed this discriminatory mechanism 'welfare colonialism'.
In public discourse the historical wrongs that have left Aborigines in
their plight and give rise to their moral right to reparation disappear
without trace in a history-less problematic about social administration
(see Rowse 1994). The new dimension of vulnerability is highlighted
by the emergence of today's unholy alliance between 'economic rationalism' and racist populism, an alliance formed in the search for
appropriate targets for welfare and general budgetary cuts, not least
targets that can be identified and stigmatised by race.

So far we have concentrated on the problem of indigenous peoples
and citizenship in the modern nation-state in order to establish its true
proportion. This proportion is entirely lost when the rhetoric of multiculturalism throws indigenous peoples into the catch-all of 'ethnic
and racial minorities'. Mutual obligations clearly exist between the
nation-state on the one hand and migrant groups and refugees on the
other. On the state's side, these obligations include recognition of cultural and racial diversity, protection of minorities and the humanitar-
ian obligations on stable, affluent nations to respond to gross human
need, political upheaval and persecution elsewhere. But here the
nation-state is not dealing with the *only* peoples whose ethnicity
derives from *its own* territory, over which they have a valid claim to
sovereignty, or with peoples whose dispossession was a condition
precedent to the nation-state's own emergence (Rowse 1994). Racial
discrimination and enforced cultural assimilation are always wrong.
But the claims of indigenous peoples and those of migrant minorities
are morally incommensurable, since the latter do not rest on dispossession and the violation of sovereignty.

Before we turn to the problem of how these incommensurable
claims might be met in a genuinely equal and inclusive citizenship, we
need to pause to consider the contemporary mechanisms and experience of racial and ethnic subjugation to appreciate how inequality and
exclusion fracture the nation today.

Race, identity and power

Race is a social construct. It is an intellectual, cultural and propagan-
distic artefact that a dominant group produces. As McConnochie,

Hollinsworth and Pettman (1989: 5–6) succinctly sum up the mechanism involved, it:

constructs racial categories or systems . . .
assigns particular traits or characteristics to those racial categories,
allocates individuals to particular racial groups, and
assumes that all individuals who have been classified within that
    racial group exhibit the traits or characteristics of that group.

Perceptions of race develop around – but simultaneously excuse or camouflage – relations of socio-economic and political *power*. Race is thus an effective reinforcement of power relations. For instance, biological racism (like biological sexism) seeks to disguise relations of power by dressing them up as a natural hierarchy. The relation of power thus appears inexorable and beyond political contestation. For European invaders, the metropolitan states that supported them and the quasi-European regimes that assert exclusive sovereignty in the lands that the invaders 'discovered' and 'settled', the idea of race became the core concept in their moral alibi and worldview. Miles (1988a: 73–7; 1988b: 13) refers to this phenomenon as 'the racialisation of populations', whereby race is constructed as a real category, a part of the natural order, and so a basic pre-social *a priori* which society and government must simply work with rather than question. Above all, it has functioned as a mechanism of subjugation and exclusion. Right from the beginning perceptive dissenters saw through the ruse (Lindkvist 1995; Reynolds 1996, 1998), but they suffered the usual fate of lone voices protesting against vested interests.

The intriguing question is why this racialisation has played such a pivotal role in the history of modern European conquest, ethnic subjugation and exclusion, when non-European and pre-modern European conquerors and dominant groups have demonstrated no such need? The citizens of ancient Athens, for instance, straightforwardly excluded from their ranks anyone who was female, not born in Athens or a slave; there was no need for an elaborate metaphysics of race in this birthplace of democracy. The literature that contributes partial and complete answers to this question is vast and covers several academic disciplines. We will have to take a short cut through it to suggest reasons for racialisation which help us understand contemporary exclusions.

Two intellectual and cultural shifts at the dawn of modernity appear significant. One was the rise of nation-states and their long depen-dence on a forced and largely mythical cultural homogeneity in the 'imagined community' they claimed in some sense to represent. The legitimacy of the state depended precisely on its claim to express a coherent folkloric soul and destiny (Anderson 1991). Clastres (1988: 54–7), who anticipated this now famous thesis, suggests that domestic ethnocide (forced cultural homogenisation within the nation-state) was the historical pre-condition to European states establishing them-selves, and they took this *modus operandi* with them in their wars of conquest outside Europe. In other words, 'the empire of uniformity' began at home before it spread to the colonies, where visible racial difference functioned as a marker of cultural difference, of the out-group which did not fit into the homogeneous community. As state power became more consolidated and European influence established the nation-state as the obligatory form of political organisation around the world, Clastres suggests, the ethnocidal imperative became less pressing.

The other important cultural shift in early modernity concerns *iden-tity*, which is the focus of much contemporary sociological, philo-sophical and psychoanalytic reflection on racism, as well as today's 'politics of recognition' (closely associated with 'the politics of differ-ence' or 'identity politics'). All human beings need a sense of who and what they are and where they belong in order to function socially and psychologically. We gain this sense of ourselves partly by perceiving who or what we are *not*. 'To assert an identity is to distinguish oneself or one's group from others', Stokes (1997: 5) writes. As Charles Taylor argues in his important contribution (1995; see also 1989b: ch. 1), iden-tity depends less on individual self-understandings than on others' *recognition* or acknowledgement of who and what we are.

In Taylor's account the denizens of pre-modern Europe founded their identities in particularisms such as status in social hierarchies, gender and locality, and their sense of self rested on a religious world-view which made them bit players in a pre-written cosmic drama. Their self-esteem (as we might say these days) resided in a sense of *honour* in the way they discharged their role in the social hierarchy and cosmic order. But modernity undermined local community, social hierarchies and religious meanings. The modern ethos, especially after the Enlightenment of the eighteenth century, expressed itself not only in secular terms but also in formally universal categories such as the self-interested 'individual' and the 'citizen'. Self-esteem now rested on the *dignity* attached to these universal categories. The problem was, where would modern identity find the oppositions or particularisms – who or what we are and are *not* in particular – to support individual and group identity?

Universal categories such as 'individual' and 'citizen' had an important political role to play in the assault on pre-modern hierarchies. But given the skewed relations of power in modern Western society, effective (and often formal) citizenship continued to be exclusive and exclusionary. The universalism of the modern categories had to be negated in practice to preserve the power of the modern social elites. Enshrining the European male as *the norm* – as what defines humanity as such – proved the way forward here. *Difference* (deviation from the norm) signified *defect*. As we saw above, non-Europeans and women were thus constructed as defective, and so excluded from citizenship, and indeed from individualship (at least in the public domain of political and socio-economic affairs). Physical and biological difference signified defectiveness, 'natural' subordination and exclusion.

Racist and sexist discourse along these lines operates among other ways through the mechanism of *recognition* and *self-recognition*: people tend to gain a self-image from the feedback they get from their social contacts. This mechanism establishes individual and group identity, and indeed an ongoing process that Stuart Hall (1994: 122) accounts for as 'identification'. Subjugated and excluded identities (or 'subjectivities') are thus continually produced and reproduced. As Taylor explains:

> our identity is partly shaped by recognition or its absence, often by the *mis*-recognition of others, and so a person or group of people can suffer real damage, real distortion, if the people or society around them mirror back a confining or demeaning or contemptible picture of themselves. Nonrecognition or mis-recognition can inflict harm, can be a form of oppression, imprisoning someone in a false, distorted and reduced mode of being. (Taylor 1995: 225)

In other words, 'the way we imagine ourselves to be seen by others' at least partially moulds our self-definition (Hall 1994: 122).

Racist identification operates on both objective and subjective levels by means of what Stokes (1997: 7) calls 'identity traps' which 'fix' a group's identity in confining and demeaning ways. He gives obvious examples of its workings on the first level; the apartheid system in South Africa or the 'protection' system deployed against Australian Aborigines. Both of these 'confined subordinate groups to a narrowly defined range of behaviours, social and economic activities or political options'.

On the cultural level, difference feeds into the construction of 'otherness', of defining the excluded groups as essential outgroups. Non-Europeans and women are characterised by their otherness to the normative group, European men. More broadly, Edward Said (1978) has shown, in his well-known contribution, how Western culture constructed 'orientalism' after the European 'discovery' of other lands. The notion of 'the Orient' sets up a fictitious compact which includes most non-European cultures and regards them as exotic, mysterious and barbarous. Orientalism does violence to the enormous range of actual non-European cultures. But by this very mechanism, European culture embellishes Western identity by 'setting itself off against the Orient as a sort of surrogate or underground self' (Said 1978: 3; see also Pratt 1992).

At its most insidious, the subjective experience of racism rests on the excluded population's internalisation of 'the imperial gaze'. Stuart Hall (1994: 122; see also Bhabbha 1994) argues that 'The way we imagine ourselves to be seen by others' becomes a significant building block in a subordinated identity, or what Taylor (1995: 226) calls 'an imposed and destructive identity'. As Franz Fanon expresses the *experience* of subjugated identity:

> I discovered my blackness, my ethnic characteristics; and I was battered down by tom-toms, cannibalism, intellectual deficiency, racial defects, slave-ships, and above all else, above all: 'Sho' good eatin' . . .

> I am overdetermined from without . . . I am being dissected by white eyes, the only real eyes . . . I am fixed. (Fanon 1968: 79, 82)

Through its imposition of subjugated identities in particular, racism can undermine resistance to the imperial project. For this reason the politics of recognition is a most important front in the struggle for just and pluricultural societies and nation-states, and for equal and inclusive citizenship.

Towards inter-cultural citizenship

Like any other grand narrative, the story about globalisation contains many mythic elements. Among them we hear how the nation is becoming irrelevant; how globalisation – some sort of inexorable metahistorical force – is stripping the nation-state of its sovereignty; and how once ethnically distinct nations have become indistinguishable multicultural polyglots, a transformation which impels the state into a benign cultural neutrality.

A moment's reflection should suffice to expose this picture as historically untenable. With the end of the Cold War, nationalist agendas and minority ethnic claims on nation-states have become the main source of international conflict. Nation-states themselves promote many of the policies and institutions that today stand for economic internationalisation and supranational co-ordination, such as the World Trade Organisation and the European Union (EU) respectively. The most salient focus of political mobilisation and of ever more numerous policy demands remains the state. For each of us, our membership of a particular nation constitutes a vital aspect of our identity. Both sexes can now be called on to join the nation's defence forces, which literally makes the nation a community to die for.

We should thus be wary of any suggestion that the nation, national identity, sovereignty and citizenship are matters of diminishing importance. On the contrary, as the burgeoning literature on nationalism suggests (see Couture, Neilsen and Seymour's 1996 survey), these matters today enjoy unprecedented salience. But we also need to be on our guard against mythic and simplistic notions of what sort of political community the nation has represented and represents today. Fortunately, none of the genocidal missions of nation-building we reviewed in the first section succeeded in creating a real 'empire of uniformity'. Indigenous peoples have resisted the imperial incursion with determination (see, for example, Reynolds 1990) and survived to press their claims today to unprecedented (though still mixed) effect. Equally unsuccessful were the strenuous efforts to impose uniformity on cultural minorities within the metropolitan powers themselves, such as Great Britain (see, for example, Colley 1992). Moreover, migration stimulated by industrialisation more than outweighs the attempts at cultural standardisation. Apart from Iceland, genuine examples of ethnically homogeneous modern nations – *ethnic nations* – are and always have been rare, no matter how fatally attractive this fantasy has proved in, for instance, the break-up of Yugoslavia and the Soviet Union.

When we turn to theories of nationhood, we discover another fantasy, one intimately bound up with modern constitutionalism. It vies with that of the ethnic nation in mythifying the political community that the nation represents and in obfuscating its historically determined character. This is the *civic* conception of the nation, which suggests, at least in its liberal version, that the nation is a voluntary collection of individuals (Couture, Neilsen and Seymour 1996: 2–10). The *civic nation* would then be a purely political and legal entity with no ethnic reference or cultural definition, and so appears to offer a culturally inclusive citizenship. But again, a moment's reflection will lead us to see that we are *born* into our national identities; they are not matters of choice. Even if we emigrate, we may not choose to abandon the national identity we are born into, or it may prove impossible to abandon.

The power of the civic myth of nationhood derives from a prevalent mode of thought known as *foundationalism*, the idea that entities like nations spring into being in a single founding moment, such as the proclamation of the American Declaration of Independence on 4 July 1776 or the proclamation of the Commonwealth of Australia on 17 September 1900. More often than not, such founding acts are mythified as social contracts whereby 'all citizens' established a constitution that once and for all constitutes the nation on the basis of just principles and effective institutions for good government.

However, any actual nation will always have a real history which extends back long before its posited founding moment and which will impel important changes after it. It is this history that determines a nation's actual ethnic, cultural and racial composition, and the ethnic distribution of wealth and power. Constituting a nation can never be a new, ethnically innocent beginning as the civic myth – aided and abetted by unreflected 'multiculturalism' – would have us believe. 'The idea that the modern state should in principle be neutral between different cultures is a liberal fantasy', Poole (1996: 417) argues; '[S]tate power in the modern world necessarily has a cultural dimension.' By suppressing reference to real ethnic inequalities and exclusions, the civic ideal actually creates a more insidious 'logic of exclusion' (Couture *et al.* 1996: 5) than the ethnic one.

With very few exceptions each modern nation does in fact have a dominant or majority culture, and a public culture – its language of political debate, administration, institutional resources and traditions – based on that dominant culture. This is not just a fact of life, but a virtual necessity for democratic governance, effective administration and the coherent dispensing of justice. This ethnically specific public culture will inevitably also provide much of the ritual, symbolism and tradition of national identity, and in this event minority cultures cannot aspire to equality (Poole 1996: 419–21).

The challenge of modern statecraft consists in working from this realistic starting point towards an equal and inclusive citizenship under conditions of cultural racial diversity. The politics of recognition rather than of assimilation then provides the key to overcoming exclusion and alienation. We can adopt Couture, Neilsen and Seymour's (1996: 47) provisional concept of the nation as 'a pluricultural political community' to encapsulate this ideal, but we will need to specify it carefully below. At the very least, this approach will demand, for instance, an education system and other public institutions that equip all citizens with the cultural skills to participate effectively in a culturally specific public life and yet continue to practicse the way of life of a minority culture into which they may have been born and in which they continue to find important roots of their identity. Beyond that, we have to enter into the specific structure of cultural diversity in each nation to identify the statecraft appropriate to it in attaining the goal of equal and inclusive citizenship.

To come to grips with how cultural diversity is structured, in each case we have to jettison the mainstream conception of multiculturalism, for two reasons. First, it abstracts and distracts us from the particular, historically determined character of the relations between ethnic groups in each nation-state, and so trivialises the particular rights of the separate groups. We have thus to go beyond the bland concept of multiculturalism to get at some of the most difficult and important questions of nationhood and a culturally diverse citizenship, as we shall do below. Second, the concept of multiculturalism falsifies what a culture is and how it relates to others. It treats cultures as analogous to billiard balls: that is, as entirely separate from one another, having definite boundaries and internally homogeneous, even to some extent static (Wolf 1982: 4–7). But the vast majority of cultures have formed and still develop *in inter-action with others* which they overlap; and there is usually a process of negotiated change going on within them (Clifford 1988; Carrithers 1992; Tully 1995: 9–10, 46–7). This alternative, *inter-cultural* view of cultures and their inter-actions has vital consequences for the politics of recognition and the issues of personal and national identity, as we shall see.

We have already touched on the connection between identity and cultural recognition in the second section of this chapter. Ross Poole nicely summarises what is becoming today's conventional wisdom about the dependence of each individual's (and citizen's!) identity on culture:

> Culture exists in the language we use, the forms of social interaction in which we are at home, the symbols we recognise as ours, even in the food we eat and the games we play. It is one of the most significant determinants of our identity . . . [T]he forms in which we interpret ourselves are those provided by our culture. We are born into a culture: we acquire it through the family, social interaction, and education . . . [O]ur cultural identity provides the context within which we choose, and sometimes the criteria on which we choose; it is not itself an object of choice. Culture in this sense is embodied in our sense of individual identity and in the social practices within which we exist. (Poole 1996: 411)

Even on a liberal view, then, the state cannot hold itself aloof from the cultural life of its citizens, for two reasons. First, the basic liberal requirement that each individual should be accorded equal respect demands *recognition of the various cultures that in effect constitute the individuals in question* (Taylor 1995). Second, there is no individual freedom without choice, and the individual relies on her or his cultural framework to set out, interpret and evaluate the choices available to her or him (see Kymlicka 1995: ch. 5).

On an inter-culturalist view, of course, individuals can be the bearers of more than one culture, and many individuals function both in a minority culture into which they were born and in the dominant public culture. But not all can or will do so, and inter-culturalism cannot relieve the state – especially its arms that regularly have dealings with the public – of its duty to communicate with its culturally diverse citizens as far as possible and necessary in the latter's community languages.

More importantly, the state must respect the collective right of each community to continue to practise and develop its culture, at least so long as this does not encroach on individual integrity and the right to forsake a particular minority culture. This requires substantial public investment in many forms of cultural survival, not least education and media. There are two bases for this imperative. First, as we have seen, nothing less can accord citizens equal dignity and effective freedom. Second, cultural diversity has attracted virtually consensual recognition in the West today as a value in itself for any national community, not least in promoting freedom by offering a greater variety of perspectives and individual choices. Cultural diversity in the West is now not just a fact but a fundamental value (Tully 1995: 207; Cope and Kalantzis 1997). As such, it should be promoted by the state as representative of the political community which both embodies and espouses it.

All these perspectives, it should go without saying, strongly condemn survivals and revivals of 'the empire of uniformity' in the guise of assimilationist policies and the rhetoric of the ethnic nation. Even more fundamentally, these perspectives place a solemn obligation on the state to combat racial and ethnic discrimination, vilification and violence energetically.

We insisted above on the need to account for the varieties of inter-ethnic relationships in each nation and in particular to attend to the historically-derived rights of indigenous peoples as separate and prior to those of migrant minorities. Our general discussion of minority rights and the state's corresponding obligations applies to indigenous peoples as well, but such minority rights and state obligations by no means exhaust the unresolved issues between them and post-colonial nation-states. These issues go to the core of what a nation-state is, what the dignity of its citizens consists in, and the basis on which it can seriously claim to be a political community.

In early modern times, Thomas Hobbes (1996) first launched the liberal foundational myth that the state arises from a pact that rationally self-interested men entered into for the purpose of securing their persons and their property. Mutual fear and individual self-love (rather than solidarity born of common origins and a common history) then provide the sole basis of loyalty. History, as we saw, is irrelevant to the founding social contract. In keeping with the individualistic spirit of our own time, the idea of the nation-state resting on foundations of enlightened self-interest enjoys a renewed modishness on the Anglo-American intellectual horizon in particular. Again, a moment's reflection will reveal the implausibility of this view. Citizenship requires all sorts of civic disciplines and personal sacrifices, such as upholding the law and paying taxes for purposes that often go beyond a given individual's self-interest. As we saw, modern nations from time to time also call on their citizens to risk their lives in wartime for the common good, a nonsensical demand to make on a citizen whose obligations are supposed to be born of – and entirely bounded by – considerations of individual survival and self-interest.

In an important argument Charles Taylor (1989a) rejects this view of the nation-state. A regime whose legitimacy rested purely on self-interest would be 'nonviable', a state that had no right to be taken seriously by its putative citizens or other nations. National identity, solidarity or sentiment – what Taylor calls 'patriotism' or 'patriotic identification' – is an essential foundation of any nation, not least a *free* nation where freedom means self-rule. 'Patriotism is somewhere between friendship, or family feeling, on one side, and altruistic dedication on the other . . . Functioning republics are like families in this crucial respect, that part of what binds people together is *their common history*' (Taylor 1989a: 166; our emphasis). Further,

> the bond of solidarity with my compatriots in a functioning republic is based on a sense of shared fate, where the sharing itself is of value. This is what gives this bond its special importance, what makes my ties with these people and to this enterprise peculiarly binding, what animates my 'virtu,' or patriotism. (Taylor 1989a: 170)

This understanding of the nation makes its history – not least its origins – the basis of national identity, of 'viability' itself.

Inevitably history-writing has always been a deeply political practice. Ursula Le Guin (1989: 83) recalls Julius Caesar's declaration, 'It was not certain that Britain existed before I went there', as an early example of the technique of 'organised forgetting'. Modern imperial cultures have similarly seen to the forgetting of non-European histories that pre-date the European 'discovery' of the lands concerned. Colin Tatz (1995, 1999) points to the significance of 'the politics of remembering and forgetting' and 'denialism' in suppressing national histories of racist atrocity. The corollary of these mechanisms is the 'organised remembering' – imperial history-writing – that Said (1978) points to. Today national histories, not least in post-colonial settler states, are thus bitterly contested.

How can national identity survive incontestable episodes that bring deep shame on the nation, as the Holocaust does for the Germans? One desperate but vain manoeuvre is to deny or trivialise it, as a handful of revisionist German historians do (Tatz 1995), thereby only compounding the national disgrace. A more honourable approach is to own the problem and deal with it head on; to confront it, analyse it, learn from it and make what practical and symbolic atonement one can in negotiation with the aggrieved group. The German philosopher

Jürgen Habermas (1989: 232–3) reflects on the meaning of the Holocaust for Germans today:

> Our own life is linked to the life context in which Auschwitz was possible, not by contingent circumstances but *intrinsically*. Our way of life is connected with that of our parents and grandparents through a web of familial, local, political and intellectual traditions that it is difficult to disentangle – that is, through a historical milieu that made us what and who we are today. None of us can escape this milieu, because our identities, both as individuals and as Germans, are *indissolubly* interwoven with it.

As Ross Poole (1996: 436) adds, questions about our individual, direct culpability or benefit from past wrongs are beside the point. It is *national identity* that links us – 'intrinsically' and 'indissolubly' in Habermas's well chosen words – to the wrongs in our national history.

Post-colonial settler nations (above all those of North and South America and Australasia) face a yet more serious problem for national identity than even the German one. Modern Germany emerged well before the Holocaust and gained nothing from it; the latter was in no way *constitutive* of the German nation, and it came to an abrupt end in 1945. But historically nations such as Australia, Canada and the USA would not exist in recognisable form without the genocides that preceded and accompanied their foundation, and which continued under the auspices of the new nation-states to the benefit of their non-indigenous citizens as a whole. Given Aboriginal peoples' continuing subjection to official practices, policies and neglect that perpetuate their drastic rates of mortality, infant mortality, violent deaths, deaths in custody, and removal of children by 'welfare' authorities, *these genocides have never really ended*. David Stannard (1992: xiii), the eminent historian of the American genocide, makes this chilling observation: '[T]he important question for the future ... is not "can it happen again?" Rather, it is "can it be stopped?" For the genocide in the Americas, and in other places where the world's indigenous peoples survive, has never really ceased.' There is no more fundamental question for the viability of a post-colonial settler state and the dignity of its citizenship.

Conclusion

In many ways, Western modernity has represented a regression in inter-ethnic contacts and cohabitation, in that it has resiled from the pre-existing principles of recognition, consent and continuity. Forced cultural homogeneity at home and imperial conquest abroad, together with their ethnocidal and genocidal impulses, mark the emergence of the modern nation-state and remain active ingredients in our national and constitutional traditions. Paradoxically, these traditions also equip us with the vocabulary and the aspiration for an antithetical, *democratic* citizenship, one based on substantive equality and inclusiveness.

If modern citizenship is to live up to its pretences, let alone up to our democratic aspirations, this paradox has to be resolved. Modern Western societies are racially and culturally diverse, and the quickening pace of migration is bound to make them even more so. Racial and cultural diversity belong to the same category of intractable difference as gender. The challenge today consists in upgrading our notions of equality and inclusiveness to make them adequate to societies characterised by difference of this order. The task will involve us in carefully rooting out all our concepts and practices based on the implicit male European norm that has driven past and present intolerance, inequalities, exclusions and subjugation.

At the same time, we need to reconceive the nation-state – the political community – in which we seek equal and inclusive citizenship. We have to understand that each nation, like all communities, has historical origins that we need to account for if the nation-state itself is to be viable. Each national history reveals a particular pattern of ethnic conflict and a consequent pattern of inter-ethnic moral claims. In post-colonial nation-states in particular, the moral claims of indigenous people are likely to be especially weighty when historical accounts are honestly rendered. Only the nation-state which duly processes all such claims, according to the demands of recognition, continuity and consent, can itself make a claim on its citizens' patriotic identification that is its lifeblood.

Notes

1   Clastres (1988: 52) distinguishes between genocide and ethnocide thus: 'Ethnocide is the systematic destruction of the modes of life and thought of people who are different from those who carry out this destructive enterprise. In short, genocide kills their bodies, while ethnocide kills their spirit. Of course, in either case it always means death, but a different death: direct physical suppression is not cultural oppression with long term effects, depending on the oppressed

minority's capacity for resistance. It isn't a choice here of the lesser of two evils.' Further, both genocide and ethnocide depend on setting up the oppressed minority as different, as 'other'. But the genocidal mind sees this other as absolutely bad, calling for complete extermination, whereas the ethnocidal one (with evangelical missionaries in the forefront) sees this otherness as redeemable by complete assimilation into the culture of the dominant group (Clastres 1988: 52–3). Clearly, though, there is a great deal of overlap between both the spirit and the practice of these two destructive impulses. See also Kuper (1981).

2   Our critique of Locke and his heritage builds on Tully (1995: ch. 3).

References

Anderson, Benedict (1991) *Imagined Communities: Reflections on the Origin and Spread of Nationalism*, 2nd edn, London: Verso.

Beckett, Jeremy (1989) 'Aboriginality in a Nation-State: The Australian Case', in M.C. Howard (ed.), *Ethnicity and Nation-Building in the Pacific*, Tokyo: United Nations University.

Burgmann, Verity (1997) 'John Howard's Assault on the Black Armband View of History', paper delivered to the Popular Education Conference, Centre for Popular Education, University of Melbourne.

Carrithers, Michael (1992) *Why Humans Have Cultures: Explaining Anthropology and Social History*, Oxford: Oxford University Press.

Castles, Ian (ed.) (1994) *Year Book Australia*, no. 76.

Clastres, Pierre (1988) 'On Ethnocide', in *Art and Text*, no. 28. pp. 51–8.

Clifford, James (1988) *The Predicament of Culture: Twentieth Century Ethnography, Literature and Art*, Cambridge, MA: Harvard University Press.

Colley, Linda (1992) *Britons: Forging the Nation*, London: Pimlico.

Cope, Bill and Mary Kalantzis (1997) *Productive Diversity: A New Australian Model for Work*, Sydney: Pluto.

Couture, Jocelyne, Nielsen, Kai and Seymour, Michel (1996) *Rethinking Nationalism* Calgary: University of Calgary Press.

Cranston, Maurice (1957) *John Locke: A Biography*, London: Longmans.

Fanon, Franz (1968) *Black Skins, White Masks*, London: Paladin.

Habermas, Jürgen (1989) *The New Conservatism: Cultural Criticism and the Historical Debate*, Cambridge MA: MIT Press.

Hall, Stuart (1994) 'The Question of Cultural Identity', in *The Polity Reader of Cultural Studies*, Cambridge: Polity.

Hobbes, Thomas (1996) *Leviathan*, Cambridge: Cambridge University Press.

Hoberman, John (1997) *Darwin's Athletes: How Sport Has Damaged Black America and Preserved the Myth of Race*, New York: Houghton Mifflin.

HREOC (1997) *Bringing Them Home: National Inquiry into the Separation of Aboriginal and Torres Strait Islander Children from their Families*, Commonwealth of Australia: HREOC.

Kuper, Leo (1981) *Genocide: Its Political Use in the Twentieth Century*, New Haven, CT: Yale University Press.

Kymlicka, Will (1995) *Multicultural Citizenship*, Oxford: Clarendon Press.

Laclau, Ernesto and Chantal Mouffe (1985) *Hegemony and Socialist Strategy*, London: Verso.

Laslett, Peter (1988) 'Locke the Man and Locke the Writer', in his edition of John Locke, *Two Treatises on Government*, Cambridge: Cambridge University Press.

Le Guin, Ursula (1989) *Dancing at the Edge of the World: Thoughts on Words, Women, Places*, New York: Harper & Row.

Lindkvist, Sven (1995) *Antirasister–Människor i kampen mot rasismen 1750–1900*, Stockholm: Albert Bonniers Förlag.

Locke, John (1975), *An Essay Concerning Human Understanding*, edited by Peter Nidditch, Oxford: Clarendon Press.

——(1988) *Two Treatises on Government*, edited by Peter Laslett, Cambridge: Cambridge University Press.

McConnochie, Keith, Hollinsworth, David and Pettman, Jan (1989) *Race and Racism in Australia*, Wentworth Falls, NSW: Social Science Press.

Mansell, Michael (1992) 'The Court Gives An Inch But Takes Another Mile: The Aboriginal Provisional Government Assessment of the Mabo Case', *Aboriginal Law Bulletin*, vol. 2, no. 57: 4–8.

Marr, David (1998) 'John Howard Has Been Walking Towards This Moment All His Life', *Sydney Morning Herald*, 4 July.

Miles, Robert (1988a) 'Beyond the "Race" Concept: The Reproduction of Racism in Britain', in Gill Bottomley and Marie De Lepervanche (eds), *The Cultural Construction of Race*, Sydney: Sydney Studies in Society and Culture.

——(1988b) *Racism* (London: Routledge).

Parekh, Bhikhu (1994) 'Superior People: The Narrowness of Liberalism from Mill to Rawls', *Times Literary Supplement*, 25 February.

Poole, Ross (1996) 'National Identity, Multiculturalism, and Aboriginal Rights: An Australian Perspective', in Jocelyne Couture, Kai Nielsen and Michel Seymour (eds), *Rethinking Nationalism*, Calgary: University of Calgary Press.

Pratt, Mary Louise (1992) *Imperial Eyes: Travel Writing and Transculturation*, London: Routledge.

Reynolds, Henry (1990) *The Other Side of the Frontier: Aboriginal Resistance to the European Invasion of Australia*, Melbourne: Penguin.

——(1996) *Aboriginal Sovereignty: Reflections on Race, State and Sovereignty*, Sydney: Allen & Unwin.

——(1998) *This Whispering in our Hearts*, Sydney: Allen & Unwin.

Rowse, Tim (1994) 'Aborigines: Citizens and Colonial Subjects', in Judith Brett, Jim Gillespie and Murray Goot (eds), *Developments in Australian Politics*, Melbourne: Macmillan.

Said, Edward (1978) *Orientalism*, London: Routledge & Kegan Paul.

Smith, Bernard (1980) *The Spectre of Truganini*, Sydney: ABC Books.

Stannard, David (1992) *American Holocaust: Columbus and the Conquest of the New World*, New York: Oxford University Press.

Stokes, Geoffrey (1997) Introduction, in G. Stokes, *The Politics of Identity in Australia*, Melbourne: Cambridge University Press.

Tatz, Colin (1987) 'Race and Inequality', in Randal Stewart and Christine Jennett (eds), *The Three Worlds of Inequality – Race, Class and Gender*, Melbourne: Macmillan.

—— (1995) *Reflections on the Politics of Remembering and Forgetting*, monograph, Centre of Comparative Genocide Studies, Macquarie University, Sydney.

—— (1998) 'Race Relations in the 21st Century', *Sydney Institute Quarterly*, vol. 2, no. 3: 40–44.

—— (1999) *'Genocide in Australia'*, Canbera: Australian Institute of Aboriginal and Torres Strait Islander, Studies.

Taylor, Charles (1989a) 'Cross-Purposes: The Liberal-Communitarian Debate', in Nancy Rosenblum (ed.), *Liberalism and the Moral Life*, Cambridge, MA: Harvard University Press.

—— (1989b) *Sources of the Self: The Making of Modern Identity*, Cambridge: Cambridge University Press.

—— (1995) 'The Politics of Recognition', in C. Taylor, *Philosophical Arguments*, Cambridge, MA: Harvard University Press.

Thompson, Janna (1990) 'Land Rights and Aboriginal Sovereignty', *Australasian Journal of Philosophy*, 68, pp. 313–29.

Tully, James (1995) *Strange Multiplicity: Constitutionalism in an Age of Diversity*, Cambridge: Cambridge University Press.

Wolf, Eric (1982) *Europe and the People without History*, Berkeley, CA: University of California Press.

5 THE CHANGING STATE AND CHANGING CITIZENSHIP

Michael Muetzelfeldt

This chapter analyses the implications for a reduced sense of citizenship and narrower sense of democratic politics in the practice of economic liberalism in the 1990s. In several English-speaking countries, privatising formerly public authorities, implementing the purchaser-provider split in benefit delivery, and contracting out diverse services has seen advocacy groups excluded from any input into public decision-making. Community service obligations in service-provision contracts rest on a much-reduced sense of what is public about public interests. In practice, ordinary citizens have borne the risk of unexpected costs and paid for differences between a holistic sense of public interests and an individualistic and aggregative sense of public interests. This anti-democratic shift in the practical working of a welfare state has therefore entailed reducing citizens to being market-oriented customers. The chapter concludes that what is most important today is to insist that any sense of citizenship and democracy must be considered political and debatable rather than an unreflective expression of either traditional welfare state or economic efficiency agendas.

There is a strong move by governments in English-speaking liberal democratic states to adopt market and contractual approaches to restructuring public management. These approaches are based on a separation of government as purchaser of goods and services from the public or private agencies that provide them. This is referred to as the purchaser-provider split. Under this model, small core government agencies purchase services from other organisations which are contracted to be providers. These providers may be government-owned businesses, non-government organisations (such as welfare agencies), or private sector businesses. In effect, the model involves setting up a market or quasi-market (Le Grand and Bartlett 1993: 10) in which potential providers compete for contracts from government, and the contracts specify exactly what goods or services are to be provided, and on what terms.

In *Reinventing Government*, Osborne and Gaebler (1992) call this 'steering not rowing'. This evocative image expresses the separation of governmental control from the work of delivering services. Despite the over-simplification inherent in this image, and the criticisms of their ideas (see Goddard and Riback 1998), this book popularised the idea that the government sector could be managed just like the private sector. In the USA, Vice President Gore headed a 'reinventing government' task force, and in the Australian state of Victoria the newly elected Kennett Government used Osborne and Gaebler as the basis for its radical restructuring of the government sector (Alford and O'Neill 1994). New Zealand and Victoria provide case studies of such restructuring. These cases are described in some detail in Boston, Martin, Palot and Walsh (1996) and Alford and O'Neill (1994). The Australian Government set up a Competitive Tendering and Contracting Branch in the Department of Finance and Administration to 'facilitate greater and more effective use of competitive tendering and contracting, maximising efficiency and reducing complexity of government purchasing, and improving business access to the government market' (Department of Finance and Administration 1998). Early moves in this direction were also taken in Britain based on the Next Steps report (HMSO 1988; Harden 1992; Hood 1996; Next Steps Team 1996). Other countries have adopted contractualism in varying degrees, and with sometimes important variations (Bouchaert and Verhoest 1999).

Government's use of market mechanisms in politics, public administration and policy-making is transforming the state. This in turn changes the notions of citizenship and democracy that are associated with state practices. The new discourse of citizens as stakeholders and clients resonates with moves throughout the Anglo-American countries to restructure public sector organisations around client focus and customer service. This market-based notion of citizenship stands in contrast to the citizenship of rights and obligations that was expressed in the bureaucratic welfare state. As notions of citizenship change, so does what counts as democratic access and influence.

The bureaucratic welfare state model and its policy practices contained taken-for-granted assumptions about democracy and citizenship. These assumptions are now up for debate for several reasons. In this chapter, I discuss the impact of the changing policy framework and the increasingly rapid and widespread restructuring of the public sector, especially through privatisation and contracting-out. This is leading to shifts in the boundaries between the public and private sectors, and between the state and civil society. The legitimacy of interest group politics is being contested, and the welfare state's patterns of politics are becoming less effective or relevant. The notion of political as well as social citizenship is being redefined. New political purposes, constituencies and rhetorics are needed, in order to engage with government's drive to minimise its responsibilities.

Citizenship and the bureaucratic welfare state

From the 1960s to the late 1970s, the welfare state was in the prime of its life. It was well established as a project but had not yet had to face the challenges of managerialism and contractualism. At this time, the welfare state was widely recognised to be a mixed blessing. On the one hand, it provided mechanisms through which governments, if they had the will, could deliver a range of universal and targeted benefits with a high degree of due process, public acceptance and perceived social effectiveness, and where states provided major universal benefits that were paid for through taxation systems that were seen to be fair in principle and in practice. This enhanced social integration, or at least social incorporation into the state and its welfare project. However, on the other hand, the welfare state was seen by its supporters to fall short of its own principled ambitions. Questions were raised about its actual effects on cross-class redistribution (Titmuss 1976) and about its capacity to become an agent for social control (Morris and McIsaac 1978; Day 1981). Many on the left came to see the welfare state as a two-edged sword, and became apprehensive about their own place working 'in and against the state'

(London Edinburgh Weekend Return Group 1980). Feminists, too, increasingly saw the welfare state as deeply patriarchal, and debated whether or not this was one of its essential features. In Australia, feminists working in state bureaucracies – 'femocrats' – opted to engage from within the state with its patriarchal biases, and achieved some apparent success (Yeatman 1990). Apparently independently of these debates about political strategy, in organisational studies the dysfunctions of bureaucracy had been recognised and seen to be important (Gouldner 1954; Merton 1957; Blau and Scott 1962).

Today the welfare state's supporters too easily disregard these problems as they close ranks in the face of the challenges from managerialism and contractualism. However, this closing of the ranks is in my view poor strategy. Supporters of a redistributive and socially integrative pluralistic society need to do more than defend an old system that they themselves know to be flawed. They need to actively debate the questions that the advocates of market and market-like mechanisms have raised, and find new ways of building state systems so as to achieve the ends that they always sought, and which they knew were not being fully delivered by the welfare state.

As part of this new debate, I consider that the welfare state's consequences for citizenship need to be considered, because these provide key tests of the socio-political effectiveness of any state system. There are some major criticisms of the ways in which the bureaucratic welfare state shaped citizenship. According to public choice theory, the welfare state is said to: favour producers rather than consumers of state services; advantage particular politically articulate interests that form alliances with (or, in the view of the neo-liberals, 'capture') those producers; and in consequence lead to uncontrolled and unwarranted growth of welfare services for so-called 'sectional' interests, which is against the so-called 'national interest' (see Niskanen 1971; Dunleavy and O'Leary 1987: ch. 3; Victorian Commission of Audit, or VCA, 1993a). The welfare state is said to undermine self-reliance and the freedom to act autonomously, which are key features of active citizenship (Saunders 1993). In their overview of the current Anglo-American literature on citizenship, Kymlicka and Norman (1994) argue that this literature now generally accepts the New Right's argument that the Marshallian programme of the post-war welfare state breeds passivity and dependence, and that this is a bad thing. They note various responses to the critique of Marshall, all of which advocate a citizenship that includes active responsibilities and virtues.

The matter is probably more complex than is recognised by either the neo-liberals or most of the proponents of the rather idealistic alternative programmes summarised in Kymlicka and Norman. The welfare state never successfully engaged with the issue of winning informed public consent to its specific redistributive programmes. While 'everyone knew' that the taxation/welfare system was redistributive, the details of which groups won what, and at whose expense, were never clear. There were two reasons for this: in part, it was because there was no perceived need for accountability at that level of detail; but it was also because the fiscal data needed for such accounting were not available. The funding of programmes from consolidated revenue, together with rolling deficit budgeting, made such detailed accounting unnecessary, unavailable, and in the end undesirable from the point of view of the nation-building policy leadership and those who thought they benefited from their decisions.

I do not question the good intentions and capacity of much of the nation-building policy leadership. Corbett is probably generally correct when he speaks of the 'careful, honest, intelligent use of regulatory power by public sector managers and staff' (Corbett 1992: 102). However, behind the welfare state's benevolence lay its paternalism. The effect was not just to reduce people's capacity to look after themselves, as simplistic rightist critics argue. Much more importantly, it reduced their capacity to consent willingly and actively to positive, redistributive and socially constructive programmes, as Saunders (1993) comes close to saying. Most individual voters and political constituencies have had their dominant political experience and political education within the frame of the redistributive taxation/welfare system. They have no background in, or knowledge about, deciding whether the specific benefits of public goods are worth the specifically stated costs. And they are not familiar with the political processes of coalition building that are necessary to mobilise public support for such public goods. Their citizenship capacities have not been developed to appreciate the possible 'win-win' benefits of specific redistributive policies, because in the welfare state specific redistributions mostly took place under the table of generalised nation-building.

So now it is difficult to mobilise and deploy voters and constituencies to support what seems to be the general good when proposed taxation cuts, crack-downs on 'welfare cheats' and Community Service Obligations (see below) are used as rhetorical political devices to attack redistributive fiscal policies and welfare provisions.

This critique of the bureaucratic welfare model does not mean that we should accept market-based policy-making: Corbett is correct when he says 'It is illusionary to suppose that reliance on market forces can mean the abandonment of reliance on government' (1992: 102). But it does mean that policy systems need to be devised that overcome the weaknesses in both the bureaucratic welfare state and the market-like policy framework that is replacing it. This chapter now examines the market-based approach, and then turns to examine possible alternatives to both.

The changing public sector

Budget-driven managerialism, dating from the late 1980s, involved establishing organisational divisions and sections as budget centres and sub-budget centres. In turn, this brought tight budget restrictions, some contracting-out, and fewer middle-level staff (often while increasing the number of senior managers). As a result, planning and day-to-day public sector operations became heavily budget-driven, and organisational practices increasingly fell outside what was generally understood to be best for the public good.

One response to this has been to adopt a customer service orientation, in which the mission of serving the public interest was replaced by the mission of satisfying clients or customers (Barton and Marson 1991; Woodhouse, Conner and Marson 1993). Some public sector managers have adopted this new market-oriented approach with enthusiasm, taking pride in their turning away from public sector values. Writing from Canada, McDavid and Marson note the 'buoyant' mood of:

> the entrepreneurial civil servant. Creativity, a willingness to take risks, responsiveness to clients, and a political flexibility were characteristics of this new breed. Such persons would have much in common with their private sector counterparts. Serving something as abstract as the public interest would not be a part of their personal agendas. (1991: 9)

These authors note that when politicians (whom they call 'elected clients') do not fit well into their model of 'the well-performing government organisation', they should not be able to stand in the way of the 'emerging cultures of service quality' (McDavid and Marson 1991: 12).

This overlaying of customer service on to budget driven management can be characterised as a shift from an organisation that is driven by funding to an organisation that is driven by its customer focus: from a partially commercial to a fully commercial organisation. In its extreme form, it involves abandoning any sense of public interest that cannot be measured by customer or client responses. And, completely in character with economic rationalist views of how and why the state should function, it involves discrediting politics in favour of the market as the only legitimate mechanism through which interests can be expressed and articulated (Muetzelfeldt 1992).

In Australia, the Kennett government in Victoria was the first to move strongly in this direction, setting a lead that other governments are following. Drawing on the approach coming from Auster and Silver (1979), the Victorian government's agenda-setting Commission of Audit Report starts from a premise that 'There is no fundamental difference between the delivery of government services and the running of a private sector company' (VCA 1993a: 184), in effect '[rejecting] social goals and social utility as factors in public spending' (Carney 1993).

This has pernicious social effects. Amongst other things, it changes and potentially diminishes citizenship and other social rights. For example, to replace heavy rail suburban trains with light rail trams might increase customer satisfaction as measured by overall patronage rates and market research of actual patrons, but it could exclude some groups of physically disabled people from using public transport. Or again, such diminution is clear in a government proposal to increase the inoculation rates of infants and children by reducing the childcare and maternity allowance payments to parents who did not have their children inoculated, and by making bonus payments to general practitioners if 90 per cent of the children they saw were immunised (Meade and Montgomery 1997; Middleton and Parsons 1997). That is, instead of the state protecting health levels through legislation, it is asking people to act in the public good in return for private financial benefits.

The use of such market mechanisms to achieve the public good involves a shift in the relationship between the citizen and the state. The state is withdrawing from situations in which it might have provided support for those citizens who need it: for example, disadvantaged parents – who, because of personal difficulties or traumas, do not keep up with the relatively complex immunisation schedule for their children – will be further disadvantaged by the state through having their financial benefits reduced.

The contested legitimacy of interest group politics

Through the policy process, the state is always involved in constructing, shaping and allocating public values and public goods. It may do this directly (for example, through regulation) or indirectly (for example, by structuring markets in particular ways); but do it, it will. This leads to the questions of how, by whom, and in whose interests public values will be chosen and public allocations will be made. That is, it leads to the question of politics. I discuss this with particular reference to the Kennett government in Victoria, which is one of the most full-blown examples of the contractual approach.

The Kennett government's programme involves denying the relevance or legitimacy of public political debate in several ways. It does this through the purchaser-provider split, through the marketisation of public-private relations and interactions, and through so-called 'best practice benchmarking': that is, making inter-state comparisons of costs and services in ways that discount the possibility of policy diversity.

The VCA proposed the purchaser-provider split as a basic tenet. According to this principle, policy-making and regulatory functions should be clearly separated from service-provision functions, and within service functions there should be a distinction between those governing service provision ('steerers') and the service providers ('rowers'). The intent is to establish a market in service outputs. Services should be identified and contracted for in terms of results, outputs or outcomes, instead of in terms of input costs. They should be purchased by government, which, through its monopoly purchaser position, has the market power to make and regulate policy. They should be provided by organisations that are clearly separate from the purchaser and wherever possible in competition with other providers (VCA 1993b: 2).

One purpose of this is to minimise the hazard of 'capture' of government decision-making by interest groups associated with service-providers who would then collaborate with client groups to demand increased services at increased cost (Dunleavy and O'Leary 1987: ch. 3; VCA 1993a: iv). Who are these interest groups? The VCA identifies the following sources of threats that the purchaser-provider split is designed to guard against: the department, in contrast to 'the interests of the government and the community as a whole'; 'providers of inputs, particularly labour inputs'; 'lobby groups seeking funding for narrow sectional interests, to the detriment of the general community'; and 'direct interference and therefore undue lobbying . . . from lobbyists (including unions)' (VCA 1993b: 3). The intent is to deny the legitimacy of, and reduce the political influence of, interest groups (including unions) that the government does not support.

Critics of the 'steering not rowing' approach argue that public interests, public values and public accountability become seriously compromised when public services are delivered by organisations that have a purely contractual relationship with government. They emphasise the distinctive requirements of public management that make it different from private sector management, and argue that those distinctive requirements cannot be met using pure private sector models.

For example, Pollitt (1993: 149–55) gives a list of key requirements of public management, and compares the different values that underlie public and private management. He also emphasises that in public sector organisations, managerial techniques such as strategy, budgeting and the rationing of services should be based on the assessment of needs through political processes of bargaining, balancing and reconciling different interests, rather than being based on maximising profit through market processes. For Pollitt, 'Public accountability goes beyond the idea of just holding to account. It requires the public manager to find ways of giving account, in many different forms and at different levels. Caution and propriety must not be allowed to stifle experiment and responsiveness to the public' (1993: 151). Advocates of contracting-out reject these criticisms. They argue that the public interest – and especially that part of the public interest that is served through smaller and more efficient government, and stronger financial and performance accountability – is strengthened through competitive performance-based contract arrangements. This view in effect ignores or denies any public interest that is more than the sum of the individual interests of people directly involved in a transaction: as John Major said, 'Public services are there for only one thing – to serve the user' (quoted in Lawson and Walker 1994: 85). The view that public interest is no more than the sum of individual interests mirrors the assumption of micro-economics that the total utility in a society is no more than the sum of individuals' utilities resulting from their transactions. In short, by downplaying any intrinsically *public* interest, advocates of contracting-out position themselves firmly within the market paradigm, using the market not just as a mechanism for implementing policy efficiently, but as the criterion by which policy objectives should be set.

Advocates of contracting-out argue that public interests – such as subsidies and protection for needy or disadvantaged client groups – can be explicitly recognised, costed and built into contracts through Community Service Obligations (CSOs), which are otherwise seen as an efficient way of achieving the 'need to regulate to obtain desired outcomes'. CSOs are delivery requirements for services or products that government has decided should be provided for a variety of social and economic public interest reasons, even though that would not happen in a purely market-driven situation. Government as a purchaser specifies these obligations in its contracts with providers and provides funding for them (Steering Committee on National Performance Monitoring of Government Trading Enterprises 1994). Examples may be: uniform standard letter postage rates throughout the country, regardless of the distance between, or isolation of, the source and destination; provision of disabled access on mass transport vehicles; interest-free deferred payment options for low-income electricity consumers who fall behind in their payments; and subsidised telecommunication rates for businesses in sparsely populated rural areas. In order to achieve desirable policy objectives, such as uniform postage rates, governments offer CSO payments to service delivery contractors in return for providing public benefits that the market by itself would not provide.

CSOs aim to provide transparent government policy intervention through clear and direct costing for clear and specific benefits. They are intended to give government explicit control over its policy decisions by avoiding historical, accidental or hidden subsidies through concealed transfers of benefits or costs. They also aim to make government more transparent by making explicit the costs and intended benefits of policy decisions. In effect they aim to subject government itself – as well as the agencies that provide services on its behalf – to greater scrutiny and accountability. They assume that market decisions about the allocation of goods and services are the norm, and that any deviation from these market decisions needs to be explicitly declared, costed and justified. In effect, they attempt to ensure that certain public interests are protected in a policy environment based on market or market-like exchange relations between self-interested individuals and organisations, rather than on the nation-building or welfare-state view that society is or should be held together by complex, implicit, multilayered and essentially political connections between citizens. However there may be broader, less obvious, but very important features of public and political accountability and public interest that remain unspecified in contracts and agreements.

One aspect of this that is beginning to be recognised is the question of risk management and risk allocation. Contracts that fail to specify which party carries which risks may end up displacing on to service users risks that previously had been carried by departments and other public agencies as part of their broad and implicit commitment to public service. For example, contracting shifts the risk of satisfactory performance from the government to the contractor. In school mainenance contracts in USA, 'The contractor's assumption of responsibility for a project's outcome far exceeds that required under a standard contract for goods and services. "Performance" means the contractor is obligated to deliver the promised savings or make up the difference out of pocket' (Engeleiter 1997).

Another aspect of this concerns the public interest in quality service not only to the direct clients, but to clients' families and the broader community. In Britain, non-government community sector organisations such as the National Autistic Society (NAS) are successfully winning human service delivery contracts on the basis of a commitment to wide-ranging quality assessment processes (covering a range of matters from staff selection and training through to surveys of staff and client satisfaction) that in effect aims to ensure that broad public interests are met (NAS 1993). NAS has grown rapidly in the last few years, winning tenders over private sector providers; these tenders are based on quality and public interest, rather than price.

The purchaser-provider split is said by its proponents to reduce costs, which in turn is assumed to be a primary aim of government in the late 1990s. Whether this model will indeed do this is increasingly open to doubt. Hodge (1996) found in an extensive review of the literature that competitive tendering and contracting-out produced significant improvement in economic performance in only a few areas, such as rubbish collection and office cleaning. He found no significant improvements in most areas of government service, such as health and education, which aimed to achieve complex objectives in a complex and unpredictable environment. In addition, any efficiency improvements that are found may result from displacing costs off budget, for example, on to staff, clients, or other public agencies (Muetzelfeldt 1995). It may well turn out that, as more of the implicit services (including risk management) previously provided by public service agencies are written into contracts, contracted private sector agencies will be even less efficient than well structured public sector agencies. A shift in emphasis from costs and efficiency to quality and effectiveness may dissolve many of the currently perceived differences between public and private service delivery agencies.

One of the basic methodologies of the VCA is the comparison of the levels of expenditure and service in Victoria against those in other states of Australia (especially New South Wales and Queensland). So-called best public sector practice – in effect, the minimum benefit that any other state has chosen to provide in any specific field – is to be striven for in Victoria. In education, 'best practice' was said by the VCA to be the lowest cost per school pupil. This in effect removes from Victoria any say in its own policy. There is no recognition that Victorians could decide that they would prefer to pay more for education, or pay less for roads, or contribute more taxes, or whatever. According to this policy-making methodology, Victoria should not aspire to more public benefit than any other state chooses to provide. Only if other states introduce policies that are more beneficial should Victoria do the same. In short, the active political choices that should be available are denied in the name of generalised managerial and economic decision-making. This removes political choice and discretion not only from community interests and interest groups, but also from the government.

The central matter here is the attempted removal of legitimacy from the political notions of interest group and constituency, and their replacement with the avowedly apolitical notion of customer. This involves a contest over concepts, legitimate knowledge, organisational practices, and hence social/political effects. At core, it is a contest over the notion of citizenship.

What is a citizen?

As part of its move towards a client focus approach to the delivery of government services, the British Government introduced a *Citizen's Charter* (1990), which has the proclaimed aim of empowering citizens in their dealings with public sector agencies. This might also be seen as a way of increasing external pressures on the public sector to improve its performance. There is a strong assumption in the *Citizen's Charter* that 'the citizen' means the individual who is directly receiving the service. It says: 'And if things go wrong? At the very least, the citizen is entitled to a good explanation, or an apology. He or she should be told why the train is late, or why the doctor could not keep the appointment' (*Citizen's Charter* 1990: 5). That is, it is assumed that the public sector is there to serve individual members of the public, rather than to serve a group of people or the public good. This involves a change to the notion of citizen: from the ideal of a fully participating member of the society to the practical function of a recipient of government services. Despite its shortcomings, the bureaucratic welfare state at least aspired to cultivate and respect the citizenship ideal, while the market-oriented contractual model has replaced that ideal with the much more mundane, limited and limiting one of efficiently delivering services to clients or customers.

The purchaser-provider split separates people in their roles as taxpaying funders of government services from (often the same) people in their roles as recipients of those services. The separation is achieved rhetorically through the political discourse that refers to and identifies the needs of 'taxpayers' as separate from those of 'clients/customers'. One effect of this separation is that citizens when positioned as taxpayers are said to – and probably do – feel their interest to be that taxation should be minimised, while the same citizens when positioned as customers or public beneficiaries are said to – and again probably do – feel their interest to be to receive the maximum service. The resulting squeeze on service providers is discursively managed through notions of 'eliminating government waste and inefficiency' and providing 'value for money'. These pressures lead government agencies to reduce costs, which may be achieved through cost displacing rather than real efficiencies (Muetzelfeldt 1995).

There are some important characteristics of citizens that are not included in the notion of government's clients or customers. Citizens are not just individuals, but also groups who collectively benefit from a service (such as the general public who benefit from the work of environmental protection agencies). Unlike customers, citizens cannot always go elsewhere: for example, taxpayers have no right to sever their relationship with their national Taxation Office, and neither of course do prisoners have any right to sever their relationship with the state. Citizens are concerned with general, and at times nebulous, outcomes (such as social equity and justice), as well as with direct outputs. They are more likely to gain or lose from transactions that they are not directly involved in (such as those who lose out if a local school closes because other parents decide not to send their children there), because public sector agencies often produce outputs and outcomes that have high externalities. And citizens have a right to be treated with due process and equity that extends beyond the rights of customers.

Most importantly, citizens are electors and members of interest groups to whom the service provider's Minister or government may be politically accountable. This political function of citizenship – the right to participate in the policy process and hold governments accountable for their decisions as well as for their service delivery performance – is systematically diminished through the client or customer focus approach to governing.

Core government business

Behind the 'steering not rowing' model there is an assumption that much of what government agencies have traditionally done is not core government business; that governments have been delivering services or products that should be done, or could be done better or more efficiently, by non-government bodies. What should or should not be core government business is now being debated. With privatised prisons and security services, many now argue that the administration of (at least parts of) the justice system is not core government business. With the contracting-out of some of the work of the Australian National Audit Office (Coleman 1993), and of some legislation writing, it would seem that not all regulatory, control and legislative services are core government business.

At its most extreme, this debate is between socio-political and economic rationalist positions. The socio-political position that government is about building the good society, and governing and enhancing the economy, social development and civil justice, leads to a conclusion that any contribution to this should be considered core government business. The economic rationalist position that government is only about providing the minimum necessary requirements for individuals and groups to pursue their own economic and social objectives leads to a conclusion that the only core business of government is to see to it that someone provides the systems and processes that will lead to those requirements being met.

The important point here is that these are basically debatable and contested positions, reflecting different notions of what citizenship is and how it should be valued. What is or is not considered to be core government business will in the end be decided politically, even if it is presented as a rational decision based on the pursuit of social justice on the one hand, or of efficiency on the other. Equally, this political decision will determine what is taken to be the prevailing notion of citizenship, and the rights, duties, obligations and individual and group identities that go with it. So, within apparently technical and managerial debates over how government services should be delivered and what is to be regarded as core government business, the notion of citizenship is up for debate. Whether and how that debate is engaged is a profoundly political matter, and the results of many other overtly political issues will hinge on its outcome.

References

Alford, J. and O'Neill, D. (1994) *The Contract State: Public Management and the Kennett Government*, Geelong: Deakin University Press.

Auster, R.D. and Silver, M. (1979) *The State as a Firm: Economic Forces in Political Development*, The Hague: Martin Nijhoff.

Barton, J.A. and Marson, D.B. (1991) *Service Quality: An Introduction*, Province of British Colombia.

Blau, P.M. and Scott, W.R. (1962) *Formal Organisations*, San Francisco: Chandler.

Boston, J., Martin, J., Palot, J. and Walsh, P. (1996) *Public Management: The New Zealand Model*, Auckland: Oxford University Press.

Bouchaert, Geert and Verhoest, Koen (1999) 'A comparative perspective on decentralisation as a context for contracting in the public sector: Practice and theory', in Yronne Fortin (ed.), *La contractualisation dans le secteur public despays industrialisés depuis 1980*, Paris: L'Harmattan.

Carney, S. (1993) 'The great audit becomes a social study that leaps the economic boundaries', *The Age*, 15 May: 19.

Citizens' Charter (1990) United Kingdom Parliament, London: HMSO.

Coleman, R. (1993) 'Some ANOA perspectives on contracting out in the public sector', in Jane Coulter (ed.), *Doing More with Less? Contracting Out and Effi-ciency in the Public Sector*, Sydney: Public Sector Research Centre, University of New South Wales.

Corbett, D. (1992) *Australian Public Sector Management*, Sydney: Allen & Unwin.

Day, P. (1981) *Social Work and Social Control*, London, New York: Tavistock Publications.

Department of Finance and Administration (1998) http://www.ctc.gov.au/ 27 August 1998.

Dunleavy, P. and O'Leary, B. (1987) *Theories of the State: The Politics of Liberal Democracy*, London: Macmillan.

Engeleiter, Susan (1997) *American City & County*, vol. 112, issue 3: 28.

Goddard, T.D. and Riback, C. (1998) *You Won – Now What? How Americans Can Make Democracy Work from City Hall to the White House*, New York: Scribner.

Gouldner, Alvin W. (1954) *Patterns of Industrial Bureaucracy*, New York: Free Press.

Harden, Ian (1992) *The Contracting State*, Buckingham: Open University Press.

HMSO (1988) *Improving Management in Government, the Next Steps*, London: HMSO.

Hodge, G. (1996) *Contracting Out and Government Services: A Review of the Inter-national Evidence*, Melbourne: Montech, Monash University.

Hood, Christopher (1996) 'Exploring variations in public management reform in the 1980s', in H. Bekke, H.J. Perry and T. Toonen (eds), *Civil Service Systems in Comparative Perspectives*, Bloomington: Indiana University Press: 268–87.

Kymlicka, Will and Norman, Wayne (1994) 'Return of the citizen: A survey of recent work on citizenship theory', *Ethics*, 104: 352–81.

Lawson, T. and Walker, H. (1994) 'Meeting the customers' needs', *Canberra Bulletin of Public Administration*, no. 77 (Dec. 1994): 85.

Le Grand, J. and Bartlett W. (1993) *Quasi-Markets and Social Policy*, London: Macmillan.

London Edinburgh Weekend Return Group (1980) *In and against the State*, London: Pluto.

McDavid, James C. and Brian Marson D. (1991) *The Well-Performing Government Organization*, Ottawa: Institute of Public Administration of Canada.

Meade, A. and Montgomery, B. (1997) 'GPs in line for $2500 immunisation bonus', *The Australian*, 1–2 March.

Merton, Robert K. (1957) 'Bureaucratic structure and personality', in *Social Theory and Social Structure*, New York: Free Press.

Middleton, K. and Parsons, B. (1997) 'Immunise or lose cash, parents told', *The Australian*, 26 February.

Morris, A. and McIsaac, M. (1978) *Juvenile Justice? The Practice of Social Welfare*, London: Heinemann Educational.

Muetzelfeldt, M. (1992) 'Economic rationalism in its social context', in M. Muetzelfeldt (ed.), *Society State and Politics in Australia*, Sydney: Pluto.

—— (1995) 'Contrived control of budgets', in S. Rees and G. Rodley (eds), *The Human Costs of Managerialism*, Sydney: Pluto.

NAS (1993) *Contract document: Contract for Care Services*, London: National Artistic Society.

Next Steps Team (1996) *Next Steps Briefing Note*, London: Office of Public Services.

Niskanen, W. (1971) *Bureaucracy and Representative Government*, Chicago: Rand McNally.

Osborne, D. and Gaebler, T. (1993) *Reinventing Government: How the Entrepreneurial Spirit is Transforming the Public Sector*, New York: Plume.

Pollitt, C. (1993) *Managerialism and the Public Services: Cuts or Cultural Change in the 1990s?*, 2nd edn, Oxford: Basil Blackwell.

Saunders, P. (1993) 'Citizenship in a liberal society', in B. Turner (ed.), *Citizenship and Social Theory*, London: Sage.

Steering Committee on National Performance Monitoring of Government Trading Enterprises (1994) Canberra: Australian Government Printing Service.

Titmuss, R.M. (1976) *Commitment to Welfare*, London: Allen & Unwin.

VCA (1993a) *Report*, Volume 1, Melbourne.

—— (1993b) *Report*, Volume 2, Melbourne.

Woodhouse, S.A., Conner, G.J. and Marson, D.B. (1993) *Listening to Customers: An Introduction*, Province of British Colombia: The Service Quality B.C. Secretariat.

Yeatman, A. (1990) *Bureaucrats, Technocrats, Femocrats: Essays on the Contemporary Australian State*, Sydney: Allen & Unwin.

6 THE SUBJECT OF DEMOCRATIC THEORY AND THE CHALLENGE OF CO-EXISTENCE*

Anna Yeatman

In this chapter, we find an unorthodox but sympathetic reading of the liberal tradition of a social contract as one, perhaps the only, modern attempt to specify the political–institutional conditions for co-existence. In this case, the relationship of co-existence concerns individuals. Liberalism offers a particular kind of compromise between the ethical demands of co-existence, on the one hand, and the desire of individuals for an unrestrained private freedom or omnipotence on the other. Generally, however, liberalism has not offered a rhetoric of co-existence for the relationship between groups and peoples. In the history of modern democratic state formation, in fact, difference has been repressed and suppressed in order to secure a shared, civic national culture. Such a culture has to be imposed from above by means of the hierarchical authorities of the modern state. To date, there are no established traditions of democratic nationalism that work with a positive acceptance of dif-

* In this reworking of a paper, 'Democratic Theory and the Subject of Citizenship', originally given as a keynote address to the Culture and Citizenship Conference, Brisbane, 30 September–2 October 1996, I have been helped considerably by the comments of Margaret Whitford.

ference, and situate it within an institutional order oriented to protocols for co-existence.

How can I coexist with him [*sic*] and still leave his otherness intact? (John Wild's Introduction to Levinas (1969: 13)

The ethical challenge of living with others

There are various ways of responding to the difficult business of living with others. The difficult business of living with others refers to the irksome reality that any one of us, or of the groups we constitute, shares the terms of species survival and social life with other co-existents. This reality grows even more irksome under the conditions of post-colonial global society where a number of trends seem to intensify the difficult business of living with others. These trends include, first, the assertion of the legitimacy of 'difference'. This follows upon the insistence of those who used to be subsumed under, assimilated within, or just denied recognition by, these established state societies that they are to be counted as having their own presence as others with whom 'we' have to live. For instance, consider this insistence on the part of indigenous peoples; of gay and lesbian individuals and communities; or of those who are constituted as ethnically or racially different in relation to the established traditions of national identity in any particular state society. Second, there is also the development of transnational standards of citizenship and rights that delegitimise the established arsenal of means (invasion, ethnic cleansing, repression, torture, and so on) by which one government or group tyrannises or oppresses others.

In this chapter I am confining my discussion to co-existents who are other human individuals and groups; those, if you will, who explicitly communicate in terms of ethical discourse. It is ethical discourse because of the point Levinas makes (as represented by Davis 1996: 48): 'the Other makes me realize that I share the world, that it is not my unique possession, and I do not like this realization. My power and freedom are put into question. Such a situation is ethical because a lot depends on how I respond.' Levinas is making the point that how I and 'we' respond is always an ethical choice: 'I am confronted with real choices between responsibility and obligation towards the other, or hatred and violent repudiation' (Davis, 1996, 49). There is a more extended discussion to be had of course as to how we should understand the co-existence of other species and life forms in relation to the human species, but I shall leave these complexities aside here.

Only one of the ways of responding to the difficult business of living with others is that of attempting a democratic, politico-ethical project of co-existence. In order to appreciate the distinctive features and challenge of co-existence, it is important to situate it in relation to the other responses that can be made. Three of these ways are historically familiar to us. The first is that of the imposition of the institutions of a national monoculture where democratic institutions of represen-tation and citizenship work on behalf of the maintenance of this national monoculture. The national culture is imposed and sanctioned by means of authoritative cultural institutions, the school system being central to these.

The second response to the challenge of living with others is colo-nialism: the colonialist imposition of alien cultural and political institu-tions on a subject people whose own ways of doing things and meeting the challenge of living with others are either forbidden or permitted a subaltern existence within the order established by the colonial power. The third response to the challenge of living with others is that of removing the challenge of the other by removing the other's presence through systemic dispossession and genocide. Australians of settler inheritance confront the difficult truth that their history has involved a virtually complete inability to embrace a politics of co-existence with the indigenous or Aboriginal peoples of the Australian mainland and Tasmania. Instead, the settler response was one of dispossession, murder and cultural genocide (see HREOC 1997; Reynolds 1998).

Co-existence as a response to the business of living with others is not unknown. For instance, for a fascinating inquiry into the condi-tions of a co-existent relationship between Jews and Poles in Poland between the fourteenth and eighteenth centuries, see Eva Hoffman's *Shtetl* (1998). Also, as we shall see below, the institutional order of lib-eralism provides, in a particular and limited way, for the co-existence of individuals. But, setting the institutions of liberalism to one side, co-existence has been a largely untried project for the national state-societies of modernity: namely, societies which have been constituted as independent states in terms of a civic-communitarian nationalism. Those traditions of democratic thought which are explicitly oriented to the development and maintenance of a national 'civic culture', to use Almond and Verba's phrase, emphasise socialisation and acculturation into this culture as the condition of democracy. Otherness is managed by reducing it as far as possible through state-centred practices of imposing a shared way of life.

National democratic governments and institutional practice have generally relied upon the consensual possibilities of a shared national culture. Here I am referring to what some theorists have called civic nationalism, namely a nationalism where secular, rationalist and democratic norms are understood as following out of and expressing the unique and distinctive virtue of a particular national community: for example, the Australian civic-nationalist traditions of mateship and 'fair go'.[1] When civic nationalism underpins the discourse of democracy, those who are authorised by the particular civic nationalism in question as subjects who belong to this particular national identity feel as though it is up to them and their kind to determine the extent to which those who do not belong are allowed to assume a presence within this civic national order. Thus, for example in the Australian case, ordinary language usage marks out who is 'an Australian' and who has to be marked as different, as a 'migrant', 'Aboriginal', 'Asian', and so on. A clear distinction is made between those who inherit the civic national-ethnic community in question, and who are thus its true sons and daughters, and those who do not enjoy access to this nativist privilege of identity and citizenship. The latter may become accepted as fellow citizens but they remain marked as different, as 'Aboriginals', 'migrants' and 'Asians' (to use Australian English again).

Historically, the management of otherness by means of the imposition of a shared ethos or way of life is so normal as to seem the only basis of social order to sociological theorists such as Emile Durkheim and Talcott Parsons. They softened the violence of imposition of a shared way of life by arguing that in most instances shared norms and values are internalised within the subject's consciousness through processes of socialisation. Socialisation, Parsons argued, begins from birth and is the process by which a social neonate is inducted into the ways of the family and society in question. The family's socialising function is complemented by an inter-familial or societally-oriented type of socialisation offered by formal and informal types of educational and cultural institutions.

Durkheim emphasises a hierarchically imposed moral education as central to the formation of the modern citizen as a subject who is trained or disciplined into the solidaristic requirements of a civic nationalism. For this to occur, it is not just cultural difference which has to disappear, but the subject's internal otherness has also to be repressed so as to permit him or her to exemplify the type of person associated with the particular civic nationalism in question. Social order is made to be contingent on a shared cultural identity.

Violence and the politics of otherness

Before we proceed, it is as well to remind us that violence is and has been a frequent, if not the usual, resort in dealing with the fact that we have to share the terms of our existence with the presence of those who are co-existent with us. In making this point, Levinas's (1994: 7) definition of violence is the relevant one: 'Violence is to be found in any action in which one acts as if one were alone to act: as if the rest of the universe were there only to receive the action; violence is consequently also any action which we endure without at every point collaborating in it.' Put like this, we realise that a good deal of our action is violent. At any point when, for whatever reason, we operate out of a need to be an omnipotent subject, this very aspiration to omnipotence leads us to act violently in relation to our co-existents. To not act violently would be to make a profound acceptance of the otherness of the other and to adapt one's sense of being in the world accordingly. This would lead on to a listening relationship to others (see Fiumara 1990) for one would be aware that one cannot know in advance or without their communication how these others understand themselves, their needs and their wants. To set aside our aspiration to omnipotence means that we are ready to come alongside the other in a manner that accepts the other in their otherness, and to listen to the other speak for him- or herself. And if others cannot speak for themselves, it means that our listening relationship to them assumes an openness to how they make their being manifest to us through other kinds of non-symbolic communication.

It is important to be aware that an aspiration to omnipotence is normal. In relation to our own selfhood, each of us needs some kind of room of our own where we can exercise this omnipotence. Moreover, in relation to others, each one of us (for either developmental or defensive reasons, or both) may see our survival as contingent on our ability to control our situation, including their presence within it. Any such effort at control is what Levinas means by saying 'violence is to be found in any action in which one acts as if one were alone to act'.

Moreover, each of us can find it extraordinarily difficult when we find our own existence to be not just partially but totally impinged upon by the existence of another. There are different circumstances of such impingement, of course. Take first those which seem by their nature benign and, to an important degree, voluntary, such as the relationships of care between mother and child, psychoanalyst and analysand, teacher and student. Winnicott, the psychoanalytic theorist/practitioner, proposes that the mother hates her baby for the very good reason that the baby's needy existence profoundly impinges on her own in ways which are not just externally but internally invasive. Winnicott (1987: 201) offers a long list of why it is a mother hates her baby:

The baby is not her own (mental) conception.

The baby is not the one of childhood play, father's child, brother's child, etc.

The baby is not magically produced.

The baby is a danger to her body in pregnancy and at birth.

The baby is an interference with her private life, a challenge to preoccupation.

To a greater or lesser extent a mother feels that her own mother demands a baby, so that her baby is produced to placate her mother.

The baby hurts her nipples even by suckling, which is at first a chewing activity.

He is ruthless, treats her as scum, an unpaid servant, a slave.

She has to love him, excretions and all, at any rate at the beginning, till he has doubts about himself.

He tries to hurt her, periodically bites her, all in love.

He shows disillusionment about her.

His excited love is like cupboard love, so that having got what he wants he throws her away like orange peel.

The baby at first must dominate, he must be protected from coincidences, life must unfold at the baby's rate, and all this needs his mother's continuous and detailed study. For instance, she must not be anxious when holding him etc.

At first, he does not know at all what she does or what she sacrifices for him. Especially he cannot allow her hate.

He is suspicious, refuses her good food, and makes her doubt herself, but eats well with his aunt.

After an awful morning with him she goes out, and he smiles at a stranger, who says: 'Isn't he sweet?'

If she fails him at the start, she knows he will pay her out for ever.

He excites her but frustrates her – she mustn't eat him or trade in sex with him.

The point that Winnicott is making is that a mother, like the psycho-analyst in the analytic relationship, 'has to be able to tolerate hating her baby without doing anything about it'. The only way she can tolerate her hate is for her to know that she experiences this hate, and that it is acceptable to hate this monster of omnipotence, the newborn baby, who not only takes over her life, but whose very being involves the use of the mother to lend her strength to make this omnipotence real (for this idea, see Winnicott 1990).

Mothering (which can be undertaken by men, of course), the psychoanalytic relationship, and love relationships in general perhaps, provide an acute version of the situation where we find our own being so profoundly impinged upon by the urgent needs of the other. Perhaps most professional-client relationships where the service in question depends upon some exchange of the self (such as teaching and learning relationships) share something of this quality. Winnicott's point allows us to see how unhelpful it is for all of these caring subjects to subscribe to sentimental discourses of care and love which require them to deny their hate for the one who is dependent upon their gift and skills of care.

There are quite different circumstances of impingement by the one on the other in ways which arouse defensive responses of the assertion of omnipotence. For instance, the history of the establishment of Israel as a home for Jews is one which proceeds by the progressive and violent dispossession of those who already inhabit the territory which becomes that of Israel: Palestine. The establishment of Israel as a homeland for Jews begins with the terrible late nineteenth-century pogroms unleashed by the Tsar against Russian Jews and proceeds through the period when European Jews sought first to flee Nazism, and later to recover from the Holocaust. There was no real alternative to Israel for the Jews. No other country was prepared to admit Jews in the tens of thousands their forced exile in the face of Nazism presented. On the other side of this relationship, the Palestinians increasingly found their homeland and way of life under threat from Jewish settlers. Once it became clear from the 1917 Balfour Declaration that the British were assisting Jewish settlement instead of pursuing the pan-Arab national ideal that the Arab alliance with the Allies against the Ottoman Empire had led the British to encourage, the Palestinians organised their resistance to this process of settlement at their expense. Zionist organisations used recruitment methods which made it appear that if Jews came to Israel they would

be settling on unoccupied land, presumably because acknowledgement of the presence of an Arab people in Israel cast doubt on the
legitimacy of Jewish settlement. Perhaps the myth of *terra nullius*,
then, is a predictable and recurrent motif in justifications of settler
colonisation where the land hunger of the settlers has its own historical rationality (as in, for example, the immigration of Irish as potential settlers in Australia after the potato famine; see Reynolds's
account (1998) of settler justifications of Aboriginal dispossession in
the Australian case). The point I am making is that the tragic history
of Palestinians and Jews in the territory of Israel/Palestine is one that
is driven by contesting historical rationalities that make sense in terms
of their respective defensive responses of asserting national-ethnic
omnipotence in the face of recent dispossession and racially-based
oppression. Perhaps there were opportunities that were not taken in
this history to attempt a politics of co-existence. Given, however, the
defensive-aggressive nationalism of Jews in the context of their persecution and genocide in Europe, it is hard to see how Israeli historical rationality could have played out differently. Given the defensive
corner into which Palestinians were driven by Israeli colonisation and
British treachery, it is hard to see how they were likely to have done
anything other than firmly reject the idea of dividing Palestine into a
Jewish and Palestinian state at the point at which it was proposed by
the United Nations in 1947. The vicious circle of defensive aggression
that now besets the relationship of Palestinians and Israel is one that
reminds us how entrenched the historical rationalities of violence as
the principal way of managing the relationship with the other can
become.

Finally, there are all the small and large, ordinary and extraordinary
instances of relationships of domination which follow upon the logic of
violence as defined by Levinas: 'any action in which one acts as if on
were alone to act; as if the rest of the universe were there only to *receive*
the action'. Domination is implicit in such action when it is undertaken
by a more powerful agent in relation to someone or something that
cannot defend itself against the passivity into which it is cast by this
assertion of omnipotence. A good deal of modern efforts of technical
mastery are structured by violence of this kind. Military organisations,
authoritarian employment relationships and patriarchal marriages are
also structured by violence of this kind. It is normal to much of our historical inheritance of how we relate to our kind and to the other species
and circumstances in relation to which we find ourselves.

Co-existence, then, is a possibility that we should consider only if we are willing to understand both how normal and how endemic violence has been as a way of managing the difficult business of living with others. We can attempt co-existence only if we understand that it is a project that requires us to tolerate and accept in ourselves all the violence (in Levinas's sense) that we find there while, simultaneously, we attempt pragmatically and democratically to work with others in ways which accept their otherness even (or especially) when their existence impinges on ours. This attempt can be made only if the institutional co-ordinates of our existence both allow and enable each of us to have what Virginia Woolf called 'a room of one's own'. There has to be, in other words, a place in which we can express our desire for omnipotence, confused as this must be with our existence as a discrete unit of existence, but which is not so large a space (relationally speaking) that the expression of this desire for omnipotence compromises that of others. For individuals, domestic-private space is sufficient to provide for this desire as long as we keep in mind that even in domestic-private space the challenge of co-existence confronts those who live together in units of domesticity. For groups, social-cultural space has to be sufficient to allow the group to express and sustain its integrity. In the case of indigenous peoples, this space has to involve land to which these peoples have original or native title. When the integrity of groupness is situated within an ethic of co-existence, then the group itself has to be constituted in such a way that it is able to respect the rights of others, including the rights of its own members to judge how far they wish to be part of this group and in what way.

Violence itself is not something we can legislate out of existence. The ethical discernment of the project of co-existence I have argued here is in part conditional on acceptance of the normality of violence within the human condition. Moreover, some expressions of violence are critical to the establishment of the need for a project of co-existence: for example the angry eruption of marginalised subjects who fiercely point out to dominant subjects, 'You do not represent me/us', is an expression of violence without which the challenge of co-existence is likely to go unarticulated and undeveloped. As for those who have been positioned as dominant subjects in the violent altercations of historical relationalities, they necessarily encounter the rebellion of subaltern subjects as disruptive of their very being. For this reason, erstwhile dominant subjects are rarely gracious in the face of the challenge to their dominance by subaltern subjects. Given the inscription of domination and oppression within the histories of human-societal relationships, it is virtually impossible for a working through of where differently positioned but related subjects have come from, and for the negotiation of new futures to occur, without these projects being threaded through by the trackmarks of violence, damage, frustrations, missed opportunities, trauma, denial and guilt.

Liberalism and co-existence

The first condition for the acceptance that co-existence is a meaningful project to attempt is a decision to view the awkward existence of the other as a fact that cannot be wished away, that cannot be phantasmatically made to disappear because it offends one's own need and desire for omnipotence. The second condition is an acceptance of the difference of the other as intrinsic to the politico-ethical relationship of co-existence. This is more than a pragmatic acceptance of the factual co-existence of the other; it is an ethical acceptance of the otherness of the other.

Here I am disagreeing with those who propose that the mere fact of finding oneself in awkward contiguity and mutual impingments with others forces an acceptance of this project of co-existence. Consider these words of Iris Young (1995: 141–2):

> There is no reason or structure for differently situated groups to engage in democratic discussions if they do not live together in a polity. In this sense, some unity is of course a condition of democratic communication. But the unity of a single polity is much weaker . . . than deliberative theorists usually assume. The unity that motivates is the facticity of people being thrown together, finding themselves in geographical proximity and economic interdependence, which means that the activities and pursuits of some affect the ability of others to conduct their activities. A polity consists of people who live together, who are stuck with one another.

Young may be right to insist that a shared polity already expresses the achievement of the people and groups concerned that they share, and want to continue to share, a project of co-existence. Moreover, against the invocation by contemporary communitarians of a shared culture as the condition of democracy, Young is offering the proposition that all people need to share is a sense of being 'stuck with one another' in order to come into a democratic polity with each other. But there is nothing in the condition of being thrown together that produces a polity.

A shared project of co-existence does not simply arise out of 'the facticity of people being thrown together'. It can be motivated by this, but this facticity of being thrown together could equally motivate a project of state-imposed normalisation through shared schooling and acculturation, a project of colonisation, or a project of reciprocal terror and extirpation. In other words, the type of motivation that leads in the direction of co-existence requires to be specified and the conditions for its possibility explained.

In prudential versions of the Social Contract, a rather similar assumption to Young's is made: instead of the facticity of people being thrown together, sovereign private property-holders discover that collective insurance makes much better sense for their survival as private property holders than anything else. Finding themselves jostling for private appropriation of the land, and having to defend themselves agains the incursions of predatory others, these subjects decide it would be a good deal safer and more secure if they all consented to establish a public authority that provided and upheld a shared rule of mutual recognition (I am using the Lockeian version of the Social Contract here provided in his *Second Treatise of Government*).

The prudential rationality of the Social Contract as a specific form of collective insurance is not to be denied, but to focus on this is to obscure the ethical complexity of what is going on in the Social Contract. This ethical complexity follows on from the peculiarity of the subjects of Social Contract theory: namely, they are individualised subjects.

What does this mean? It means that the subject is constituted as a distinct and unique being whose agency is its own. To put this differently: this is a subject whose being in the world is predicated upon the ownness of its actions and speech. To paraphrase David Levine's words, it is a subject who has the ability to make its life its own (Levine 1996: 115).

The possibility of this individualisation is conditional upon others according recognition to the ownness of a particular subject's actions and speech – that these are its own; that being so, they are expressions

of its distinctive and unique being. The acceptance of individualisation is simultaneously an invitation for individualisation to occur.
Neither is possible without an elementary acceptance of difference or
otherness.

Of course, the subject's distinctness and uniqueness are thoroughly
imbued with the situated worldliness, relationships and connections
of this subject. However, just because the subject's speech and actions
are both imbued by circumstance shared by others and are indebted
to the influence, impact and impingment of others, does not mean
that such speech and action are reducible to such circumstances and
impact. Not in the least: they are the subject's *own* because they reflect
and express its distinct and unique subjectivity as this has been relationally constituted by means of the history of this subject's individualisation in relation to its particular others (this account is an
over-simplified version of insights offered by post-Freudian psychoanalysis, and for some suggestion of this, see Elliott 1994: 18–27).

The central point is that a subject cannot show its distinctness and
uniqueness without the recognition of this ownness by others. Such
recognition carries, if you will, the consent of others to let the subject
be its own subject.

Here we see that the relational terms of individualisation harbour
the project of co-existence. For, as Social Contract theory shows us, as
the individualised subject comes to awareness that its individualised
being is predicated upon the recognition and consent of others, it also
comes to awareness that it has to give this recognition and consent to
the existence of these others.

Just how this awareness is achieved is surely a complex process
subject to disruption by the historical vicissitudes of being thrown
together. What Social Contract theory tells us about this achievement
is certainly useful but not the whole story. It tells us that individualised
subjects first attempt a solipsistic fantasy of omnipotence. They discover quickly that this fantasy withdraws recognition and consent by
one as to the existence of the others as individualised subjects. The
decisive problem with this is that it means the subject's own individualised existence is at risk. For if it has withdrawn, or in fact never
given, recognition of and consent to the existence of other individualised subjects, they withdraw from it the actuality or possibility of
their recognition of and consent to its own existence.

In other words, Social Contract theory provides a story of the logic
by which individualised subjects discover their dependence for the

condition of their (individualised) being on an ethical relationship of mutual recognition which needs to be institutionalised into the public rule of law upheld by a public authority. Put differently, this is a story by which omnipotent subjects discover that the very condition of their omnipotence – their capacity to own private property – is dependent on a relationship of mutual recognition which inscribes the boundedness and thus the relativity of these subjects' omnipotence. In this particular and (as we shall briefly discuss) limited way, Social Contract theory discovers and works with a project of co-existence.

This is not something that commentators on the Social Contract tradition have appreciated. The critical enabling feature of Social Contract theory for a project of co-existence is that it starts not with a way of life or sociality that is already shared, but with the absence of this. It begins with the condition of individualisation.

In this way, Social Contract theory draws attention to, even while it constitutes, the 'difference' that makes any ethical project of co-existence the only sensible response to the existence of such difference. The project of co-existence, then, is not driven by a prudential pragmatics: that is, by a rational calculation that since others exist, we had better reckon with their existence. Rather, it is driven by the ethical acceptance of the existence of others, and in this way it reflects a remarkable achievement.

This ethical acceptance is possibly only to the degree that the subject becomes an individualised subject: that is, a subject whose individualisation or difference is to count. This is not a subject whose capacity to live with others is dependent upon an internalised collective conscience. Instead, this is a subject who can accept (for most of the time and when it really counts) the existence of others upon whose recognition it is dependent for its own individualised being.

The extraordinary elegance of the theoretical or fictional device of the Social Contract is that it manages to do two things: it affirms the omnipotence of individualised subjects through upholding their private propertied status as individuals who own their own subjectivity and a space in which this subjectivity can be expressed; simultaneously, the Social Contract shows how these omnipotent individualised subjects depend for the security of their being on a relationship of mutual recognition with other such subjects. In other words, the Social Contract does not introduce social order at the expense of individualised and omnipotent being.

Social Contract liberalism is an ethically complex account of individualised being, but the terms on which these individuals practise co-existence turn out to be very limited, and, arguably, to be at the expense of the otherness or difference of the other. The account of co-existence which liberalism offers is predicated on a sameness of individuated status. All these individuals have to be mature (adult), rational actors who are oriented to each other not as fellow co-existents but as potentially rivalrous private property owners. Theirs is the same kind of individuality, the type that is best expressed through the competitive private property relationships of a market economy. Indeed, by the terms of the liberal account of co-existence, it is all too easy to hand over the political challenges of co-existence to the terms of market competition. Assuming, in other words, a market economy in which lawful transactions are upheld and protected by law, the dynamics of choice and competition in the market sort out how these individuals are to co-exist in ways which, theoretically anyway, as committed private property owners they are supposed to accept.

Liberalism, in short, works with an exceedingly limited conception of difference, one that turns out to be containable within the one type of individualisation. As individuals, these are all the same kind of individual for whom the same kind of institutional design makes sense and works.

Conclusion

Modern democratic institutional design, to date, has been largely confined to two types: first, the democratic nationalist communitarian institutions of the modern nation-state. I have argued that this kind of democratic nationalist communitarianism is not reconcilable in any degree with the contemporary challenges of co-existence and a politics of difference. Second, the liberal institutions of contract, representative government, private property and the market economy do make some provision for difference or otherness in the form of individualisation. In any liberal institutional design, explicit attention has to be given to how these different individuals will and can co-exist. However, this is an institutional design which works from a monocultural conception of individualisation, one which privileges a rational, calculative, adult and independent private property owner (for some further elaboration of these points, see Yeatman 1994: ch. 4; Yeatman 1998). In other words, because liberalism works with such an undeveloped conception of individualisation it does not have to work in any extended or intensive way with the challenges of co-existence. These challenges require their own democratic institutional design and theory, and one of the urgent tasks of our shared present will be to contribute to the development of these.

Note

1   See Yeatman (1994: 252), especially this passage: 'In this context, multiculturalism is read in terms of a tolerance for difference which is containable within any one specific jurisdictional version of civic nationalism. Accordingly, it is perfectly possible for a specific national jurisdiction to proclaim a commitment to multiculturalism as central to its particular tradition of civic nationalism. The problem with this is this kind of nativism that lurks in civic nationalism. France or the United States or Australia are all made to stand for the apogee of civic nationalism because there is something special in their civic history which explains their special and distinctive attachment to the virtues of civic nationalism. Thus Kristeva invokes the French Enlightenment; American nativists invoke the unique and founding new-world status of the USA and the manifest destiny that follows from this; such Australian nativists as Donald Horne and Paul Keating invoke the tradition of the "fair go"; and New Zealand post-colonial Pakeha and Maori invoke the Treaty of Waitangi as the founding constitutional origin of New Zealand civic nationalism.'

References

Almond, G. and Verba, S. (1965) *The Civic Culture*, Boston: Little, Brown.

Davis, C. (1996) *Levinas*, Cambridge: Polity.

Elliott, A. (1994) *Psychoanalytic Theory: An Introduction*, Oxford: Basic Blackwell.

Fiumara, C. (1990) *The Other Side of Language: A Philosophy of Listening*, London and New York: Routledge.

Hoffman, E. (1998) *Shtetl: The History of a Small Town and an Extinguished World*, London: Secker & Warburg.

HREOC (1997) *Bringing Them Home: National Inquiry into the Separation of Aboriginal and Torres Strait Islander Children from Their Families*, Commonwealth of Australia: HREOC.

Levinas, E. (1969) *Totality and Infinity: An Essay on Exteriority*, Pittsburgh: Duquesne University Press.

——(1994) *In the Time of Nations*, Bloomington and Indianopolis: Indiana University Press.

Levine, D. (1996) *Wealth and Freedom: An Introduction to Political Economy*, Cambridge: Cambridge University Press.

Reynolds, H. (1998) *The Whispering in Our Hearts*, St Leonard's: Allen & Unwin.

Winnicott, D.W. (1987) 'Hate in the Countertransference', in *Through Paediatrics to Psychoanalysis: Collected Papers*, London: Karnac Books.

——(1990) 'The Theory of the Parent-Infant Relationship', in *The Maturational Processes and the Facilitating Environment*, London: Karnac Books.

Yeatman, A. (1994) 'Multiculturalism, Globalisation and Rethinking the Social', *Australian and New Zealand Journal of Sociology*, vol. 30, no. 3: 247–53.

——(1998) 'Models of Individualised Personhood: the challenge of reconciling self-determination with dependency', paper prepared for Constitutional Law, Administrative Law and Institutional Ethics: the Role of Feminist Values, University of Sydney, 16–18 April 1998.

Young, Iris (1995) 'Communication and the Other: Beyond Deliberative Democracy', in M. Wilson and A. Yeatman (eds), *Justice and Identity: Antipodean Practices*, St Leonards: Allen & Unwin; Wellington: Bridget Williams Books.

7 DEMOCRACY, CLASS AND CITIZENSHIP IN A GLOBALISING WORLD

Alastair Davidson

This chapter links some of the arguments in Part I with the case studies in Part II. It points out that since ancient times, citizens' empowerment, autonomy and government from below have required establishing institutions for controlling the arbitrary power of both kings and external forces. This requirement of the rule of law for the achievement of democratic citizenship has today been radically transformed. Networked computers have greatly empowered capital while the decline of welfare states has undermined working-class consciousness. The resurgence of economic liberalism has seen the emergence of an under-class of migrant and part-time workers in the West. New social movements for women's liberation, environmentalism, gay and lesbian liberation, anti-nuclear power and anti-racism have also failed to counter the resurgence of economic liberalism within the old nation-states. Some form of global citizenship, possibly developed within the principle of subsidiary democracy such as that in the EU, offers only a faint possibility of countering international economic liberalism.

Men and women seek to be empowered against the daily threats and risks that their natural and social world imposes on them. Against the arbitrariness of the slings and arrows of outrageous fortune, they wish to establish the regularities of a rule of law. This at least allows some predictability and security and thus, as Rousseau pointed out, makes them free from the anxieties that the arbitrary brings.

This fundamental desire for empowerment over the context within which men and women live is consistent – as the long history of political societies shows – only with political institutions where all the individuals living in a particular context make the laws under which they live. If only one person, a monarch, makes those laws then predictability is greatly reduced for each individual. This is also the case if the few, or oligarchs, rule. Only where political power is equal for all inhabitants of a particular world can the desire for empowerment be achieved.

Since the ancient Greeks, it has always been accepted that citizenship, or the power to make the laws under which we live, can really only exist where all individuals have equal decision-making power. This can be expressed most clearly through each person having a vote of equal value. Having this guarantees the right to be heard in the debate over which laws are to be agreed upon for the benefit of the entire collectivity.

To this prior will to empowerment, which drives citizenship and democracy, we can now add a second and equally basic presupposition: that there is always a pre-existing context – which affects us – over which we wish to be empowered. To the degree that we attain such empowerment, we establish a state, the Janus-face of citizenship. It is the place where our rule of law runs, as the French words *état de droit* make explicit.

So, what we do to achieve power from below (Kelsen 1945) depends on the context. A context is an intellectual construct. We never know for sure the origin or source of the forces that influence our lives. With the acquired reason we inherit, we make calculations about the nature and extent of the context we want to get under our control, so that it has patterns and is feasible. The ancient Greeks who first formulated our notions of democracy and citizenship still believed that wrathful Gods decided much that took place in a human realm and they left a large space for fate. Moreover, the worlds that they thought affected them were limited to tiny city-states and their inter-state relations. It was not beyond the bounds of rationality to believe that democratic decision-making within such spaces could take the form of direct law-making by all citizens. A host of direct democratic procedures evolved.

Similarly, when the vastly larger nation-state system replaced earlier forms after the fifteenth century, and above all since 1900, new and more appropriate procedures had to be evolved to guarantee a modicum of power from below. These were those of a popular majority choice between at least two parties whose elected members would represent the popular sovereign in a Parliament. Here the representatives would debate for the populace who had once had the right to do so directly in the agora of Athens. The elected majority party would control the even more restricted government that would apply the laws made by the Parliament (Strasbourg Consensus 1983).

Both ancients and moderns understood that all of a context could not be controlled (Zeus had no chains). A community only had the strength to create a rule of law over certain spaces and activities. Beyond them lay the relative chaos of a war of all against all. This was kept at bay by strong borders, fiercely defended against the barbarism of the outside and the Other. International law as something more than the imposition of power took centuries to evolve, and the first national 'peoples' popularly endorsed war as the extension of politics. It is enshrined in the words of the Marseillaise.

Both ancient and modern sets of procedures exist today, though the first tradition is vestigial (in Switzerland, for example). The dominant context is that of the 191 nation-states which make up the global community and whose inter-state relations are governed more and more by convention and agreement. The latter is not a democratic space as many states are not democratic. Even when democratic states reach agreement to be ruled by law it is a state-to-state agreement and not the result of democratic choice.

Overall, then, a discussion of what democracy and citizenship mean and require today depends on what context we believe we are living in and what procedures are required to cope with that context.

It is a commonplace that the new context we face is that of the globalising market. Every day we are told how its imperatives require our adaptation to particular demands and challenges. These are frequently portrayed as uncontrollable and unpredictable, creating a new world of risk with which we must learn to live. Since citizenship, and in particular its democratic form, grew out of a wilful refusal to accept such a life, we can only expect new forms of democratic citizenship to emerge to meet the new challenge.

Globalisation

We may sum up the relevant dimension of globalisation for our topic in the following fashion. The world capitalist market system has existed for at least two centuries and as a world economy for five (Braudel 1979: 18–19), and it has been radically transformed by the increased rapidity in communications. The qualitative change came with computers and the Internet. This ended the constraints of space and time that conditioned all earlier human transactions, practices and therefore identities.

Effectively, what has happened is dual. First, the world capitalist market – after a short blip of nationalist protectionism – has reasserted its *telos* towards free trade, especially after 1945. Increasingly and incrementally, capital, goods and labour have moved to the places where the most profit and well-being can be produced and these movements have become ever less constrained by trade barriers corresponding with national borders. This does not mean that most economic life does not take place within former national borders.

The growth of free trade emerged unevenly in different regions, and the oldest and most developed European capitalisms took the lead, promoting the growth of regional free trade spaces such as the EU. There the nature of nation-state sovereignty was radically reduced. Those states, notably in Asia, which benefited from free trade but refused to move in the direction of regional polities and refused to adopt the requisite social and political transformations, went into crisis as a result in 1998.

By itself the growth of free trade as the norm throughout the globe was not novel. What was novel was the impact of the computer revolution which made information the most important mode of production. This allowed competitive advantage and higher rates of profit. The people who had or could process the information became the decision-makers of the global capitalist system. They concentrated in a few global cities – London, New York, Tokyo, Sydney – and lesser satellites (Castells 1989, 1998; Sassen 1991). What the Internet meant was the end of the need for production to be located in one site where capital, goods and labour concentrated (typically a factory). Instead, it could be disaggregated over vast spaces. Moreover, since instantaneous knowledge of conditions became possible the sites could be shifted at will *ad infinitum* in many areas of production. New types of plug-in-as-required workforces without traditional skills have emerged (Castells 1989). The overall effect is the relative decline of the percentage of workers in centralised production points and the vast growth of distribution and service employment in the capitals of world finance. Workers no longer work together full time.

The end of class

The implications for the category of class are enormous. They impact greatly on any notion of democratic citizenship. At the risk of tele-scoping class theory, we can affirm that its basic notion was that all previous loyalties based on difference were transformed in the crucible of the factory into a solid shared sense of class consciousness. By the late nineteenth century the 'workers' were born. Whether that consciousness was transformed into a political force depended on the organising force, which could range from British Labour Party trade unionism to Leninist bolshevism. These organisations built on the objective realities of a working class, or proletariat, that was united in its suffering and through its combined political practice (Davidson 1998). Within the nation-state, the workers and their parties became one of the factors that had to be examined in any discussion of politics.

The most influential Anglo-Saxon theorist of citizenship, T. H. Marshall (1950), argued that it was this class that forced the rights of citizenship in Britain beyond the attaining of limited, male-only civil rights in 1884 and also beyond the universal political rights attained in 1928. In order to meet the requirements of an autonomous active citizen for any democratic participation, they extracted from a reluctant capitalism some economic, social, health and educational rights. These minima of well-being were the pre-condition for participation in political life. With an over-optimism common in post-Second War Britain, Marshall assumed that all those rights had been won and full democratic citizen participation guaranteed. Later commentators, starting with Bryan Turner and Anthony Giddens, pointed out that it was a continuing battle as capitalism sought to roll back such third-generation rights (Giddens 1985; Turner 1986).

The bedrock of such a theory of welfare-state democratic citizen-ship was the unquestioned presence of a self-conscious working class that presented a solid political force within any nation-state. That class certainly exists as a dwindling proportion of the world population, especially in the centres. Today, it is found mostly in Third World countries to which traditional production techniques have been exported. Everywhere its political attitudes have been affected by another effect of globalisation. This is the arrival of new workforces from other nation-states, often former colonies, to supply the market for labour in the growth areas of world capitalism. Overall, it is a small percentage of the working class but in the global cities it often constitutes more than half.

The arrival of these multi-ethnic workforces has shattered working-class unity in a new way. The arrival of such workforces had always taken place. They had worked in the factory alongside the 'old' workforce, lived in its neighbourhoods (although not without friction and violence), and gradually joined its unions and parties. In sum, they were transformed in 'the struggle' into people whose over-riding loyalty was to their 'class'. Today, the transformation and transfer of identities no longer takes place in the same fashion.

It is this transformation of identities that we must insist on. It is clear – as Castells (1998: 344–6) has recently pointed out – that the structure of the working class and the social relations of production have changed. In particular, he identifies in the latter a tendency towards increased social inequality and polarisation, which arises from:

> a) a fundamental differentiation between self-programmable, highly productive labour and generic, expendable labour; b) the individualisation of labour which undermines its collective organisation, thus abandoning the weakest sections of the workforce to their fate; and c) under the impact of the individualisation of labour, globalisation of the economy, and de-legitimation of the state, the gradual demise of the welfare state, so removing the safety net for people who cannot be individually well off. (Castells 1998: 344)

The result is social exclusion for large numbers of people who are irrelevant from the point of view of the logic of globalisation.

Castells (1998: 348) concedes that these objective factors are what make cultural battles the power battles of the Information Age. To use traditional terms, a global hegemony is almost complete, with no oppositions easily identifiable. It is significant that he has to use the Zapatistas of Mexico, a tiny and ever-menaced movement, as an illustration of a globalised left opposition to the system. The effect of migrating global workforces at the level of minds, or self and identity, is what is important for class consciousness.

With no intention to stay or settle, rapid and regular returns 'home', and the maintenance of contact through phone and Internet, they are never obliged to leave or to identify with a new place. They hold multiple passports and have multiple allegiances that over-ride those acquired in the factory, even if they work in such a place. The maintenance of their multicultural associations means that even into the second generation there is no transfer of allegiance (Eade 1997: 159). They are denizens, with no aspiration to be citizens if this means renouncing old identities and ties. As disembedded and distanciated beings (Giddens 1990), they are, emotionally speaking, in many places at the same time.

Class consciousness has therefore collapsed or retreated into ultra-nationalism and racism among some of the old working class. Fearful of newcomers' apparent threat to their economic and social conditions, they become ever more ready to exclude them from such benefits. Denial of rights in California, France, Australia and elsewhere goes beyond the increasing difficulty newcomers have obtaining nationality. They are excluded from legal employment and from unemployment benefits in many cases. As their numbers increase, their exclusion from citizenship means a decline of democracy and human rights within even formerly open republics. The capitalist state can successfully roll back the welfare state necessary for the Kantian citizen.

Such working-class nationalism is not new. But the tendency of the movement to internationalise and universalise rights, if only to build solidarity, has certainly also been a feature of the working class. It has become much less obvious in the last two decades as workers defend national economies against the inroads of globalisation and economic rationalism.

Therefore, in a global world the central role of class as traditionally conceived in promoting and extending democratic citizenship has to be challenged. New practices and new civic values have to be proposed to substitute for it as a driving force behind the extension of citizenship rights.

Social movements

For some two decades it has been suggested that the new social movements could replace or are already replacing the single unified working class as the promoters and defenders of third- and, indeed, fourth-generation rights. These social movements are coalitions of people built around certain issues: the women's movement, the ecologists, anti-war movements, gay and lesbian rights movements. It was expected that after their initial successes, especially among Greens, and their transition into more than single-issue political parties, they would defend and promote new rights.

Indeed, if we observe the extension of rights to hitherto ignored categories such as women and children, the handicapped, and in defence of nature and the environment in both UN conventions and those of, say, the EU, their success on paper has been great. If we add to those achievements the everyday activities of Amnesty International, Oxfam, *Médecins sans frontières*, and other organisations, they certainly fill some of the gap.

However, overall they have not been as successful on a political level as right-wing nationalist forces and they have not managed to build long-lasting political unity across their corporate interests. Above all, they have not succeeded in preventing the roll-back of the welfare state and an enormous increase in workers' alienation from citizen activity. Except in countries of compulsory voting and in the EU, participation in the democratic process has declined quickly.

Put bluntly, the global context requires a new citizen subject to ensure power from below: a global citizen. The old national and progressive working class has either melted into air or is no longer sufficient. To assert its democratic power this new subject requires a new combination of procedures. Some of these have already emerged in regional polities and further proposals for global governance.

Global citizenship

Where threats wider than those arising in a national context are faced jointly and not regarded as the problem of the other nationality, policies promoting regional and global citizenship already exist. In the EU they function through semi-federal structures which rest on the principle of subsidiarity. This is where decisions are taken as close as possible to the problem. Local government by smallish communities makes most decisions; a vastly reduced nation-state level makes others and a regional or global (EU or UN) level makes a very few where problems are truly supranational. In other words, a new structure is proposed to replace the representative systems of nation-state liberal democracies, which sought to establish a direct relationship between the individual citizen and the legislature and frowned on intermediate associations as weakening the common commitment. Through developing on a federal model it is hoped that this will establish more democracy in more places. While still representative and not true direct democracy, community and democracy will be made to coincide more, whether the community is a city or locality, or even an ethnic minority.

Thus the power from below which once was expressed through a working class – and which undoubtedly constituted the majority and therefore often arrogated to itself the leading role among the sovereign people – is replaced in the new global world by the power of different communities. The working class as a social movement still remains one of these, together with others such as the women's movement, ecologists and so on.

The effect of democratic devolution is supposedly to put management into community hands. These communities sometimes correspond with cultural or ethnic minorities who now can govern themselves according to their community values. This, however, only displaces the problem of democracy. It is easy to envisage how that would work in a shared community of values. It becomes problematic at the frontiers with the larger Other or Outside, where it links up federally. There, community values cannot apply because there must be some negotiated universal or common procedures and norms. The nature of these values is enormously difficult to envisage.

Nevertheless, regional citizenship along the lines established by the Maastricht Treaty seems a relative success. Despite vestigial hostility to foreigners, who today have a right to work alongside old nationals and enjoy a host of other rights including the vote and candidacy in local and European elections, without even speaking the national language, overall Europeans accept other Europeans as equals. There are certainly still borders against non-Europeans. Islam, above all, is still the object of practical discrimination. Self-government at a local level has not ended racism, as the *Lega Nord* actions reveal daily. So extensive education programmes designed to complement practical education in democracy, which attaches people to the public, have been introduced in the EU and more generally in the UN. These preach new virtues of tolerance and a mild approach to the Other. They battle against the racism and new nationalism which the clash between the feeling of national ownership and new global workforces provoke.

The picture is less rosy when we leave the relatively homogeneous European commitment to democracy and human rights, which is a century old and rests on a common memory of tyranny based on nationalism. Once we leave regions long committed to citizenship principles, the compromises that have to be made across cultures are so enormous that little common ground is easily found for the establishment of regional polities. This is doubly so when the procedures for ensuring freedom are discussed. The bulk of the world's population is in Asia (including Central Asia) and Africa. The leaders of the former – with the significant exception of Japan, the Philippines and Thailand – mostly reject the notions of democratic citizenship as inappropriate to human well-being. The condition of Africa is aptly summed up in the title of a recent book, *Africa in Chaos* (Ayittey 1998). Viewed worldwide rather than from a European perspective, the sense of global civic virtue is spread so thin that commentators such as Richard Falk (1996) wonder whether a global citizenship can have meaning.

Consequently, to promote a sense of civic commitment to a common public realm in a context where all states are necessarily made up of culturally different minorities, and are expected to remain that way, requires a practical education in working together. To achieve this, the Global Commission of the UN proposes the democratisation of its decision-making bodies to promote a global sense of empowerment (Global Commission 1995). While praiseworthy, such a proposal runs into the problem already addressed by the EU, which has broken the nexus between nationality and citizenship rights, so that foreigners are empowered in spaces that formerly belonged only to nationals. The problem is that is impossible to conceive a representative system that ends up with a Parliament of 1000 or more members encompassing a regional and global constituency. This is a problem that would exist even in a system where only a few general matters are dealt with at the top of a semi-federal system (Davidson 1997).

While suggestions about substituting electronic democracy are seductive and certainly seem apposite for decision-making at local levels, their development is embryonic [as we will see in the Chapter 19]. The use of computers to reintroduce direct democracy – long regarded as a pipe-dream by theorists of democracy in large states –

might allow the re-emergence of a popular sovereign who no longer feels increasingly disempowered in the complex global world. It is, however, only a possibility for the 6 per cent of the world on the Internet and therefore only viable in the most 'developed' regions of the world.

Such pessimism may appear a counsel of despair. It is important, therefore, to reaffirm that whatever the prospects for 'global citizens', the promotion of regional arrangements like those of the EU should be encouraged. Despite the limitations of such enlarged meta-polities, they have successfully expanded both the list of human rights and the obligations of their citizens to one another and to the polity.

References

Ayittey, G. (1998) *Africa in Chaos*, London: Macmillan.

Braudel, F. (1979) *Civilisations materielles, economie et capitalisme xv–xviii siècles*, Paris: Colin, III.

Castells, M. (1989) *The Informational City: Informational Technology, Economic Restructuring and the Urban Regional Process*, Oxford: Basil Blackwell.

—— (1998) *End of Millennium*, Oxford: Basil Blackwell.

Davidson, A. (1997) 'Regional politics: the Euroopean Union and Citizenship', *Citizenship Studies*, vol. 1, no. 1: 33–55.

—— (1998) 'New global mode of production: achievement and contradiction', *Dossier 2 Le Manifeste communiste 150 ans après Rencontre internationale*, Paris, 13–16 May.

Eade, J. (1997) *Living the Global City: Globalisation as a Local Process*, London and New York: Routledge.

Falk, R. (1996) 'The decline of citizenship in an Age of Globalisation', Paper at the Globalisation and Citizenship Conference, Geneva, 9–11 December; UNRISD/Swinburne.

Giddens, A. (1985) *The Nation-State and Violence*, London: Macmillan.

—— (1990) *The Consequences of Modernity*, Cambridge: Polity/Basil Blackwell.

Global Commission (1995) *Our Global Neighbourhood*, Oxford: Oxford University Press.

Kelsen, H. (1945) *A General Theory of Law and the State*, Cambridge, MA: Harvard University Press.

Marshall, T. (1950) *Citizenship and Social Class and other Essays*, Cambridge: Cambridge University Press.

Sassen, S. (1991) *The Global City*, New York, London, Tokyo, Princeton, NJ: Princeton University Press.

Strasbourg Consensus (1983) *The Strasbourg Consensus*, Strasbourg: Council of Europe.

Turner, B. (1986) *Citizenship and Capitalism: The Debate over Reformism*, London: Allen & Unwin.

PART II
NATION-STATE CASE STUDIES

8 CITIZENSHIP AND DEMOCRACY IN GERMANY: IMPLICATIONS FOR UNDERSTANDING GLOBALISATION

Robert van Krieken

As we have seen in Chapter 4, the Holocaust and the tradition of citizenship through ethno-kinship ties poses particular issues for understanding what German experience has to say about citizenship and democracy in a global era. In this chapter, van Krieken rejects Dahrendorf's well-known arguments about Germany's inadequate modernisation in favour of Eley's thesis that despite the country's rapid modernisation it lacked an institutional capacity to cope with rapid political and economic change imposed by the rest of the world. Van Krieken follows Brubaker's contrast between the French state's tradition of territorially bounded political identity (jus soli) *and the German* Volk *tradition of an imagined national community of descent, culture and ethno-kinship ties* (jus sanguinis). *He concludes that German history exemplifies the importance of considering how state and nation, institutions and cultures, interact in practice.*

The history of the German nation and state has always had an important as well as profoundly ambiguous relation to liberal conceptions of both citizenship and democracy. On the one hand, both the social insurance schemes of Bismarck and the municipal welfare programmes of German cities served as models for state-sponsored social policy and for the non-government organisation of social work and social welfare. In relation to the social policy and welfare dimensions of citizenship, then, Germany has since the middle of the nineteenth century stood as a prototype of the way in which the relationship between individuals and the state could best be organised (de Swaan 1988: 187–92; Steinmetz 1996), and this is also true of the post-war welfare state in the Federal Republic of Germany.

The rise of fascism in Germany and the Holocaust have, on the other hand, also worked as the example against which liberal democracy since 1945 has measured itself. It has become the best example of what democratic citizenship should *not* be, the ideal-typical mistake which liberal democracies should take every measure to avoid. Above all, the German case has offered a seemingly overwhelming argument for the dangers of too much democracy, of granting too unrestricted a range of powers to 'the masses', who inevitably became a violent, brutish 'mob' without the civilising restraints of an educated (bourgeois) political elite retaining the lion's share of real political power. Although Joseph Schumpeter's (1987, but originally 1943) arguments against the 'classical doctrine of democracy' as government *by* the people was framed in general terms [as was discussed in Chapters 1 and 3 above], the 'elitist' or 'realist' conception of democracy which emerged in political science after mid-century was constructed as a direct response to the 'failure' of liberalism as well as democracy in the German Weimar Republic and the rise of German fascism (Pateman 1970: 2; see also Almond and Verba 1963; Verba 1965: 131; Bachrach 1967; Thompson 1970; Verba and Nie 1972: 299–344).

More recently, the German experience of the central features of intensifying globalization – increased migration, the movement of peoples across state boundaries – also highlights the problems which the concept of multicultural citizenship (Kymlicka 1995) can encounter. This is particularly so when seen against the backdrop of the German National Socialist experience. The German experience offers some suggestions as to how multicultural citizenship might be best realised. The aim of this chapter is to outline the particular character of the development of the German nation and state, of German citizenship and democracy, to chart the problems and issues which this history has produced, and to highlight the ways in which the specificity of this history helps us come to a better understanding of the various ways in which citizenship, democracy, nation and state interrelate, particularly in a period where they are undergoing the tremendous transformations being wrought by intensifying social, political and economic globalization.

I will organize the discussion around two related issues: German fascism and the Holocaust, and the peculiarity of the German treatment of immigrants. Much of the liberal-democratic response to the Holocaust has revolved around the idea that it is possible to guard against the repetition of such events through the development of appropriate democratic institutions. The significance of a deep understanding of fascism and the Holocaust – and this is why it continues to fascinate social scientists – is that there may be features of advanced capitalist, modern societies other than their overt political forms which produce such 'civilized barbarism', which only a more complex and detailed historical, sociological and psychological analysis of German fascism can reveal (see Elias 1996).

The overall argument concerning the significance of the German case will have two elements: first, that the tendency in political theory generally and citizenship debates in particular to see the two elements of the couplet 'nation-state' as *naturally* linked together, with citizens automatically sharing culture, language and way of life, prevents us from seeing many of the complexities of the operation of citizenship and democracy in real historical and geo-political contexts;[1] and second, that we need to come to a better understanding of how and why 'nation' and 'state' can rub up against each other as often as they work hand in hand, especially if we are to understand the effects of globalization and postmodernisation on contemporary social life. This is particularly important in coming to grips with the operation of ethnic and cultural differences among any particular grouping of citizens, in relation to both migrants and indigenous populations (Kymlicka 1995).

The 'Dahrendorf thesis' and its problems

Unlike his discussion of social policy, Marshall's analysis of the historical development of citizenship was focused on the British example, although it was possible to extend his observations to other countries such as France and the USA (Marshall 1964). What was left out of the picture was the implications for a sociological theory of citizenship and democracy of their most spectacular failure, namely the rise of fascism in Germany, Italy and Spain, and especially the most dramatic example of the removal – let us say 'extermination' – of citizenship rights in the Holocaust (Noakes 1987; Peukert 1987). Ralf Dahrendorf engaged with this problem in *Society and Democracy in Germany* (1968, originally 1965), and set out to establish some answers to 'the German question', the most important part of which was 'How was Auschwitz possible?'

Dahrendorf's answer to this question was essentially one of 'uneven development': a disparity between economic modernisation and political traditionalism, and a 'failure' on the part of the German bourgeoisie to assert its social and political position in Germany society, which in turn led to the weakness of the 'liberal' component of liberal-democracy. As he put it, in a chapter titled 'The Faulted Nation':

> Just as the economy of Imperial Germany became industrial but not capitalist, the German society of the time did not become bourgeois, but remained quasi-feudal. Industrialization in Germany failed to produce a self-confident bourgeoisie with its own political aspirations . . . As a result, German society lacked the stratum that in England and America, and to a lesser extent even in France, had been the moving force of a development in the direction of greater modernity and liberalism. (Dahrendorf 1968: 52)

Although Bismarck's social policy initiatives did bring about a welfare state concerned with the needs and well-being of its members, it was an 'authoritarian' welfare state which excluded the transformation of subjects into citizens. Dahrendorf spoke of Imperial Germany as having 'missed the road to modernity', and he saw its early social policy programmes as preventing rather than encouraging the development of 'the citizen role'. The *combination* of industrialisation and technological modernisation with the continued ideological and political centrality of traditional military and aristocratic elites, which the German middle classes were unable or unwilling to displace, produced the paradoxical structure of 'an industrial feudal society' (Dahrendorf 1968: 61). It was this paradox which, for Dahrendorf, formed 'the explosive core of a society in which the liberal principle could settle only haltingly and occasionally' (Dahrendorf 1968: 48).

His explanation of the failure of the Weimar Republic's democracy and the rise of the Nazis thus rests on a deep-structural analysis, one of a 'fault' inherited by twentieth-century German society from the ways in which industrial modernity combined with political traditionalism in the nineteenth century. For these 'unmodern men in a modern world', pre-democratic forms of conduct persisted throughout the German population, and 'this could all too easily turn into the anti-democratic behaviour of a nostalgic demand for the nest warmth of the closed society' (Dahrendorf 1968: 387), which was precisely the fertile ground in which Nazism grew. So powerful was this deep-structural legacy that Dahrendorf felt it persisted in German society into the 1960s, arguing that citizenship rights were still not generalised, and observing the continued presence of 'second- and third-class citizens who are lacking many requisites of civilized life and chances of full development'; he found it 'hard to dispute the suspicion that the ability to distinguish not only between men of different classes but also between men and "submen" is still slumbering in many Germans' (Dahrendorf 1968: 82).

For Dahrendorf, then, the significance of the German experience of democracy and citizenship was that the kind of development of citizenship rights charted by Marshall was heavily dependent on an effective *liberalism* within modern industrialised societies, and that this was in turn dependent on the social and political strength of the bourgeoisie. Many other commentators have agreed with this overall view, referring the significance of the absence of a bourgeois revolution in Germany, and developing a similar linkage of the failure of parliamentary democracy in Weimar Germany with the political weakness of the bourgeoisie compared to military and aristocratic elites (most prominently, Moore 1966). To guarantee the proper development of genuine citizenship, then, one needed the development of a particular political culture, which in turn depended on the ideological and political dominance of the bourgeoisie. The association he established, and which has been taken up in many subsequent interpretations of the German case, was: weak bourgeoisie = weak liberalism = weak citizenship, and in the case of German fascism, the elimination of citizenship rights as they have usually been understood. Is this interpretation correct?

According to much of the German historiography since the 1980s, it is not, for two reasons. First, there is no basis for assuming that the bourgeoisie are always and everywhere liberal, and that authoritarian ideas only reside in the breasts of landed aristocrats, army generals and navy commanders. Geoff Eley points out that all the supposed 'traditional' limitations on democracy and citizenship in Imperial Germany were typical for Europe at the time. Even more telling, rather than constituting a paradoxical 'industrial feudal society', Imperial Germany 'was more frequently regarded as an exemplary "modern" state', because of the technical efficiency of its bureaucracy, government and army, the active role of the state in both economy and civil society, its advanced social policy and social welfare system, and its early introduction of universal male suffrage (Eley 1996: 93).

It was in fact the very *modernity* of Imperial Germany, argues Eley, which produced anti-democratic and imperialist policies rather than its supposedly 'recalcitrant' traditional character. The radical nationalism which fostered the rise of the Nazis was not a nostalgic image of the past but an active vision of the future, and in this respect 'it harnessed the cultural aspirations of many who were comfortably placed in the emerging bourgeois society, the successful beneficiaries of the new urban-industrial civilization, whose political sensibilities were offended by the seeming incapacitation of the establishment before the left-wing challenge' (1986: 266–7). Rather than seeing the bourgeoisie – or any social group for that matter – as the natural 'bearers' of liberalism, as Dahrendorf and others have, Eley prefers to allow for the possibility that they can also be profoundly illiberal and authoritarian, and that the problem becomes one of identifying the particular circumstances of state- and nation-formation which produces outcomes like Nazism and the Holocaust.

Very crudely, the gist of the position taken up by Eley and historians such as Detlev Peukert is to acknowledge the significance of historically and geo-politically specific conjunctures, especially economic and political crises, which need to be viewed alongside the supposed deep structures underlying whatever we call 'the state' and 'civil society'. Eley suggests that 'traditional' concepts retained their power in Weimar Germany not because they had somehow 'persisted' as 'relics', but because they appeared to offer more *effective* solutions to the problems facing the country, particularly the effects of the Versailles Treaty, the 'crisis of reproduction' that followed the end of the First World War (Peukert 1991; Hong 1996), and of course the general economic crisis of the Depression years. As Eley puts it:

the pace of social change outstripped the adaptive capabilities of the existing
political institutions, particularly when the latter were called upon to be responsible to new social forces – agricultural populations concerned for their future
in an economy increasingly structured by industrial priorities, urban populations demanding a more rational ordering of their hastily improvised city environment, a potential chaos of private economic interests, the mass organizations
of the industrial working class, and the more diffuse aspirations of the new professional, administrative and managerial strata of the bourgeoisie and petty
bourgeoisie. (1986: 265)

Educated German citizens turned to a radical nationalism which
emphasised national allegiances and priorities organised around a
tightly defined *Volk* not because they simply failed to give such ideas
up, but because they perceived the existing political system – liberal,
parliamentary democracy – as ineffective and impotent. This political
position then in turn had the effect of self-fulfilling prophecy, further
undermining the ability of the Weimar Republic 'to organize a sufficient basis of consent among the subordinate classes to permit stable
government to continue' (Eley 1986: 266).[2]

Peukert also stresses the particularity of the period between 1918
and 1933 in Germany, pointing out that it was characterised by a
'feverish succession of events' as well as 'vast convulsions and violent
changes in political culture and society' which generated 'a deep-
seated sense of unease and disorientation' (1991: 275). The Weimar
period was one of tension, not between tradition and modernity as
Dahrendorf would have it, but between the development of a new,
modern social, political and economic system and the simultaneous
strangulation of its real ability to deliver on its promises, and actually
to provide the benefits which were meant to compensate for its
costs. There was virtually no growth in wealth to redistribute, and
reductions in wages and welfare benefits made disputes over them
increasingly bitter, further encouraging 'social fragmentation and
polarization' (1991: 276). Given that the introduction of parliamentary democracy coincided with all these developments, it is hardly surprising that there was a strong tendency – among both elites and
non-elites – to attribute Germany's woes precisely to the Weimar constitution itself, correspondingly increasing the attraction of radical,
authoritarian nationalism. Modernisation, argues Peukert, 'took a
more brutal, uncompromising form in Germany in the twenties than
it did in other countries' (1991: 280), and its 'dark side' made it difficult for many Germans to retain their faith in the ability of liberal

democratic institutions to steer their way through the crisis. Although Peukert acknowledges the significance of the political relationships between the traditional elites and the bourgeoisie within the new parliamentary democracy, this alone does not explain the collapse of Weimar democracy, which can only be properly understood by placing its development within the context of a string of very particular historical circumstances, ones which would have tested (and which *will* test) *any* form of democratic rule within *any* cultural and ideological context.

We cannot quite leave matters here, though, because there are other things that can be said about German history, which tell us more about the particular form of the response to these crises, and the specific way in which citizenship was conceived and practices of exclusion from citizenship were mobilised. As Eley remarks, all modern societies are cobbled together with pre-modern elements, making the crucial question not simply one of tracking down 'feudal relics', but of establishing 'how certain "traditions" became selected for survival rather than others – how certain beliefs and practices came to reproduce themselves under radically changed circumstances, and how they became subtly transformed in the very process of renewal' (1986: 261). To answer this question, we need to turn to the work of Rogers Brubaker and others on the disjunction between the German 'nation' and the German 'state'.

The 'Brubaker thesis'

Brubaker concerns himself primarily with a different problem – namely, the differences between the French and German models of the relationship between immigration and citizenship – but in the process of examining this question, he also casts light on the question of the 'failure' of citizenship and democracy in Germany. His thesis is that France and Germany can be regarded as two contrasting ideal-typical models of how particular nation-states, formed under different historical conditions, are differently disposed to accept immigrants as citizens.

On the one hand, France serves as a model of a 'state-centred, assimilationist, essentially political' (1990: 380) understanding of citizenship, which allows, even demands the transformation of immigrants – as well as peasants – into Frenchmen (Weber 1976). The

French understanding of national identity is a political-territorial one, following the principle of *jus soli*, established in 1889. On this principle, French citizenship was, and continues to be, granted to everyone born and domiciled in France, partly in order to ensure that all French residents, no matter what their ethnocultural origins, would enter military service (Brubaker 1990: 395). The French elite were so confident, suggests Brubaker, of the capacity of French social and political institutions – especially the school and the army – to assimilate any foreigner into Frenchness that they dismissed the dangers of different ethno-cultural nations within the French nation. This meant that by the second generation everyone within the territorial boundaries of France was regarded and treated as a French citizen with full citizenship rights, and conversely there were no ethnic French outside the boundaries of the French state who could make a claim on French nationalism. French citizenship and democracy was thus based on a close alignment of ethno-cultural nation and political-territorial state, reflecting the particular trajectory of French nation-state formation. This does not mean that the two always overlap perfectly, as French conduct under the Nazis as well as the more recent history of ethnic hostility shows, but such ethno-cultural understandings of national identity and citizenship rights always have to work against the *jus soli* foundations of citizenship, rather than being able to call on a legal tradition of ethno-cultural exclusion. There is still a strong institutional tendency towards defining the nation as a 'nation of citizens'.

The German experience, on the other hand, 'reflects an ethnocultural understanding of nationhood as prior to and independent of the state' (1990: 380), and the German model revolves around a ethno-cultural 'community of descent', which is extremely resistant to the absorption of new members. German law has since 1913 conferred citizenship according to the *jus sanguinis* principle, that of kinship ties and descent. The German nation, as Ulrich Preuß observes, is conceived as 'a prepolitical community of individuals who are bound to each other by the commonness of either their "nature" (their blood) or their culture (their language, literature, religion, and history)' (Preuß 1996: 542). Preuß suggests that the origins of this conception may lie in the dispersion of Germanic tribes on the outskirts of the Roman Empire, whereas the Gauls were included within the territorial boundaries of the Empire. At the very least, most commentators (such as Halfmann 1997: 267) also note the fact that German state-formation followed, very belatedly, German nation-formation.

For Brubaker, the foundations of this detachment of nation and *Volk* from the state had three origins. First, western Germany was traversed by Europe's 'city belt', a dense belt of 'cities, ecclesiastical principalities, and other small but autonomous political jurisdictions' (1996: 113) all of which obstructed the development and consolidation of a territorial state encompassing all Germans. Second, a number of significant waves of German migration eastward since the Middle Ages had produced a presence of ethnic Germans throughout Central and Eastern Europe which also made it impossible for ethno-cultural and political boundaries to coincide. Third, the experience of Polish-German citizens in East Prussia, and the clear failure to assimilate them into German culture, underlay the elites' reluctance to pursue assimilation as an overall nation-building strategy (Brubaker 1990: 397). None the less, while the German state was perceived as effective and powerful, it remained possible to harness this *Volk* nation conception to the state, and Bismarck's ambition was always to present the German territorial state as the expression of the German *Volk*. This changed dramatically with the outcome of the First World War. The territorial and institutional boundaries of the state were highly contested by both the left and the right, and 'the Weimar Republic proved unable to "embody" the nation or to "contain" nationalism' . . . within the territorial frame of the state' (Brubaker 1996: 117). In Brubaker's words:

> Because the state had lost much of its binding, integrative power, nationalism was partially de-territorialized and de-institutionalized. Nationhood, which had become firmly, though never exclusively, identified with the prestigious and 'successful' state in the Bismarckian and Wilhelmine eras, was now detached from the devalued frame of the defeated state, and again identified primarily with the state-transcending, institutionally amorphous ethnocultural nation or *Volk*. (1996: 117–18)

The result was a conception of the 'imagined community' of the nation, not as a 'nation of citizens', but as a '*Volk* nation', bound together not by shared citizenship rights within the state, but by ties of blood and culture which were regarded as more fundamental, more 'sound' and of a 'higher order' than political-territorial ties, especially those revolving around liberal conceptions of individual rights.

This had a number of important consequences for both the operation of citizenship and democracy and the fate of liberalism in Germany. As Rainer Lepsius puts it:

The folk is conceived as a prepolitical essence; the individual is subsumed under this collectivity on the basis of the identity ascribed to his properties. The nation does not develop as a politically constituted solidarity association of citizens. On the contrary, it appears as a prepolitical essence which has a higher status than the individual. The attribution of an essential nature based on natural law rests on the value of the collectivity of the people, not on the value of the individual . . . there is no necessity for legitimizing political order through equal rights for citizens and democratic rights of participation. (1985: 49)

Liberal conceptions of individual rights are then constructed as alien to the organic unity of the *Volkgemeinschaft* (folk community), and both democratic procedures and citizenship rights become susceptible to erosion in the name of the interests of the *Volk* as interpreted by ruling elites (Lepsius 1985: 50). Most importantly, the idea of *opposition* which is so fundamental to liberal conceptions of democracy has no place within this German Romantic organicist conception, and tends to get constructed as 'treason' or an attack on the *Volk* as a whole; in addition, the organisation of citizenship rights around an ethno-cultural definition of nation-membership has what Lepsius calls a 'latent potential for degrading other peoples as inferior' (1985: 51; see also Peukert 1987; Noakes 1987; Sünker and Otto 1997). The Janus-faced character of the concept of the *Volk* detached from the state was that it *included* those Germans outside state territorial boundaries within the definition of Germanness, but *excluded* those German subjects who did not form part of the German community of descent. This exclusionary tendency in *Volkish* thought could take malign forms, so that we need to see the Nazis as having constructed it in a very particular way (there had never been, for example, an argument for the *removal* of citizenship rights from German subjects: Brubaker 1992: 166) but the basic tendency towards an *internal selectivity* in allocating citizenship rights had still been established. As Lepsius points out, 'the detachment of the concept of the nation from all constitutional foundations and nominal operational characteristics made possible the disenfranchisement, exclusion, and ultimate annihilation of German citizens of Jewish belief or origin without the recognition that this also abolished the civil rights and freedoms of all German citizens' (1985: 52). Once those rights have been stripped from *some* citizens, they have in effect been destroyed for *all* citizens, for there is no longer any secure foundation for the protection of any individual or group should they be defined

as lying outside that organic ethno-cultural abstraction which is the
Volk nation.

The kinds of 'tradition' which were drawn upon in response to the
crises of the Weimar period, then, were ideas which centred on ethnicity and cultural homogeneity, an organic conception of the nation
which was detached from the state in a way which one did not find in
the Western European and North American experience. Although any
conception of nationhood and citizenship will contain both ethno-
cultural and territorial-political elements, in the countries most frequently referred to in discussions of citizenship and democracy, such
as France and Britain, the two are relatively integrated, whereas
'in the German tradition ... political and ethno-cultural aspects of
nationhood have stood in tension with one another, serving as a basis
for competing conceptions of nationhood' (Brubaker 1990: 391), and
this competition leaves relatively little space for liberal understandings of citizenship. In times of particular socio-economic and political
crisis, such as the Weimar period, this instability in the understanding
of citizenship and nationhood certainly made it much easier for an
ideology of the *Volk* community, which stripped some members of
society of all their citizenship rights, to flourish.

Conclusion

Jürgen Habermas (1992) has identified three important features of
current developments in the relationship between citizenship and
national identity: first, the question of the future of the nation-state
itself following German re-unification and the ethno-national conflicts
breaking out throughout Eastern Europe; second, the implications of
the supranational entity of the EU for democratic processes based on
autonomous nation-states; third, the increasing waves of migrants and
asylum-seekers from the poorer regions of Eastern and Southern
Europe to the rest of Europe. The third process, in particular, 'exacerbates the conflict between the universalistic principles of constitutional democracies on the one hand and the particularistic claims of
communities to preserve the integrity of their *habitual* ways of life on
the other' (1992: 1).

What does the German case tell us about these three problems, in
a context of globalisation, with greater migration across state boundaries reproducing the very features which made its experience differ-

ent from the Anglo-French pattern of state-formation? States are bounded *territories* (Weber 1978), but nations are *imagined communities* (Anderson 1991), and the challenge posed by globalisation is how we are to respond to changed relationships between the two. The German experience of fascism indicates that there can be a profound tension between the ethno-cultural 'imagined community' of the *Volk* nation, and liberal conceptions of citizenship and democracy; it suggests that the best possible 'shell' for the latter may be a 'cool' and 'thin' (see Turner's discussion of 'cosmopolitan virtue' above, Chapter 2, as well as Elias's (1987) discussion of 'detachment') political-territorial conception of both state and nation, rather than a 'hot' and 'thick' idea of a national or cultural identity. This is especially true in conditions where increasing migration makes it ever more difficult to maintain very much of the 'fit' between nation and state, as is usually assumed in the conception of the 'nation-state' in most discussions of citizenship.

Will Kymlicka (1995) has recently suggested that the conception of liberalism which tries to deny cultural difference and treat every citizen as more or less equivalent individuals has become – if it was not already – 'incoherent' in the face of the real polyethnic and multicultural character of contemporary social life. An engagement with the German experience tells us that if we go beyond simply 'explaining away' the Nazi regime and the Holocaust in terms of German 'exceptionalism', and turn instead to understanding German history in terms of what it tells us about the different ways in which 'nation' and 'state', 'culture' and 'citizenship' can relate to each other under particular social, political and economic conditions, then we will have moved a considerable distance towards addressing what may be the most serious challenge facing our understanding of citizenship and democracy in a global era: that of formulating the social, political and economic bases of democratic and humane unity within societies composed of diverse ethnic, cultural and national forms.

Notes

1   It would be fair to say that there is a strong Anglo-French bias in citizenship theory, ranging from Marshall himself through to examples such as the recent collection titled *Citizenship, Identity and Social History*, edited by Charles Tilly (1995), which says hardly a word about Germany. The Western European and North American experience is then treated as the norm for nation-state

formation and cases such as Germany treated as exceptions or deviations from the 'Western' route to modernity, at enormous analytical cost.

2   Eley (1984) remarks that if the British bourgeoisie was more 'liberal' than their German counterparts, this was because 'In Britain liberalism reaped the benefits of a 'corporate' working class and a poorly developed socialism; in Germany its options were severely restricted by the risks of co-operating with a relatively more advanced and vigorously independent party of the working class' (1984: 122). The ties between the bourgeoisie and the landed aristocracy arose from 'a rational calculation of political interest in a situation where greater levels of parliamentary democracy necessarily worked to the advantage of the Socialist left. In Britain in this period of parliamentary forms proved an admirable means of containing socialism; in Germany they threatened to work in its favour' (1984: 125).

References

Almond, G.A. and Verba, S. (1963) *The Civic Culture: Political Attitudes and Democracy in Five Nations*, Princeton, NJ: Princeton University Press.

Anderson, B. (1991) *Imagined Communities*, London: Verso.

Bachrach, P. (1967) *The Theory of Democratic Elitism*, Boston, MA: Little, Brown.

Brubaker, R. (1990) 'Immigration, citizenship, and the nation-state in France and Germany: a comparative historical analysis', *International Sociology*, vol. 5, no. 4: 379–407.

Brubaker, R. (1992) *Citizenship and Nationhood in France and Germany*, Cambridge, MA: Harvard University Press.

——(1996) *Nationalism Reframed: Nationhood and the National Question in the New Europe*, Cambridge: Cambridge University Press.

Dahrendorf, R. (1968) *Society and Democracy in Germany*, London: Weidenfeld & Nicolson.

de Swaan, A. (1988) *In Care of the State*, Cambridge: Polity.

Eley, G. (1984) 'The British Model and the German Road: rethinking the course of German history before 1914', in D. Blackburn and G. Eley, *The Peculiarities of German History: Bourgeois Society and Politics in Nineteenth-Century Germany*, Oxford: Oxford University Press: 39–155.

——(1986) *From Unification to Nazism: Reinterpreting the German Past*, Boston, MA: Allen & Unwin.

——(1996) 'German history and the contradictions of modernity: the bourgeoisie, the state, and the mastery of reform', in G. Eley (ed.), *Society, Culture, and the State in Germany, 1870–1930*, Ann Arbor, MI: University of Michigan Press: 67–103.

Elias, N. (1987) *Involvement and Detachment*, Oxford: Basil Blackwell.

——(1996) *The Germans: Studies of Power Struggles and the Development of Habitus in the 19th and 20th Centuries*, Cambridge: Polity Press.

Habermas, J. (1992) 'Citizenship and national identity: some reflections on the future of Europe', *Praxis International*, vol. 12: 1–19.

Halfmann, J. (1997) 'Immigration and Citizenship in Germany: contemporary dilemmas', *Political Studies* 45 (2): 260–74.

Hong, Y.S. (1996) 'World War I and the German welfare state: gender, religion, and the paradoxes of modernity', in G. Eley (ed.), *Society, Culture, and the State in Germany, 1870–1930*, Ann Arbor, MI: University of Michigan Press: 345–70.

Kymlicka, W. (1995) *Multicultural Citizenship*, Oxford: Oxford University Press.

Lepsius, M.R. (1985) 'The nation and nationalism in Germany', *Social Research*, vol. 52, no. 1: 43–64.

Marshall, T.H. (1964) *Class, Citizenship and Social Development*, Chicago: University of Chicago Press.

Moore, B. Jr (1966) *Social Origins of Dictatorship and Democracy*, Harmondsworth: Penguin.

Noakes, J. (1987) 'Social outcasts in the Third Reich', in R. Bessel (ed.), *Life in the Third Reich*, Oxford: Oxford University Press: 83–96.

Pateman, Carole (1970) *Participation and Democratic Theory*, Cambridge: Cambridge University Press.

Peukert, D.J.K. (1987) *Inside Nazi Germany. Conformity, Opposition, and Racism in Everyday Life*, New Haven, CT: Yale University Press.

——(1991) *The Weimar Republic: The Crisis of Class Modernity*, London: Allen Lane.

Preuß, U.K. (1996) 'Two challenges to European citizenship', *Political Studies*, vol. 44, no. 3: 534–52.

Schumpeter, J.A. (1987) *Capitalism, Socialism and Democracy*, London: Unwin.

Steinmetz, G. (1996) 'The myth of an autonomous state: industrialists, Junkers, and social policy in Germany', in G. Eley (ed.), *Society, Culture, and the State in Germany, 1870–1930*, Ann Arbor, MI: University of Michigan Press: 257–318.

Sünker, H. and Otto, H.-U. (1997) '*Volk* community: identity formation and social practice', in H. Sünker and H.-U. Otto (eds), *Education and Fascism: Political Identity and Social Education in Nazi Germany*, London: Falmer: 15–35.

Thompson, D.F. (1970) *The Democratic Citizen*, Cambridge: Cambridge University Press.

Tilly, C. (ed.) (1995) *Citizenship, Identity and Social History: International Review of History*, Supplement 3, Cambridge: Cambridge University Press.

Verba, S. (1965) 'Germany: the remaking of political culture', in L.W. Pye and S. Verba (eds), *Political Culture and Political Development*, Princeton, NJ: Princeton University Press.

Verba, S. and Nie, N.H. (1972) *Participation in America*, New York: Harper & Row.

Weber, E. (1976) *Peasants into Frenchmen: The Modernization of Rural France, 1870–1914*, Stanford: Stanford University Press.

Weber, M. (1978) *Economy and Society*, Berkeley, CA: University of California Press.

9 CITIZENSHIP AND CULTURE IN CONTEMPORARY FRANCE: EXTREME RIGHT INTERVENTIONS

Katrina Gorjanicyn*

In the previous chapter, Brubaker's comparatively positive picture of French notions of citizenship served to reinforce criticism of German citizenship this century. In this chapter, however, Gorjanicyn disputes the usefulness of Brubaker's thesis for understanding more recent developments in France. As a former colonial yet nuclear-armed power, post-colonialism and the end of communism and the Cold War has created problems of cultural identity. The French Communist Party led the resistance against the Nazis during the Second World War and so after the War it became the watchdog of French politics, for example, leading the opposition to the French Army's suppression of the Algerian liberation movement. However, during the 1970s and 1980s, the Nouvelle Droite *inverted the Gramscian communist tradition of cultural studies, and* Front National *became the watchdog of French politics. Looking at the well-known headscarves affair, Gorjanicyn's chapter illustrates Turner's point about the inadequacies of T. H. Marshall's social-liberal model of citizenship in a multicultural society, It arguably also demonstrates*

*I wish to thank Dr Philomena Murrray for sharing sources and commenting on this chapter and Dr Derek McDougall and Carolyn O'Brien for recommending additional articles and Internet addresses.

the inadequacy of Rawls's model of tolerant citizenship in a just society. Gorjanicyn shows how the left and the right of post-war politics suffered internal splits over the new problems of unity and difference, secular values and religious multiculturalism, assimilation and contained separatism. She concludes that the French Revolutionary tradition of universal citizenship and jus soli *has in part shifted to the conservative tradition of* enracinement *or rootedness and* jus sanguinis.

The idea of citizenship in contemporary France is a site of discursive contestation. Competing definitions of citizenship reveal schisms in French politics regarding what constitutes culture, race and identity. Citizenship is determined not only by nationality laws which provide the formal status of membership in France; it is also defined through elaborate discursive devices which establish forms of cultural belonging to the national community. These discourses have the power to include or exclude groups of people on the basis of their 'culture' regardless of whether or not they are legal citizens of France. An inclusionary discourse accepts diversity and acknowledges the economic and cultural contribution of immigrants to the host society; a counter discourse premised on exclusion portrays immigrants as putting strain on the economy and unable to assimilate on the basis of cultural difference (Brubaker 1992: 76). A case study of citizenship in France demonstrates the need for discursive analysis of how 'culture' has become the linchpin for the meanings various groups attach to 'citizenship'.

In this chapter, I focus on how the French extreme right political party, the *Front National*, and the culturalist new right, the *Nouvelle Droite*, have shaped debate on nationhood. They have done this by making discursive interventions into the realm of culture to construct citizenship in racially specific terms. In particular, I am concerned with how the left-wing discourse of *la droite à la différence* (the right to difference) has been appropriated by the extreme right to exclude non-European immigrants from the cultural criteria on which French citizenship is predicated. Moreover, I analyse the extent to which French political parties of the traditional left and right have borrowed from the extreme right's discourse to produce definitions of French citizenship based around the notion of a European 'race'.[1] I locate these approaches to citizenship within the historical framework of French Republicanism which, with its emphasis on assimilation and cultural unity, has structured recent debates on identity and membership in the French community (Favell 1998).

Notions of citizenship in contemporary France revolve around various concepts of cultural identity which are linked to perceptions of national community. A discursive struggle is ensuing over what it is to be 'French'; ultimately, it is a struggle over the creation and legitimation of a dominant culture and identity against which otherness can be measured. Following Turner (1997, and this volume, Chapter 2) I see these competing discursive formations of culture as challenging Marshall's theory of citizenship in that they bring cultural, religious and linguistic diversity into the idea of what constitutes citizenship. Marshall recognised social class divisions but did not take account of cultural multiplicity (Marshall 1950); his theory was based on the premise that modern societies are ethnically and culturally homogenous (Roche 1992). Yet it is largely because France has become a heterogeneous society in the twentieth century, particularly since the Second World War, that the meaning of citizenship is disputed. It is this articulation between culture and citizenship that I wish to explore.

Cultural heterogeneity and the challenge to French Republicanism

The cultural heterogeneity which now characterises French society is not unique to France and neither is it a new phenomenon. Migrant labour and the arrival of political and economic refugees have marked the history of most West European countries throughout the twentieth century. It is how immigration has been problematised and politicised in France during the 1980s and 1990s, particularly in relation to economic conditions and the principles of republicanism, that has turned cultural heterogeneity into a salient issue.

The national mood regarding immigration is closely aligned to shifts in the economic climate. When migrant labour was sought in France during the 1970s to boost the labour force, immigration did not trigger a national debate but, in the 1980s and 1990s when economic conditions deteriorated, immigration was converted into a major dilemma in France (Favell 1998: 22–3). Moreover, the issue of cultural difference which permeates debates on French citizenship can be viewed as a new phenomenon related to a crisis of the nation-state, which has occurred in an era of postmodernity. Contrary to the principles underlying republicanism, fragmentation and plurality are evident in French society (Silverman 1994).

In response to these economic and social developments, the French are reviewing the cultural space accorded to immigrants and their children by the French state. Immigrants' presence in France has been the trigger for a questioning of what constitutes the substance of French nationality, culture, and hence citizenship. Debates about citizenship hinge on who should be included or excluded from cultural membership of the French nation-state. Of central concern in this process is the extent to which France can accommodate cultural difference. However, 'cultural difference' is a rubbery concept that is subject to shifts in meaning and significance in discursive constructions of citizenship.

As the French have been confronted by a range of issues which have prompted them to reconsider the meaning of culture and national identity there has been a parallel rise in xenophobia. However, fear and intolerance of 'otherness' has been apparent in other periods of French history. In the late nineteenth century 'peaceful invasion' and 'depopulation or denationalisation' were terms used to register dissatisfaction with the arrival of European immigrants in France. Nevertheless, there was an assumption that European immigrants could be assimilated and become part of the *creuset français* (the French melting pot) in line with republican values of assimilation. This emphasis on cultural homogeneity underpinned the reform of the Code of French Nationality in 1889 which was intended to make 'Frenchmen from foreigners' (Wihtol de Wenden 1991). While it was believed that European immigrants could be absorbed into the dominant culture of France, non-European immigrants were seen as being resistant to integration.

Since the 1930s North African immigrants have been the primary target of racism in France; they have been widely depicted as foreigners who cannot become 'French'. However, North African immigration has been problematised in different ways during the twentieth century. In the 1930s, North Africans were stereotyped as primitive, delinquent, libidinous and diseased. While their arrival in France during this period was referred to as an 'invasion', Islam was not constructed as a threat to national identity at this point (Wihtol de

Wenden 1991). Algerian emigration to France increased from 1947 when a new statute enabled Algerians to move freely between North Africa and France. But this did not feature as a major concern in French politics at the time because post-war reconstruction and modernisation dominated the political agenda. Another wave of North African immigration occurred during the 1960s when, following the independence of Algeria, Morocco and Tunisia, citizens from these countries could easily reside in France. Throughout most of this decade, immigration was not perceived as a problem by the state because North Africans provided a pool of cheap, unskilled labour in the secondary labour market which stimulated development of the French economy.

In the 1970s the world economic recession changed the way in which North African immigrants were received in France. The government and trade unions reacted to the sharp rise in unemployment by reserving jobs for French nationals. New discursive arrangements were introduced to problematise the presence of guest workers in France. During the economic boom, when extra labour was required, migrants who sidestepped official government regulations and entered France without work and residence permits were seen as partaking in *immigration spontanée* (spontaneous immigration). This discourse conveyed that immigrants were welcome in France even when they did not adhere to official procedures relating to the immigration process. However, when such spontaneous immigration ceased to be of economic benefit to France these same guest workers were placed in the category of *immigration clandestine* (illegal immigration) which marginalised their status within the workplace and society. Further restrictions on immigration were imposed by the Marcellin-Fontanet circulars of 1972, which limited access to work and residence permits and facilitated the expulsion of illegal immigrants. In 1974, primary immigration was suspended and the French government made unsuccessful efforts to introduce measures to cut back on family reunion and encourage voluntary repatriation. The distinction between legal and illegal immigrants has been further politicised in the 1990s with the extreme right, followed closely by parties of the traditional right, excluding illegal immigrants from the economic, social and political dimensions of citizenship rights. Attempts to address illegal immigration have often stalled due to major differences amongst the political parties in how they problematise the issue (de Brie 1997; Lochak 1997; Vaillant 1997). Consequently, many immigrants continue to be 'de facto citizens' of France; they participate in society but are not officially recognised as belonging to it (Layton-Henry 1996).

The economic climate and pressures on the welfare state continue to shape the way in which North African immigrants are perceived in France. The *Front National* and the political parties of the traditional left and right have contributed to a discourse which portrays North Africans as draining scarce resources. However, the preoccupation with economic insecurities is not the only factor linked to anti-immigration sentiment. Islam has become a problem for those who construct North Africans as 'others' and 'culturally different'. This has prevented the granting of equal citizenship. The idea that North Africans are outside French culture was demonstrated in 1984 when a poll taken in France showed that 81 per cent of respondents thought that Italians and Spaniards had integrated well while 70 per cent held the view that Algerians were badly integrated (Hargreaves 1989: 154). Discourses which separate out 'non-Europeans' have been extended by the extreme right's frequent claim that France has been 'swamped' by North African immigrants. This language plays on – if not produces – fears that cultural homogeneity and social security are threatened by 'others'. Yet the number of people living in France without French nationality at the present time, around 7 per cent, is the same as it was in 1930. What has changed has been the percentage of Europeans and non-Europeans settling in France with the number of North African immigrants increasing and European immigration decreasing. In 1946 Europeans made up 88.7 per cent of the foreign population in France and North Africans constituted 2.3 per cent. By 1982 European immigrants had fallen to 47.6 per cent of the foreign population while North Africans had risen to 38.5 per cent (Hargreaves 1989: 148). Furthermore, there has been a ghettoisation of Muslims and Blacks in poorer urban areas of France, which contributes to the idea that France is being 'swamped' by immigrants.

If common cultural membership, based on the dominant culture, is a criterion for being French then it is apparent that North African immigrants and their children are excluded from full citizenship rights. The granting of legal citizenship and participation in economic and political spheres does not guarantee cultural rights. These perceptions of North African immigrants are not, however, necessarily fixed and final. Although simplistic perceptions of Muslims in Europe prevail in political and popular discourses, negative perceptions of cultural otherness may well be on the brink of change as the second and third

generations of North African immigrants carve out a place for themselves in French intellectual and social life (Ramadan 1998).

Insecurities concerning national identity that inform debates on
citizenship in France have a specific historical context. The French
are struggling to reconcile new approaches to citizenship that have
arisen in an era of post-colonialism and immigration from North
Africa with traditional notions of citizenship that are steeped in
republican and revolutionary history. There is a clash between, on
the one hand, discourses of plurality and difference which have
been emerging in recent decades and, on the other hand, concepts
of belonging to a nation which, rooted in the revolutionary and
republican tradition of the eighteenth century, revolve around discourses of centralisation, universalism, cultural unity and assimilation
(Silverman 1991, 1994).

The stark contrast between historical and contemporary discourses
of citizenship became the basis of a national dilemma in 1989 when
three girls were suspended from their school for wearing Muslim
headscarves to class. A lengthy and prominent national debate based
on different interpretations and usages of the discourse of *la droite à
la différence* followed the incident of *l'affaire du foulard* (the headscarves affair). The headscarves affair elicited polarised views on the
wearing of religious adornments to state schools (officially banned for
all religions to ensure the republican principle of separation of state
and religion), falling into the categories of secularism and difference.
Both the left and the right of the political spectrum were divided in
their response to the headscarves affair and an uneasy discursive
alliance formed between left and right in regard to the issue of cultural difference. Secularism was supported by assimilationist republicans and members of anti-racist and feminist groups who all argued
that this approach protected liberty and neutrality; yet this was a discourse that appealed to groups on the right who embraced secularism
and assimilation because it would assist in halting what they believed
to be the Islamicisation of France. Similarly, the argument in favour
of the right to express difference incorporated elements from the left
and the right. Sections of the left supported the decision of Lionel
Jospin, then Minister for Education, who permitted the girls to wear
their headscarves to school on the basis that they had a right to display
cultural difference, but this discursive terrain was simultaneously
occupied by members of the *Nouvelle Droite* who took the position
that different cultures should be marked out and function separately

from each other (Silverman 1994: 111–18; Favell 1998: 174–83). Moreover, the intersection of these discourses of difference juxtaposed ideological constructions of culture, race, nation and gender. The headscarves affair raised issues of how these constructs are rolled into a notion of 'otherness' to produce specific definitions of nationhood and cultural citizenship.

Other historical factors relating to France's position in world politics have contributed to shifts in discourses of citizenship. France's leading role in shaping European defence initiatives through the strategy of nuclear deterrence, as played out in Cold War politics, has become redundant. Narratives of national grandeur and glory, which were integral to the political discourse of Gaullist France, have lost their poignancy. Consequently, the nation's relative position of power in world politics has frayed. Colonisation is no longer perceived as bringing advantages to France; North African immigration to France is more often presented as being a social, economic or cultural problem than an asset. These shifts in world order and the legacy of Empire, which have contributed to a crisis of national identity, have been exploited by the extreme right in its efforts to assemble a monolithic definition of French citizenship.

Also framing the debate on citizenship and what it means to be French is the effect that the demise of the nation-state is having on the national psyche as the French position themselves within a borderless EU. With European integration and globalisation comes the prospect of a lack of control over national sovereignty and a further intermeshing of cultures, presenting a challenge to the universalism of the Enlightenment that traditionally has underpinned notions of citizenship in France. While digesting the political, economic and cultural changes that European integration imposes, the French are being forced into re-evaluating nationhood in the context of globalising processes.

The concept of 'cultural difference'

A specific discursive use of 'cultural difference' forms the basis of what has been termed the 'new racism'. The new racism does not directly employ the language of biological difference but the assumptions underpinning this form of racism, based on essentialist notions of the community in which cultural differences are fashioned as

natural and commonplace, are very closely aligned to the racist discourse of biological determinism. According to the theory of the new
racism, cultural discourse becomes the vehicle through which 'nation'
is imagined. This concept of cultural difference is the central plank in
the French extreme right's discursive strategies (Barker 1982; Seidel
1986).

The discourse of cultural difference is more than just a new
vocabulary; it has played a major role in formal political debates about
French citizenship. Attempts to change French citizenship laws have
incorporated ethno-cultural concepts of nationhood which echo the
German criteria for citizenship. I would argue that this point has been
understated by Brubaker (1992) in his comparison of French and
German nationhood. Brubaker claims that a clear distinction continues to exist between the French assimilationist and the German dif-
ferentialist constructions of citizenship. According to him, the French
have largely adhered to a political understanding of nationhood which
is predicated on assimilation and cultural unity, while the German idea
of nationhood remains based primarily on cultural particularism with
German citizenship ascribed on the basis of descent (Brubaker 1992).
While Brubaker acknowledges that the French extreme right has challenged the traditional notion of French citizenship by promoting policies of exclusion that pivot on the idea of cultural difference and are
more closely attuned to the German model of citizenship than the
French, this point requires elaboration (Brubaker 1992: 13–14). A discursive analysis of the French extreme right and its effect on the established political parties of the left and right shows that concepts of
citizenship have been moving closer to the German model of descent
than Brubaker concedes in his analysis.

The legal criteria of French citizenship, traditionally based on a
combination of *jus soli* (citizenship by birth in the territory) and *jus
sanguinis* (citizenship by bloodline), has been challenged by the traditional right-wing parties on the basis that citizenship ought to be
determined primarily by descent. The French Nationality Code, which
automatically transformed children born on French territory of
foreign parents into French citizens at majority, was reviewed in 1986.
Members of the political parties of the traditional right argued that
second and third generation immigrants should not automatically
acquire citizenship. Harsh anti-immigration measures accompanied
the newly elected right-wing coalition's stance on nationality laws.
New immigration policies were packaged in a discourse which empha-

sised a need to preserve national community and national identity (Silverman 1994: 141–2). While the Chirac Government succeeded in clamping down on immigration laws, its proposals to change the Nationality Code were blocked by strong opposition and political circumstances. Although the territorial component of French citizenship laws remained intact and the acquisition of French citizenship retained distinct features which set it apart from the German ascription rules (Brubaker 1992: 81), the idea of belonging to the French community was, nevertheless, reconceptualised in political discourse with nationality overtly linked to ethno-cultural understandings of community. This occurred largely in response to the extreme right's definition of nationhood which is based around a concept of culture transmitted by descent. The *Nouvelle Droite* and the *Front National* have been instrumental in placing these discursive constructions of nationhood on the political agenda.

Concepts of the 'other' which underscore debates concerning cultural difference are central to the approach taken by the *Nouvelle Droite* in its invention of French national identity. The *Nouvelle Droite*, of which GRECE (Research and Study Group for a European Civilisation) is the key group, is comprised of right-wing intellectuals who promote racism through cultural study and 'metapolitics'. In making interventions into culture, the *Nouvelle Droite* has inverted the left-wing strategy of counterhegemony developed by the Italian Marxist, Antonio Gramsci (Seidel 1986). Members associated with the *Nouvelle Droite* work within the cultural sphere, with the aim of determining the way in which race and national identity are defined. Racism is transported through academic language and pseudo-scientific theories in an effort to exclude 'non-Europeans' and members of the Jewish community from French citizenship. However, the *Nouvelle Droite* does not directly refer to 'race'; it takes 'culture' as its reference point. Central to the racist discourse of the *Nouvelle Droite* is the idea that French culture is linked to 'enracinement' (rootedness). This concept was developed by the overtly racist *Action Française* of the 1920s, which assembled and prized the notion of Indo-European roots (Seidel 1986; Simmons 1996: 207–15). The interconnection between race and culture has been made explicit in *Identité*, a magazine which focuses on national theory, where it has been argued that the purity of France's Indo-European roots connects it to the 'white world' (*Guardian Weekly*, 1/12/91).

Jean-Marie Le Pen, leader of the *Front National*, clearly couches his anti-immigration policies and racist definition of citizenship within the discursive framework of cultural difference. Le Pen's approach to shaping perceptions of otherness is grounded in populist language rather than the 'respectable' discourse of the *Nouvelle Droite*; however, both discursive strategies inter-relate in their construction of race and nation as hereditary. It is primarily North African immigrants, including second and third generations, who are excluded from the *Front National's* definition of French citizens. Le Pen portrays 'non-Europeans' as culturally different from the 'French' and argues that it is natural and common sense to exclude and expel 'others' from France: I adore North Africans. But their place is in the Maghreb ... I am not racist but national. ... For a nation to be harmonious it must have a certain ethnic and spiritual homogeneity' (cited in Silverman 1994: 167). The slippage between biological and cultural formations of race and nation is clearly evident in Le Pen's concept of heritage in which culture and nationality are consanguineous: 'We cannot share the heritage of France with anyone. Our heritage is our nationality transmitted by our ancestors' (cited in Ogden 1991).

Despite claiming that the *Front National* does not espouse racism, Le Pen and other members of his political party have stated that they do not believe in the equality of races (Agence France Presse 18/2/97). This was articulated in detail by Catherine Megret of the *Front National* who, shortly after she was elected as mayor of the southern town of Vitrolles in 1997, was reported as saying that blacks are genetically different from whites (Agence France Presse 25/3/97).

Le Pen's public speeches are littered with references to differences between the French person and the non-European other, and these references both create and play on xenophobia among electors (*Le Monde*, 1998). This discourse attracted 15 per cent of the vote in the 1995 French presidential elections and over 20 per cent of the vote in a large number of towns (Shields 1995). However, these electoral coups cannot be directly translated into an anti-immigration sentiment. Popular support for the extreme right's policy of keeping cultures separate and limiting the criteria for citizenship to a consanguineous notion of nationality is tied to instabilities and perceptions of a wider set of social, political and economic 'problems' than immigration alone. Le Pen links his anti-immigration policies to economic conditions and law and order concerns. His solutions to problems are based on giving priority to the French over foreigners in employment, housing and welfare (Shields 1995: 24–5; Agence France

Presse 1/5/97). This discourse has resonated in the south of France where anti-immigration and xenophobia have occurred in a context of high unemployment, rapid urbanisation, increasing inequalities, disaffection from politics and a loss of a sense of solidarity (Gaspard 1995: 149–53). The *Front National* has developed polices which focus on the major issues dominating the French political agenda and it trades on offering an alternative to the political parties of the traditional left and right (Front National 1998). Le Pen's foray into mainstream politics has posed a major dilemma for the established political parties in terms of how they incorporate immigrants into the notion of citizenship and how they discuss national identity and cohesiveness.

French political parties and the construction of citizenship

The *Front National's* racist discourse has had a major influence in setting the political agenda on immigration. The extreme right's interventions into culture have shaped the way in which definitions of citizenship and national identity have been moulded by the French political parties of the traditional left and right. The established parties have woven elements of the *Front National's* definitions of culture and otherness into their discourses on immigration as they struggle to win back the share of the vote which the extreme right has taken from them at both national and local elections. It is the *Front National* rather than the French Communist Party which now fills the role of the 'watchdog' of French politics.

A 50-point plan designed by the *Front National* in 1991 details policies that are intended 'to protect the French'. The fundamental goals of the extreme right include abolition of all non-European immigration to France, definition of French nationality on the basis of descent, and giving preference to French nationals for jobs, social security and political rights. Although the traditional parties of the left and right have not directly endorsed the *Front National's* agenda they have contributed to discursive formations that promote racism in order to play 'catch up' politics. It is primarily the neo-Gaullist RPR and the liberal right, the UDF, which have lost votes to the *Front National* and have since engaged with the extreme right in order to reconnect with the electorate. This collaboration has occurred at two levels. First, within the political sphere the traditional right has formed alliances with the

Front National in local elections, particularly in the south of France. Second, in the discursive arena the traditional right has invented culture and nationhood using a similar language to that of the extreme right.

When Jacques Chirac was Prime Minister of France he made a clear distinction between French nationals and immigrants based on the notion of cultural difference:

> When a Frenchman living in the Goutte-d'Or and working with his wife to earn 15000 francs a month, sees a family [of immigrants] crowded into the apartment across the landing consisting of a father, three or four wives and a score of kids drawing F50000 in social welfare payments, and add to that the racket and the smells, it just burns him up. (Cited in *The Guardian Weekly*, 30/6/91)

Chirac's preference for a national identity based on 'European culture' has been evident in his policies concerning rights and access to citizenship. As Mayor of Paris, Chirac clearly intended to boost the birth rate of Europeans in the city by introducing a special family allowance which was available only to French and European Community nationals. A similar programme to produce 'European babies' has since been on the Front National's agenda (Agence France Presse 17/4/98).

Definitions of French nationality based on 'European culture' were again narrowed by the RPR when in 1986 the Chirac Government proposed changes to the Nationality Code to prevent children born in France to foreign parents from automatically acquiring French nationality. Again the notion of citizenship was linked to the idea that culture is inherited and cannot be obtained through residency. The 'Pasqua laws' of 1993 and Debré Bill of 1997, which increased restrictions on immigrants' entitlements, consolidated this ethno-cultural approach to citizenship.

More recently however, as President of France, Chirac has dissociated himself from the extreme right. During the run-up to the 1998 regional elections Chirac denounced the *Front National* as 'racist and xenophobic', and he urged the traditional right to abstain from electoral pacts with the extremists (Agence France Presse 23/3/98 28/3/98).

Valéry Giscard d'Estaing of the UDF has modelled French citizenship around a theory that nationality and culture are welded together; he has advocated a policy of *jus sanguinis* (nationality determined by descent) over *jus soli* (nationality determined by where a person is born). Giscard d'Estaing's position on culture was further outlined in an article he wrote for *Figaro Magazine* in 1991 in which he described immigration to France as an 'invasion'.

Despite recent attempts by the RPR to isolate the *Front National* in the March 1998 regional elections, members of the 'moderate right' have openly collaborated with the extreme right. In a number of southern regions of France the RPR and UDF have continued to join forces with the *Front National* in order to govern. Moreover, former French Prime Minister, Edouard Balladur, proposed setting up a commission – which would include members of the *Front National* – to look into restricting welfare benefits to French nationals. This proposal accords with the extreme right's policies of 'national preference' (Bacqué 1998).

To some extent the French Socialist Party has also been lured by the discourse of the extreme right. From the late 1980s, as support for the *Front National* increased, there was a clear shift towards the right in the Socialist Party's approach to immigration and citizenship. The Socialists developed a harder line on immigration by placing tighter restrictions on the rights of residency during President Mitterrand's administration. In 1989, Mitterrand crossed into the extreme right's territory when on French television he used the phrase, coined by the right in the 1970s, *seuil de tolérance* (threshold of tolerance) in his discussion of immigration.

The Socialist Party has been implemented in creating the idea that Muslim immigrants are unassimilable. This was evident in the words of Gaston Defferre, former Socialist Interior Minister:

> When Poles, Italians, Spanish, and Portugese live in France and decide to naturalize, it matters little whether they are Catholics, Protestants, Jews, or atheists ... But the rules of Islam are not simply religious rules. They are rules of living that concern ... marriage, divorce, the care of children, the behavior of men, the behavior of women ... these rules are contrary to all the rules of French law on the custody of children in case of divorce, and they are contrary to [French rules on] the rights of women with respect to their husbands. What is more, in France we don't have the same habits of living. (Cited in Brubaker 1992: 149)

In 1997 the Socialist Party's campaign promises to repeal the harsh anti-immigration legislation, introduced by the previous right-wing government in the Debré Bill, were short lived. The Jospin Government's proposals for new immigration laws were surrounded by controversy on the basis that it was seen to be shifting towards the right's anti-immigration policies (Agence France Presse 26/8/97).

The French Communist Party (PCF) reinvented its approach to immigration and citizenship in the early 1990s. Although blatantly anti-immigrant in the 1970s and 1980s when immigrant workers entered working-class areas, the PCF has now developed policies which promote social, political and economic rights for immigrants. The PCF does not tie cultural conformity to the criteria for French citizenship; membership in the French community is linked to residency, equality and human rights (Parti Communiste 1990, 1991: 5). These policies set the PCF apart from the other political parties but, as the party is no longer a dominant force in French politics (attracting fewer votes overall than the *Front National*), the Communists have limited ability to shape the debate on immigration and citizenship.

Conclusion: reconceptualising citizenship

Cultural diversity has become a feature of the modern nation-state and it challenges the conceptual boundaries of citizenship. The mosaic composition of French society and the ways in which it has been problematised point to a need to develop a wider perspective on citizenship that takes account of the linkage between ethnicity and national identity. As the case study of contemporary France reveals, discursive formations of identity, belonging and nationhood can be soldered to a notion of cultural conformity which is constructed in racist terms. The interventions of the French extreme right demonstrate that the meaning of 'cultural difference' is a site of discursive struggle which has the potential to include or exclude those who do not partake in the formation of the dominant culture on which nationality is moulded.

Racist notions of citizenship which use 'culture' as a platform are not, however, the preserve of the extreme right. The French political parties of the 'moderate' right and the left have been implicated in creating the frontiers of citizenship by making verbal concessions to the extreme right and introducing stringent laws pertaining to immigrants. It is possible that these culturally-specific definitions of citizenship could be reinforced at the supranational level with the abolition of internal border controls between EU states under the terms of the Maastricht Treaty of 1995. This has the potential to create a 'Fortress Europe' whereby 'non-Europeans' are excluded from the idea of community (Weil 1996: 83–6). However, the EU may provide a new public space where multiple understandings of citizenship emerge (Meehan 1996).

Although the French extreme right has used 'culture' as its tool in formulating an exclusionary definition of citizenship, notions of culture need not be attached to racist constructions of national community. There are other means of fashioning citizenship around the concept of culture which decouple national identity from ethnic homogeneity. A more expansive and inclusive citizenship criteria premised on cultural rights would redirect the debate on culture and citizenship. Such rights would encompass cultural resources such as education, knowledge, religion and language (Turner 1997: 6) within a framework of tolerance, cultural promotion, recognition of diverse lifestyles, and legitimate, dignifying representation whereby 'difference' is not marginalised from the dominant culture (Pakulski 1997: 77, 80). Merging cultural rights with French citizenship would create a new discursive space that incorporates immigrants into the fabric of the national community. This discourse of cultural rights challenges the French extreme right's monopoly of the discursive terrain of culture; 'culture' and its connection with national community can be conceptualised through different ideological lenses. The idea of citizenship, as based on culture, is a malleable concept.

Note

1   For further analysis of the extreme right's discourse and how it has shaped the debate on immigration within French politics see Gorjanicyn (1998).

References

Agence France Presse:
  'French group to attack Front leader over racist comments', 18/2/97.
  'National Front mayor to face law suit over race remarks', 25/3/97.
  'Far rightist Le Pen kicks off campaign in French election', 1/5/97.
  'French Socialist premier dithers on new immigration law', 26/8/97.
  'President Chirac to address French Monday night', 23/3/98.
  'Thousands march in France against far-right National Front', 28/3/98.
  'Court ends National Front cash bonus for European babies', 17/4/98.

Bacqué, Raphaëlle (1998) 'Balladur tilts towards the National Front', *Guardian Weekly*, 28 June.

Barker, Martin (1982) *The New Racism, Conservatives and the Ideology of the Tribe*, Frederick, Maryland: Alethia Books.

Brubaker, Rogers (1992) *Citizenship and Nationhood in France and Germany*, Cambridge, MA, and London: Harvard University Press.

de Brie, Christian (1997) 'Aux frontières des libertés: la politique française d'immigration mise à l'épreuve', *Le Monde Diplomatique*, November.

Favell, Adrian (1998) *Philosophies of Integration: Immigration and the Idea of Citizenship in France and Britain*, London: Macmillan.

Front National (1998) 'Qui sommes-nous?', http://www.front-nat.fr/qui.htm.

Gaspard, Françoise (1995) *A Small City in France: A Socialist Mayor Confronts Neofascism*, Cambridge, MA, and London: Harvard University Press.

Gorjanicyn, Katrina (1998) 'Race, Culture and Identity: The "Other" in French Political Discourse', in Stephen Alomes and Michael Provis, *A Changing France in a Changing World*, rev. edn, Clayton, Victoria: Institute for Study of French Australian Relations.

Hargreaves, Alec G. (1989) 'The Beur generation: integration or exclusion?', in J. Howorth and G. Ross (eds), *Contemporary France: A Review of Interdisciplinary Studies*, vol. 3, London, New York: Pinter.

Layton-Henry, Zig (1996) 'Citizenship and Migrant Workers in Western Europe', in P. Murray and P. Rich (eds), *Visions of European Unity*, Boulder, CO: Westview Press.

Le Monde (1998) 'Le Front national, c'est ça',
http://www.lemonde.fr/elections/regionales/cestca/index.html.

Lochak, Danièle (1997) 'Bons "étrangers" et mauvais "clandestins"', *Le Monde Diplomatique*, November.

Marshall, T.H. (1950) *Citizenship and Social Class*, Cambridge: Cambridge University Press.

Meehan, Elizabeth (1996) 'The Debate on Citizenship and European Union', in P. Murray and P. Rich (eds), *Visions of European Unity*, Boulder, CO: Westview Press.

Ogden, Philip (1991) 'Immigration to France since 1945: myth and reality', *Ethnic and Racial Studies*, vol. 14, no. 3 (July): 294–318.

Pakulski, Jan (1997) 'Cultural Citizenship', *Citizenship Studies*, vol. 1, no. 1: 73–86.

Parti Communiste (1990) Extrait du Programme du PCF voté au 27ème Congrès en décembre.

——(1991), *L'Humanité*, 12 July.

Ramadan, Tariq (1998) 'Immigrations, Intégration et Politiques de Coopération: L'islam d'Europe sort de l'isolement', *Le Monde Diplomatique*, April.

Roche, M. (1992) *Rethinking Citizenship: Welfare, Ideology and Change in Modern Society*, Cambridge: Polity Press.

Seidel, Gill (1986) 'Culture, Nation and Race in the British and French New Right', in Ruth Levitas (ed.), *The Ideology of the New Right*, Cambridge: Polity Press.

Shields, James G. (1995) 'Le Pen and the Progression of the Far-Right vote in France', *French Politics and Society*, vol. 13, no. 2 (Spring): 21–39.

Simmons, Harvey Gerald (1996) *The French National Front: The Extremist Challenge to Democracy*, Boulder, CO: Westview Press.

Silverman, Maxim (1991) *Race, Discourse and Power in France*, Aldershot: Avebury.

——(1994) Deconstructing the Nation: Immigration, Racism and Citizenship in Modern France, London and New York: Routledge.

Turner, Bryan S. (1997) 'Citizenship Studies: A General Theory', *Citizenship Studies*, vol. 1, no. 1: 5–18.

The Guardian Weekly, 30 June 1991.

The Guardian Weekly, 1 December 1991.

Vaillant, Emmanuel (1997) 'De l'usage des régularisations', *Le Monde Diplomatique*, November.

Weil, Patrick (1996) 'Nationalities and Citizenship: The lessons of the French experience for Germany and Europe', in David Cesarani and Mary Fulbrook, *Citizenship, Nationality and Migration in Europe*, London and New York: Routledge.

Wihtol de Wenden, Catherine (1991) 'North African immigration and the French political imaginary', in Silverman (1991).

10 GENDERED CITIZENSHIP IN BRITAIN: FROM MOTHER-CARER TO WORKER*

Linda Hancock

In this chapter, Hancock looks at the way both class and the gendering of citizenship have shaped social policy shifts that were initiated by the Thatcher–Major Conservative governments. Under Blair, the basis of women's citizenship entitlements has shifted from mother–carer to paid worker. While committed to inclusion and participation of previously marginalised groups, Blair's Welfare to Work and income tax credit reforms for lone mothers have been controversial, and his childcare initiatives slow to be implemented. However, change driven by EU supranational Directives may trigger faster reform at the national level, signalling the significance of new forms of citizenship. The argument and themes of this chapter resemble those of the case studies of Australia and Japan in Chapters 15 and 16.

Debates on equality and democratic participation for women in political, civil, social and economic life have been advanced through drawing on notions of citizenship and rights. Mainly developed at the level of the individual's interface with the nation-state, and more

* I am grateful to the British Council for assisting travel for the UK-based research for this chapter.

recently with supranational and transnational entities, citizenship usefully encapsulates the inter-mixture of rights and duties that flow from
membership of a polity. However, citizenship does not necessarily
enhance democratic participation or egalitarian outcomes, and historically it has been a gendered site of contested meanings and divergent practices. Much of the recent thinking on citizenship (relevant in
particular to OECD countries in the West) grapples with reconceptualising citizenship in ways that cater for choice and diversity of roles
across genders, the public/private divide, and the carer/worker distinction. This thinking also grapples with reconceptualising citizenship
in ways that reformulate people's rights and obligations at national,
regional and global levels.

The first section of the chapter analyses citizenship as a gendered
site in Britain under Thatcher and the Conservatives, and the second

This chapter is about what citizenship has meant and might mean
in the future for women in Britain. My analysis draws on feminist critiques of liberalism and social contract theory (Held 1989; Pateman
1989; Meehan 1991, 1993; Vogel 1991; Lewis and Åström 1992; Carlson
1994; Everingham 1995; Lister 1997). These authors criticise the
supposedly gender-neutral and abstract notions of citizenship under
liberal and contract theories and the more recent 'citizen-as-worker'
model, in which citizenship rights flow through a person's status as
paid worker. Women's participation in political, civil, economic and
social spheres is mediated through the family (marriage, children and
men) and the private sphere (through caring for children, the dependent or disabled), rendering women's citizenship typically derivative
and relational (see Hancock 1999). Moreover, women's participation
in society, although far from passive, has been concentrated in generally devalued, informal and community spheres and at subordinated
levels of public life. In terms of citizenship, women have been
marginalised and excluded from dominant male centric notions
of citizenship, public participation and rights. Central to such marginalisation is the devaluing of women's caring roles.

The first section of the chapter analyses citizenship as a gendered
site in Britain under Thatcher and the Conservatives, and the second
section looks at more recent developments under the Blair Labour
government. Fractured along lines of class and race, the picture
of women's citizenship under neo-liberalism and Thatcherite policies
favoured a general model of women as citizen/mother/carer, rather
than as citizen/worker or a combination of the two. Thus, in the deeply
divided society that emerged from 17 years of Conservative rule, more
women than ever were working, but increasingly in part-time and

casualised work, and for lower wages in the secondary labour market. Women rank high among the poorest in a society that has seen the post-war welfare state whittled away. This chapter takes the view that maintaining beneficiaries at below subsistence levels, or as the 'working poor', does little to enhance active participation as citizens and does little to create the conditions for citizens to exercise their citizenship rights. Under neo-conservatism, the rhetoric of formal equality is strongly contrasted with the reality of a lack of substantive equality and substantive citizenship for women. This is starkly illustrated in the Conservatives' approach to key areas of social policy. Under Blair, reforms point to a strong endorsement of citizen as worker. This has prompted criticism of women's policy reforms, in light of Blair's renewed commitment to Britain's full membership of the EU. In the context of a general strengthening of equality provisions up to and including the Treaty of Amsterdam, the final section deals with Britain's interface with the EU. It is now increasingly difficult to dismiss the impact of European integration at the national level. The interface of national and supranational citizenship rights and national obligations are more stringently enforced by the EU as a supranational entity. This could bring a more integrated approach to gender equality and new forms of citizenship.

Mother-carer: women's citizenship in Britain under the Conservative legacy

Britain has the formal institutions and mechanisms for equal opportunity and participation in political, social and economic life but much of the debate about citizenship and gender in Britain notes the gap between formal equality and the substantive inequality (based on gender, class, and race) that arose during 17 years of Conservative government. In general terms, this period was noted for a growth in inequality (Atkinson, Rainwater and Smeeding 1995; Joseph Rowntree Foundation 1995; McRae 1997), a fall in income share for the poorest, an exponential rise in the incomes of the rich (Goodman and Webb 1994: 66) and a general polarisation of those on high and low incomes (Jenkins 1994: 46), along with a whittling away of the welfare state. Social policy has been described as being 'more like an ambulance' sent out to pick up the victims of economic downturn (Evans, Paugam and Prelis 1995: 33). Rising unemployment and precarious employment increasingly became linked to income poverty, household debt, bad housing, poor neighbourhood, weakened social ties and social exclusion (Evans, Paugam and Prelis 1995: 8). Much has been written about New Right liberalism under the Conservatives, the predominance of economic justifications of the state's role (Le Grand 1995), the pursuit of labour market deregulation, decreased social contributions, decreased public spending, increased labour market flexibility and the privileging of individualism over collectivism (King 1988; Evans, Paugam and Prelis 1995; Walker and Walker 1997). As Evans, Paugam and Prelis (1995: 13) remark on this period: 'British concepts of citizenship, partnership and community are seen as an aggregation of individual action rather than an expression of social solidarity.'

In terms of policies on income redistribution and social security, this period was characterised by concerns to contain public expenditure. This was manifested in tighter conditions and increasingly means-tested benefits targeted at the most disadvantaged, moves to encourage a shift for the better off from state to private provision, reduced benefit levels, and more policing of claimants. What Lister (1997: 183) refers to as 'liberalist residualist philosophy' accentuated disparities along racial or ethnic lines, with changed rules, welfare curtailment, stricter immigration controls and reductions in welfare benefits and services (Bloch 1997: 121). Towards the end of the Conservative era there were changes to the relative differences between unemployment, aged and illness benefits, removal of entitlement for 16 to 18 year olds (unless lone parents, disabled or in severe hardship), cutbacks in assistance for one-off needs and moves to less comprehensive coverage (Evans, Paugam and Prelis 1995: 16; Howard 1997).

On the other hand, the 1970s and 1980s saw new non-contributory benefits for the disabled, carers and single parents (who were discouraged from registering as unemployed). Social assistance was provided for lone parents, without the obligation to work until the youngest child was 16. However, these moves, which were ostensibly supportive of women's caring roles, heralded no major breakthrough for women. They were low paid, reinforced the perception of care for the aged and children as essentially a private and not a state responsibility, and generally served to entrench women's economic dependency (Lister 1996, 1997: 173). They also maintained women in traditional roles within the family. As Cass (1994: 110) observes, state support for women as carers – especially at low rates – undermines their claims to equitable participation in the paid workforce. At the same time, those on welfare were increasingly derogated as members of a dependent under-class; lone mothers and the unemployed bore the brunt of this with ' "(b)laming the victim" reaching new heights' (Millar 1997: 108).

While a full assessment of the impact of all policies on women is beyond the scope of this chapter, the discussion below canvasses some implications of Conservative governments' labour market, childcare and social security policies as policies central to social citizenship for women. The British labour market exhibits strong gender differences in a sex-segregated labour force, with over 90 per cent of women participating as employees. Although the employment rate of women in Britain was less than that of men (Eurostat, 1997; using 1995 figures), women's employment patterns were different, with about 40 per cent of women (compared to 7.6 per cent of men) employed part-time in 1997 (OECD 1998: 206). Public sector employment has been a key source of professional jobs for a small proportion of women in more 'protected' employment although the main growth in women's employment has been in part-time work, particularly in clerical and service sectors. Growth in employment opportunities has been higher for white women who enjoyed an increase from 59 to 68 per cent from 1984 to 1995, while opportunities for ethnic women only increased from 44 to 46 per cent over the same period (Bloch 1997: 113) and the unemployment rate for ethnic women is higher: 18 per cent, compared with 8 per cent for white women (Minister for Women 1999: 103).

A UK study of pay and gender in private and public sectors found that the devolution of pay determination, performance appraisal, merit pay and market forces impacted more on women than men and that such reforms have widened the gender gap in pay (Equal Opportunities Commission 1992: 11). British free market reforms to the labour market – marked by deregulation of wages, temporary contracts, hire and fire, extension of part-time work and low pay – have resulted in changes in the terms and conditions of women's work. These include growth in casualised work opportunities available to women, abolition of the Wages Council (setting minimum rates of pay), the failure to achieve equal pay for men and women, the impact of privatisation of services on job losses for women, and worse conditions and pay for those re-employed after privatisation (Millar 1997: 107).

Women accounted for seven out of ten low-paid workers in 1996. Based on individual incomes, 52 per cent of married women compared with 11 per cent of married men were below the poverty line (Davies and Joshi, cited in Millar 1997: 102–3). Over the last 20 years in Britain, the two groups characterised by highest risk and longest duration of poverty are older women living alone and lone mothers (Millar 1997: 99–100). To these could be added the poor women partners of unemployed and low-paid workers. Millar presents a picture of the combined austerity of declining real incomes and living standards and declining access to services, with privatisation, higher service charges, and increased targeting of welfare benefits. She argues that positive policies (such as extension of maternity leave, extension of family credit to part-time workers and childcare subsidies and vouchers for nursery school age children) benefited only a minority of working women.

This scenario to a large extent reflects Conservative approaches to family policy, reasserting the traditional family and the notion of individual responsibility. It firmly places the onus of unpaid caring work on to the family. Some argue that men have probably gained more than women from increased subsidised opportunities to opt out of state systems and from changes in tax policies, thus reducing the tax burden on the higher paid (Millar 1997). Average men's paid working hours above the EU average could also be argued to have precluded a significant involvement in the care of children for some men.

Childcare provision has been central to women's workforce participation patterns (Figes 1994). Government provision of childcare is fundamental to women's ability to participate in full-time and, to some extent, part-time paid employment. Britain has had one of the lowest levels of public provision of childcare in the EU.[1] Towards the end of Conservative rule, government provided childcare for those under 3 years old in the UK and Ireland stood at 2 per cent in 1993, compared with 23 per cent in France, 33 per cent in Sweden and 48 per cent in Denmark. The UK provided services at a level similar to Spain and Greece and ranked amongst the lowest in the EU for children aged 3 to 6 (European Commission Network on Childcare and Other Measures 1996). In the UK, the concentration of women's labour market participation in part-time work, high in comparison with other EU members,[2] provides further indication of the Conservatives' pursuit of policies that reinforced traditional family ideology.

For a combination of reasons, the UK has one of the lowest rates of full-time employment of lone mothers (Lewis 1998: 10). Under the Conservatives, the UK had no parental leave as a right of workers and, on grounds of the costs of implementation, sought an exemption from the June 1996 Council directive on parental leave. They also negotiated a 10-year period of grace, delaying the implementation of the Working Time Directive's 48-hour maximum working week.

In the area of social security benefits, state-provided benefits have characteristically worked via the labour market to cater for the predominantly male, regularly employed (Lewis and Åström 1992: 63). This has worked against those more peripheral to full-time work, such as women and ethnic minorities. In general terms, women's rights to welfare have either been indirect (in relation to household income) or in terms of their roles as carers. As Miller (1997: 106) argues, women's combined roles as mother-carer-worker have rendered them particularly vulnerable to changes in state policies. She cites various illustrations of this from the Conservative era, including:

* freezing child benefit throughout most of the 1980s;
* reductions in benefits (for example, through linking basic pensions to prices rather than to earnings);
* cutbacks to SERP (state earnings-related pension scheme) and changes to pension entitlements from 'best 20 years rule' to lifetime's earnings (see also Bloch 1997: 114);
* freezing the one-parent benefit and income support premiums for lone parents post-1996 budget; and
* abolition of reduced rate national insurance contributions in 1986, thus excluding many women from National Insurance benefits.

With regard to payment of carers and single mother pensions, the state recognised carers' roles but did not reward the actual work they do (McLaughlin and Glendinning 1994).

Thus, the twin objectives of conservative family policy were to cut expenditure and to reinforce the family's responsibility to care. At the ideological level (since in reality non-traditional family forms increased), the Conservatives reinforced a traditional family-centred notion of women's citizenship and of women as citizen carer-mother, even if women were working in increasing numbers.

Citizen-as-worker: women's citizenship in Britain under the Blair government

Blair's landslide victory in 1997 improved the political representation of women (from 9 per cent to 18 per cent) in the British Parliament, although Britain is still lagging behind countries such as Sweden, Denmark and Finland, with over 33 per cent. Blair also established an office of Minister for Women, although as an afterthought.[3]

The Blair government is committed to three major policy areas for Cabinet action on women: a National Strategy on Childcare (£300 million over 5 years to create up to one million extra out-of-school childcare places), freedom from violence, and family-friendly working conditions (Harman 1998). In terms of major policy process priorities, Labour is committed to opening up new dialogue with women and women's organisations (such as citizens' juries to open up community consultation processes). It is also committed to mainstreaming (where Ministers take responsibility for women's issues within their portfolio areas) and to encouraging more women into public life (Ruddock 1997; Coote 1998).

However, Labour has allowed the perception that dependence on state benefits encourages passivity and dependency to continue. 'Welfare to Work' and 'Active Labour Market Strategies' have involved the widely criticised implementation of pre-existing legislation to cut single parent pensions by removing their special benefits on the grounds that single parents would be better off under Active Labour Market Strategies, a minimum wage, tax credits, wages top-ups (leaving it to families to decide which parent receives the extra cash), childcare allowances (up to 75 per cent of childcare costs) and labour market support.

Lewis (1998: 4) criticises the emphasis on making welfare recipients engage in paid work on the grounds that it devalues unpaid caring work, mostly performed by women. She and others are critical of the shift from structural analysis to individual failings that comes with the discourse of 'dependency culture'. In many respects, the state's approach to single parents is a litmus test of its approach to women as citizens in relation to the welfare state and the carer–worker dichotomy reinforced under the Conservatives. Whereas the Conservatives supported lone parents as citizen-mothers and approached reduction of state pensions expenditure through pursuit of fathers under the Child Support Scheme, they did give some recognition of women's unpaid work as carers. New Labour has redefined women as citizen worker-providers, drawing on arguments of reversing exclusion by integration into society through paid work, especially for lone mothers. This policy raises the thorny issue of 'care as work', and as Lewis (1998: 10) suggests, the much larger issue of how care work is valued and shared in society. She argues that 'stakeholder welfare' is about paid employment and 'ignores the contribution of unpaid care work' (Lewis 1998: 11).

Despite its commitments to mainstream women's policy and to address women's inequalities, the Blair Government's decisions in December 1997 on controversial lone parent benefit cuts[4] meant new claimants would receive £5 less in benefits from April 1999, representing government savings of over £400 million pounds over 3 years. 'Pushing through this cut was vital for new Labour as a step towards replacing welfare benefits in their entirety with workforce schemes' (*International Worker* 1997).

It can be argued that New Labour has put in place a framework for child care with the National Childcare Strategy (Green Paper 1998). However, central to its success in facilitating more women's participation in the labour market is a substantial government commitment to funded centres and childcare places. One obvious issue confronting delivery of labour's policy promises is Blair's election commitment to remain within public expenditure limits. In the broader scheme of things, tax credits to parents favour those in employment and overlook policies that foster broader opportunities, such as education and training for women.

In assessing the Blair Government's performance some commentators are silent about its strategies regarding women as citizens (Gray and Jenkins 1998). They focus on what might be perceived as big picture issues, which exclude women. High on Blair's reform agenda are the Social Chapter of the EU, the Low Pay Commission and a minimum wage, devolution of Wales and Scotland, education and health initiatives, new approaches to youth crime, administrative constitutional and parliamentary reforms, and strengthening accountability and policy coordination across departments. These reforms could, however, have implications for women, but little attention has been paid to what the gendered implications of these changes might be. There could be a new era for women in the UK, especially employed women, heralded by the Blair government's vocal commitment to women in its response to CEDAW (Minister for Women 1999); in particular, its commitment to implementing the Social Chapter of the Amsterdam Treaty, The Parental Leave Directive, the European Works Council Directive, the Part-Time Work Directive, the Working Time Directive and the Directive on the Burden of Proof in Sex Discrimination Cases.

Britain and the EU

Historically, Britain has been a weak partner in EU determinations on worker-related rights. It sought exemption from the Social Protocol incorporated into the Maastricht Treaty in 1991 (including the right to parental leave for men and women and equal rights for part-time and full-time workers). Under Blair, it decided to join the Social Protocol, including provisions on social policy, education, training and youth.

The EU has been an important influence on improving the status of women in Member States. However, some see the equal pay, social security and other provisions as benefiting some women over others and as primarily directed towards women as workers rather than addressing broader issues of unpaid care and family roles (see Meehan 1991; 1993). The Equal Opportunities Action Plan (1996–2000) incorporates the principle of mainstreaming, defined as 'mobilising all general policies and measures specifically for the purpose of achieving equality' and taking account at the planning stage of the possible effects of various policies and measures on women (Commission of the European Communities 1996). One example of how mainstreaming provides means of tackling inequalities between women and men is to tie EU 'structural funds' to demonstrated outcomes from specific initiatives to address inequalities and equal opportunity initiatives, and to make pursuit of these outcomes a condition of funding. The European Structural Funds are regrouped under the New Objective 3 of Agenda 2000, marking increasing recognition of the complex patterns of disadvantage and gender relations and the need for transnational co-operation to fight the discrimination and inequality that prevent access to employment (Flynn 1998: 1; Hough 1998: 16).

As part of a joint effort to promote employment, Member States were required to submit National Action Plans for employment to the

European Commission in June 1998. These have raised the importance of implementing mainstreaming and equal opportunity objectives, particularly with respect to gender and disability (Women of Europe 1998: 1). The Treaty of Amsterdam (The European Commission 1997; put into force on May 1 1999) set out to address the social needs of the EU and the fight against social exclusion and poverty. With regard to social policy, the Treaty provides for equality of opportunity and equal treatment for men and women at work. More broadly, it enables the adoption of EU-wide measures to combat discrimination in all forms, whether related to gender, race, ethnic origin, religion, political or other convictions, physical handicap, age or sexual orientation. One of its four main objectives is to place employment and citizens' rights at the heart of the Union. Enshrining equality within the Treaty has given it pre-eminent importance as primary law. This has implications for a broadening of equality rulings in the European Court of Justice and for its binding effect on member states' national courts and laws (Sanjuan 1998).

Conclusion

Central to assessing the Blair government's success will be its attention to those groups previously excluded from substantive, active citizenship, principally through low income, social exclusion, and lack of opportunity. Reforms for inclusive citizenship will need to address:

- poverty;
- indirect discrimination;
- lack of financial independence;
- gender inequalities that traditionally flow from marriage;
- social security tied to contributions through paid work when access to decent jobs is limited;
- lack of state-provided childcare;
- concentration of women in casualised and precarious jobs;
- the gender pay gap;
- low pension levels paid to carers; and
- generally the question of how to rethink citizenship in ways that combine working with caring.

Both Britain and the EU have been criticised for their emphasis on market reforms and weak real commitment to substantive 'equality in practice'. Although the EU has implemented specific action programmes since the 1980s, the European Council meeting in Essen (December 1994) declared the promotion of equal opportunities for women and men a key priority for the EU and member states. It was put on a par with the problem of unemployment (Commission of European Communities 1997: 1). The Fourth Action Plan on Equal Opportunities for Men and Women (for 1996–2000) endorsed the policy of mainstreaming (*Women of Europe Newsletter* 1998). Incorporating equal opportunities for women and men into all community policies and activities is a strong aspect of the Treaty of Amsterdam. Commitments to more inclusive citizenship for women at the supranational or EU level may bring leverage at national levels, encouraging governments to implement policies that develop more gender-sensitive notions of citizenship in ways that relate to both paid work and the unpaid caring that is still borne largely by women.

Notes

1   In the UK, the paid-work participation of mothers with one child was considerably lower compared with women without children, because working mothers in Britain were more likely to work part-time rather than full-time. Participation in the UK labour force was lower than for mothers (with children under 10) in Belgium, Denmark, Finland, Austria, France, Portugal and Sweden. Barring Austria, these countries all have significant provision of publicly funded childcare (Commission of the European Communities 1997: 52).

2   The percentage of women employed part time (as a percentage of all employed women) is 44.8 compared with an EU average of 31.5 and 34.5 for Denmark (Eurostat 1998: 121–2).

3   After all the paid ministerial posts had been filled, Harriet Harman was appointed belatedly to the position in addition to her other role as Social Security Secretary, with Joan Ruddock appointed as deputy, positioned outside Cabinet, with no additional salary and no designated department (David 1998). Harman was dropped in the first Cabinet reshuffle, her credibility shaken with women's groups after cuts to lone parent pensions (discussed below).

4   Forty-seven MPs voted against the cuts and, later, the Minister for Women undertook to ensure compensation to lone parents on benefit or in work to more than compensate for cuts (Ward, Perkins and White 1998).

References

Atkinson, A.B., Rainwater, L. and Smeeding, T. (1995) *Income Distribution in OECD Countries: Evidence from the Luxembourg Income Study*, Paris, France: OECD.

Bloch, Alice (1997) 'Gender', in A. Walker and C. Walker (eds), *Britain Divided: The Growth of Social Exclusion in the 1980s and 1990s*, London: Child Poverty Action Group.

Carlson, Soren (1994) *Experience from Work on the Danish Government's Action Plan for Equal Status*, European University Institute: European Forum, Workshop on Company Strategies, Family Strategies, Differences in Conceptualisation, Common Ground for Mutual Understanding, November.

Cass, Bettina (1994) 'Citizenship, work and welfare: the Dilemma for Australian Women', *Social Politics*, vol. 1, no. 1: 106–24.

Commission of the European Communities (1996) *Incorporating Equal Opportunities for Women and Men into All Community Policies and Activities*, COM (96) 67 final, Brussels: Office for Official Publications of the European Communities.

—— (1997) *Annual Report from the Commission: Equal Opportunity for Women and Men in the European Union – 1996*, COM (96) 650 final 12.02.97, Brussels: Commission of European Communities.

Coote, Anna (1998) *Women at the Heart of Government: Address to Emily's List*, victoria: Parliament House, April.

David, Miriam (1998) *The National Child Care Strategy: New Directions and New Dilemmas for New Labour*, Paper presented at the Politics Seminar Series, University of Melbourne, July.

Equal Opportunities Commission (1992) *Annual Report 1992: The Equality Challenge*, London: Equal Opportunity Commission.

European Commission Network on Childcare and other Measures to Reconcile Employment and Family Responsibility (1996) *A Review of Services for Young Children in the EU 1990–1995*, Brussels: D.G.V.

Eurostat (1997) *Eurostat Yearbook, Office for Official Publications of the European Communities*, Luxembourg.

—— (1998) *Eurostat Yearbook*, Luxembourg: Office for Official Publiciations of the European Communities.

Evans, Martin, Paugam, Serge and Prelis, Joseph (1995) *Chunnel Vision: Poverty, Social Exclusion and the Debate on Social Welfare in France and Britain*, Welfare State Program, Discussion Paper 115, London: The Toyota Centre, London School of Economics.

Everingham, Christine (1995) *Individuating 'Other': Re-defining the Citizen of the Liberal State, American Feminist Studies*, 22 (Summer): 99–120.

Figes, K. (1994) *Because of Her Sex*, London: Macmillan.

Flynn, P. (1998) ' "Mainstreaming" a radical new approach to equal opportunities for the future Structural Funds', *Women of Europe Newsletter*, no. 78 (March–April): 1.

Goodman, A. and Webb, S. (1994) *For Richer, For Poorer: The Changing Distribution of Income in the United Kingdom 1961–91*, London, Institute for Fiscal Studies Commentary No. 42, June.

Gray, A. and Jenkins, B. (1998) 'New Labour, New Government? Change and continuity in public administration and government 1997', *Parliamentary Affairs*, Oxford: Oxford University Press, 8 May: 111–31.

Green Paper (1998) *A National Childcare Strategy: a framework and consultation document*, Cm 3959, London: HMSO.

Hancock, Linda (1999) 'Citizenship on the Margins: the case of divorce in Western Europe', in Leslie Holmes and Philomena Murray (eds), *Citizenship and Identity in Europe*, Aldershot: Ashgate.

Harman, H. (1998) *Harriet Harman Speaking at the European Parliament's Women's rights Committee on 2 February*, UK Government: WWW, Women's Unit.

Held, Virginia (1989) 'Liberty and Equality from a Feminist Perspective', in N. MacCormich and Z. Bankowski (eds), *Enlightenment, Rights and Revolution*, Aberdeen: Aberdeen University Press.

Hough, Jane (1998) *The Reform of the European Structural Funds and the Cohesion Fund*, Research Paper 98/92, London: House of Commons Library.

Howard, Marilyn (1997) 'Cutting Social Security', in Walker and Walker (1997): 84–96.

International Worker (1997) 'Lone Parents hammered by New Labour', no. 242 (Dec./Jan).

Jenkins, S. (1994) 'Income Inequality and living standards: Changes in the 1970's and 1980's', *Fiscal Studies*, vol. 12, no. 1: 1–29.

Joseph Rowntree Foundation (1995) *Inquiry into Income and Wealth, Vol. 1*, York: Joseph Rowntree Foundation.

King, Desmond S. (1988) *The New Right: Politics, Markets and Citizenship* London: Macmillan Education.

Le Grand, J. (1995) 'The market, the state and the distribution of life cycle income', *The Dynamic of Welfare: The Welfare State and the Life Cycle*, ed. J. Falkingham and J. Hills, Hemel Hempstead: Prentice-Hall/Harvester Wheatsheaf.

Lewis, Jane (1998) '"Work", "Welfare" and Lone Mothers', *The Political Quarterly*, vol. 69, no. 11: 4–13.

Lewis, Jane and Åström, Gertrude (1992) 'Equality, Difference and State Welfare: Labour Market and Family Policies in Sweden', *Feminist Studies*, vol. 18, no. 1: 59–87.

Lister, R. (1996) 'Back to the family: family policies and politics under the Major government', in H. Jones and J. Millar (eds), *The Politics of the Family*, Aldershot: Avebury.

——(1997) *Citizenship: Feminist Perspectives*, London: Macmillan.

Mc Laughlin, E. and Glendinning, C. (1994) 'Paying for care in Europe: Is there a feminist approach?', in L. Hantrais, and S. Mangen, *Family Policy and the Welfare of Women*, Loughborough: Cross-national Research Group.

McRae, Susan (1997) 'Household and labour market change implications for the growth of inequality in Britain', *British Journal of Sociology*, vol. 8, no. 1: 384–405.

Meehan, Elizabeth (1991) in Ursula Vogel and Michael Moran, *The Frontiers of Citizenship*, London: Macmillan.

——(1993) *Citizenship in the European Community*, London: Sage.

Millar, Jane (1997), 'Gender', in Walker and Walker (1997): 99–110.

Minister for Women (1999) *United Convention on the Elimination of all Forms of Discrimination Against Women*, Fourth Report of the United Kingdom of Great Britain and Northern Ireland, London: Women's Unit of UK Government.

OECD (1998) *Employment Outlook*, June 1998, Paris: OECD.

Pateman, Carole (1989) *The Sexual Contract*, Oxford: Polity Press/Basil Blackwell.

Pimlott, Ben (1997) 'New Labour, New Era?', *The Political Quarterly*, vol. 68, no. 4: 325–34.

Ruddock, Joan (1997) 'New Dialogue', Paper presented at IPPR Conference, London, 3 July.

Sanjuan, Teresa Freixes (1998) 'Women in the new European society', *Women of Europe Newsletter*, No 79 (May): 1.

The European Commission (1997) *Amsterdam June 17, 1997, A New Treaty for Europe*, Luxembourg: Office for Official Publications of the European Communities.

Vogel, Ursula (1991) 'Is Citizenship Gender Specific?' in Ursula Vogel and Michael Moran, *The Frontiers of Citizenship*, London: Macmillan.

Walker, Alan and Walker, C. (1997) *Britain Divided: The Growth of Social Exclusion in the 1980s and 1990s*, London: Child Poverty Action Group.

Ward, Lucy, Anne, Perkins and Michael, White (1998), 'Child Care Cash Boost for poor', *The Guardian*, 26 February.

Women of Europe (1998) 'Employment: National Action Plans fall short on equality', *Women in Europe*, No. 81, Brussels: 1–4.

11 'SWEDISH MODELS' AND ECONOMIC CITIZENSHIP

Andrew Vandenberg*

Sweden is often cited as an example of a country where social citizenship has been developed more fully than anywhere else. This chapter points out that a local social democratic theory of political, social and economic citizenship pre-dates Marshall's arguments about legal, political and social citizenship. However, the history of class conflict and Social Democratic achievements and setbacks supports Turner's and others' criticisms of the shortcomings of the Marshall's scheme of unilinear, one-directional, continuous and inexorable developments towards the present. The defeat of the union movement's campaign for economic citizenship in the 1970s and 1980s also illustrates Hindess's critique of the conceptual inadequacies and slippages in any choice between democratic realism and participatory radicalism.

Sweden is well known for its progressive social policies, high taxes and exceptionally extensive welfare state (Dow 1993). Since the 1930s, the country has often been seen as a model of successful social liberal politics (Stråth 1998), providing handy defences against the fatalistic arguments of either economic liberalism or some versions of Marxism. Early examples of these 'Swedish models' include the views of Marquis Childs (1936) and Anthony Crosland (1956). Childs visited

* Thank you to Winton Higgins, Timothy Tilton, Geoff Dow and Jonas Pontusson for reading and commenting on the arguments developed here.

Sweden in the mid-1930s and took home with him to the USA arguments about a middle way between Soviet communism and depression capitalism, which implicitly favoured Franklin D. Roosevelt's New Deal programmes. When Crosland visited in the mid-1950s, he took home to Britain lessons about how responsible union leaders could help parties of labour in government to combine low inflation with permanent full employment. These lessons reinforced the view of the Labour Party's leaders as against their Marxist critics on the left (see Anderson 1962, 1963). Childs and Crosland founded the minor industry that Sweden-watching and model-building has become (see Martin 1984; Bosworth and Rivlin 1987; Swenson 1989; Fulcher 1991, 1994; Misgeld, Molin and Åmark 1992; Pontusson 1992a, 1992b; Clement and Mahon 1994; Lachman *et al.* 1995). This chapter addresses the failure of these models to regard social cohesion, solidarity or citizenship as a *political* achievement that was opposed within Sweden by groups similar to those that oppose comparable objectives elsewhere.

There is a common myth that Sweden is populated by an almost superhuman race of calm and rational people. They are supposed to be inclined to peaceable negotiation of all political, social and industrial problems and to enjoy the benefits of considerable ethnic and cultural homogeneity. These suppositions are the reverse side of the coin in Swedish models. Those who dislike the social-liberal politics of Swedish models argue that they cannot be imported into other countries because they could not work among more ordinary people elsewhere in the industrially advanced West. This chapter disputes the assumptions of both Swedish models and the usual arguments against them. In a short chapter, I cannot go into all the aspects of culture, gender, race or ethnicity, and class in the considerable social solidarity that Sweden has indeed achieved in the twentieth century. Like Marshall (1950), in his schematic picture of a gradual accumulation of civil, political and social rights of citizenship among ever wider circles of adult permanent residents in Britain, I too limit myself to the divisiveness of class and capitalism (though this is a conscious choice on my part). I dispute the Whig view of history (as a story of unilinear, one-directional, continuous and inexorable developments towards the present) that is intrinsic to Marshall's liberal scheme. I argue that social cohesion is a political achievement marked by struggle, detours, setbacks and breakthroughs, defeats and triumphs (see Turner 1986).

The chapter has four parts. In the first part, I look briefly at representative aspects of Swedish political history in the twentieth century. In the second and third sections, I look at an important debate between those who argue in favour of the political possibilities of social democratic reforms and those who argue that capitalism imposes harsh limits upon reformism. This debate focuses on the political struggle that is notably absent from the social liberalism of the usual Swedish model. In the fourth part, I briefly advance an argument that defeat of the Swedish union movement's campaign for economic democracy raises an important political paradox.

Background

In 1928 the leader of SAP,[1] Per Albin Hansson, stood up in the *Riksdag* and delivered an impromptu speech that has come to be widely regarded as the founding expression of social citizenship, cohesion or solidarity[2] which inspired SAP's policy-making for the next 60 years or so:

> The foundation of a home is a common sense of belonging. A good home knows no distinctions between the privileged and the under-privileged, between favourite children and stepchildren. No one looks down upon anyone else; no one seeks to gain advantage at someone else's expense; the strong do not repress and plunder the weak. In the good home equality, consideration, co-operation, and helpfulness are the order of the day. Applied to the great home of the people, this would mean breaking down all social and economic barriers that now divide citizens into the privileged and the under-privileged, the rulers and the dependent, the rich and the poor, the propertied and the destitute, the plunderers and the plundered. . . . Swedish society is still not a good home of the people. There is a formal equality between people, an equality of political rights, but in society, matters of class and elite dictatorship are still the order of the day. If our society is to become a good home for the people, class differences must be eliminated, social welfare must be expanded, an economic equalisation must take place, and the employed must be granted a part in economic administration. Democracy must also be implemented and applied in its social and economic aspects.[3]

Like the other Scandinavian and Germanic parties of labour, SAP has strong roots in the Marxist political legacy of the German SPD.[4] The Swedish social democrats' sense of a good 'home of the people', or *folkhem*, opposed to the bourgeois state, resonated with the contemporary German sense of a *volk* and a culture distinct from the nation and the state [as we have already seen in Chapter 8].

SAP has an ideological affinity with the other Scandinavian and Germanic parties of labour, but unlike them it has some affinity with the history of the Anglo-Saxon parties of labour. The way one generation of party activists passes practices on to the next has never been interrupted by civil war (as in Finland), invasion (in Austria, Holland, Denmark, Norway), or Nazi dictatorship (Germany: see Therborn 1992 for a good discussion of the continuity and other dimensions of SAP's exceptional parliamentary predominance). This organisational and political continuity in the predominant party of government, and in the democratic traditions of the country during the twentieth century, has provided ample illustration for various proponents of Marshall's vision of a gradual accumulation of civil, political and then social rights of citizenship.

At the risk of overly simplifying complex developments, two key reforms – one in 1933 and the other in 1959 – can serve to illustrate how SAP secured strategic positions from which it could build a large and popular welfare state around the social solidarity of a *folkhem*.[5] The first reform involved public subsidies for the trade unions' unemployment insurance funds. These funds were first raised at the turn of the century to protect officials against blacklisting by employers. Subsequently in Belgium, Holland, Norway, Denmark and finally Sweden, liberals supported public subsidy of the unions' funds as a comparatively cheap means of encouraging people to protect themselves against the financial insecurity of unemployment (Lewin 1985). They worried that the public subsidies might strengthen unionism in the long run, but figured that public control and regulation of access to the funds would ensure that public benefit would outweigh possible partisan political consequences. As it turned out, both their worries and their expectations were fulfilled. After the Second World War, the countries that introduced public subsidisation of union unemployment insurance funds saw unionism become markedly more popular among white-collar workers and public sector workers than elsewhere (Wallerstein 1989; Rothstein 1990). A surge in white-collar unionism contributed strongly to the Swedish union movement presiding over the most densely organised workforce in the world.[6] After the Second World War, the public subsidisation of the unions' unemployment funds contributed (along with several other economic and political factors) towards making employment a right of citizenship. The power of the Swedish union movement is a most important factor in the exceptional predominance of SAP and the extent of progressive social policies it has instituted (see Martin 1984; Higgins 1985a, 1996; Tilton 1990).

The second reform dealt with retirees' incomes. In 1946–50 and again in 1952–55, public inquiries investigated the complex issues of how to finance retirement pensions and eliminate the class-based differences between professionals, managers and upper-level white-collar workers who retired on superannuation benefits and all other wage-earners who retired on a simple old-age pension. In 1956, the SAP-Agrarian League coalition government collapsed over SAP's decision to opt for a pension scheme involving compulsory and universal contributions to publicly controlled investment funds, which would finance generous pensions. SAP was convinced that making contributions compulsory and universal was the only way to eliminate class injustice among the retired, while publicly controlled investment funds was the only way to ensure that pensions increased apace with the increases in productivity and living standards among the currently employed (see Heclo 1974; Esping-Andersen 1985; Lewin 1985).

In the 1930s, the liberals supported the public subsidisation of unions' unemployment insurance schemes; however, in the lower house elections of 1956, a referendum on the issue in 1957, upper house elections in 1958, and lower house elections in 1960 they led the opposition to compulsory contributions and public control over very large capital investment funds. In a dramatic conclusion to the struggle to institute an important aspect of social citizenship, SAP's scheme finally passed into law on the strength of a single liberal parliamentarian's abstention in 1959. At the 1960 election, SAP won a resounding victory, the opposition parties abandoned their criticism, and the public pension funds proceeded to firmly establish social security as a right of citizenship comparable to schooling or the vote.

In the 1970s and again in the 1990s, the deeply popular schemes for unemployment insurance and retirement pensions funds were a primary cause of large increases in the total outlays of government, which peaked at 64 per cent of GDP in 1979 and then at 73 per cent of GDP in 1992 (Bosworth and Rivlin 1987; Ryner 1994; Lachmann *et al.* 1995).

The democratic class struggle and social citizenship

In the widely influential argument of Walter Korpi (1978, 1983), a dramatic and fundamental shift in Swedish industrial relations took place after SAP's narrow electoral victory in 1932 and then landslide victories in 1936 and 1940, which saw it establish itself as the predominant party of government. After the First World War, Sweden and Norway endured volumes of industrial conflict that were proportionately greater than anywhere in the world. But in Sweden in the 1930s, industrial conflict dropped off quite suddenly. The balance of power in industrial relations shifted away from the employers as a result of what Korpi dubs 'the historic compromise' between labour and capital (1978: ch. 3, ch. 4). This class compromise did not, however, imply any dissolution of the social democrats' ideological resolve. The dramatic decrease in industrial conflict arguably rested instead on a 'balance of terror' between powerful organisations of labour and capital. This balance of class forces contributed both to economic expansion and a 'flow of issues' from the market arena of conflict into the political arena of conflict, which benefited the working class and shifted the whole spectrum of political opinions to the left (Korpi 1978: 40, 47–8). Industrial conflict returned in the early 1970s when unions challenged the continuing relevance of the class compromise between labour and capital and put first industrial democracy and then economic democracy on the political agenda (Korpi 1983: ch. 10).

Gøsta Esping-Andersen (1985) has filled out Korpi's general argument for the possibility that parties of labour can cumulatively institute one reform after another and strengthen their own socioeconomic foundations. He argues that SAP has managed to grasp both horns of the dilemma of electoral socialism. According to this dilemma, parties of labour *either* pursue socialism *or* seek to win elections; socialist policies mobilise core working-class voters but put middle-class voters off, whilst catch-all policies attract the middle class but disappoint working-class voters. SAP has been able to avoid impaling itself on either horn of that dilemma by instituting welfare policies that generate social solidarity, transform what it means to belong to the working class, and identify with social democracy. Welfare reforms of social solidarity have thus generated stable electoral majorities for the party of labour (Esping-Andersen 1985: 6–11).

The social and political effects of the pension reform in the 1950s went hand in glove with the great expansion of white-collar unionism. However, Esping-Andersen argues that if SAP was to continue insti- tuting welfare reforms which generated social solidarity amongst larger socio-economic classes of voters then it faced an imperative in the 1980s. It had to move on from the post-war strategy of socialising 'stocks' of capital to provide public services, and pursue a strategy of socialising the 'flows' of capital in private industry. It was time to expand on the collectivisation of capital flows in the pension scheme and take a fundamental step from social democracy on to economic democracy. At the end of the 1970s and beginning of the 1980s, such an imperative directly confronted the emerging agenda of economic liberalism in Anglo-Saxon countries. Rather than socialise the flows of capital, social democrats faced the task of defending the stock of capital in public authorities against privatisation. Defeat of the union movement's campaign to institute economic democracy was therefore a serious setback, to which I return at the end of the chapter.

The limits of reformism

Korpi's and Esping-Andersen's sociological focus upon institutions and political developments has been criticised by those who insist that the economics of capitalism impose harsh limits upon how far welfare reforms can go within a capitalist economy. Critics such as Jonas Pon- tusson (1984, 1987, 1992a, 1992b), Gregg Olsen (1994) and Magnus Ryner (1994) argue that in the 1970s the conditions under which SAP and the union movement had flourished for so long changed funda- mentally. The credibility of Keynesian public policies declined. The Swedish Employers' Federation departed from its traditions of prag- matic industrial relations in favour of a new-right militancy. The large Swedish corporations became much more involved in international trade and global capitalism. High unemployment became common- place again in the industrially advanced countries of the OECD, though full employment remained in Sweden until 1991. These critics of Korpi's approach have a strong point when they argue that however successful labour has been in Sweden, capital has also been particu- larly successful.

A close look at *Fortune Magazine*'s annual lists of the world's top 500 corporations shows that per head of population in 1976, 1980 and 1985, Sweden consistently ranked at the top of the list of the number of non-US industrial corporations in a country (*Fortune International*, August 1976: 242; 11 August 1980: 201; 19 August 1985: 179; United Nations, *Demographic Yearbook 1985*, New York). Switzerland ranked consistently second to Sweden because it too has a small population and several large international corporations (in pharmaceuticals). Since the mid–1980s, a wave of amalgamations has swept through the very large multinational corporations but Sweden continues to host the headquarters, and research and development activities at least, of about 20 *Fortune Five Hundred* industrial corporations. These corporations are, however, owned by a small band of exceedingly wealthy and powerful men, among whom Peter Wallenberg is the most prominent. Through a network of interlocking directorships and shareholdings centred on the Wallenberg family's bank, Wallenberg controls 20 of Sweden's largest corporations (Olsen 1994: 200–3). Links between the wealth and power of these corporations and the pro-business corporate tax policies of Social Democratic governments led one critic to observe that Electrolux and other large corporations 'clean up' in supposedly socialist Sweden (Israel 1978).

Against the economic basis of arguments about the limits of reformism advanced by Pontusson, Olsen and Ryner, Francis Castles (1987) and Göran Therborn (1985) have advanced important arguments about the social limits of capitalism. Sweden's small economy is particularly open to foreign trade but this can be thought to underscore rather than undermine arguments such as Korpi's and Esping-Andersen's about the importance of political choices and social achievements. The erratic nature of earnings from exports provides the basis for a plausible argument that Sweden has been able to encourage its export corporations precisely because it has a large public sector that provides comprehensive social security to all residents. Through high taxes, high unemployment benefits and extensive retraining programmes, the costs of rapid economic restructuring (of, say, the shipping industry that boomed in the 1960s only to collapse dramatically in the 1970s) are borne collectively by everyone. The costs of international economic fluctuations and necessarily rapid economic restructuring are not suffered individually by retrenched employees and bankrupt employers. Economic restructuring can proceed all the more quickly because the social costs are distributed fairly and the social benefits of high employment rates in the long term are maximised. The large public sector can therefore be regarded as a vital contribution to the systemic efficiency of a high employment economy, rather than as a 'burden' on the private sector (Castles 1987).

In his study of *Why Some Peoples are more Unemployed than Others*, Göran Therborn (1986: 17) concluded that there was little or no statistical correlation between the usual explanations of unemployment and the divergence between low and high unemployment countries in the 1974–76 and the 1979–81 recessions. Developments in labour forces, such as ageing populations and increased female participation, were of only minor importance. Dependence upon exports and vulnerability to international economic cycles were of minor importance. Levels of unemployment bear no statistically significant relationship to general price inflation, labour costs inflation, taxes, social expenditure or unemployment benefits. Wage restraint leads to neither improved employment rates or greater international competitiveness. Finally, Therborn concluded that political and cultural independence appeared to have been decisive for the maintenance of low unemployment. Unemployment had been kept low in countries that speak languages other than English, were not members of the EU, refused to follow the tenets of international economic liberalism, and had long-standing institutions for maintaining high employment well before 1974. Such institutions include both labour market retraining programmes and export finance schemes. After 1974, the institutionalised commitment to high employment was supplemented in various ways. Austria and Switzerland resorted to expelling their immigrant guest-workers. Norway spent the proceeds of its nationalised oil industry on public sector employment. Sweden undertook a very large devaluation of its currency in 1981–82.

It is interesting to note that, on the one hand, Sweden, Norway and Austria have strong labour movements with Marxist beginnings, large public sectors, and states that have long been governed by parties of labour. On the other hand, Switzerland and Japan have insignificant labour movements, small public sectors, and states that have always been governed by parties of capital. The predominant parties of government in these countries have no common ideology or class representation, but (along with several countries in East And South-East Asia [as Scott Burchill argues in Chapter 18]) they do share a degree of cultural and political independence from the Anglo-Saxon dogma of free markets, comparative trading advantages and international economic liberalism in general. They therefore tend to see the nation-state as having an integral role to play in supporting the international success of their industry. If the class loyalties of the predominant party of government cannot readily explain either a commitment or lack of commitment to maintaining employment, what other explanations can there be for Sweden's dramatic abandonment of its long-standing commitment to full employment in 1991–93?

Basically, SAP has abandoned its Germanic traditions of mobilising wide popular support for reforms and campaigning for them against the predictable opposition of the large corporations, their employer confederation, and their political representatives in Parliament. Instead, SAP has begun to think in terms of a 'Swedish model' of gradual, largely uncontroversial reformism. The sharp increase in unemployment happened during a period of bourgeois government but the decline in political independence, or increased subservience to the international orthodoxies of economic liberalism, began during the 1982–91 SAP government. The dramatic 16 per cent devaluation of October 1982 was something of a last hurrah for SAP's post-1930s tradition of public policies that defied the precepts of economic liberalism. During the 1980s, the SAP government managed to balance its budget and maintain full employment without cutting welfare programmes, and this attracted praise by visiting economists from the Brookings Institute, Washington (Bosworth and Rivlin 1987; Vandenberg 1990, 1991; Ryner 1994). However, in 1986–88 the SAP government abolished the foreign exchange regulations that made devaluation a possibility. This deregulation followed the orthodox international view that currency controls no longer matter. Since 40 per cent of world trade takes place within the large transnational corporations, they can use transfer pricing of goods bought and sold by national divisions to bypass regulations. In 1989–91, a series of fiscal austerity measures saw the SAP government move decisively towards joining the EU. Then in 1992 the new bourgeois Government faced revelations that the publicly guaranteed and part-owned *Post-Kredit Banken* had made huge losses on central business district real estate loans and money market transactions. The government was forced to raise capital abroad to keep the bank afloat. Consequently when the value of the Swedish Krona declined, the public budget went into spectacularly large deficit along with the balance of payments. The bourgeois party leaders began to cut welfare spending heavily and scale down the labour market retraining scheme in the belief that the reduced public outlays would allow the private sector to generate more so-called 'real jobs'. Unfortunately, public sector retrenchments reduced the taxation base, while they increased outlays on unemployment benefit payments. The cuts cost more than they saved (Lachman *et al.* 1995).

In 1994, the social democrats were returned to government and at a referendum a majority of people voted to join the EU. Sweden has since become a full member. Since then the SAP government has managed to balance its budget and has also reduced the trade deficit to reasonable proportions. But it has made little headway in its attempts to restore expenditure on welfare programmes and the long-established labour market programmes. It has been hamstrung by an aspiration to keep inflation, interest rates, and the value of the currency within the narrow range required to join the countries that use the European Currency Unit, in case Britain does opt to join and Sweden needs to follow suit quickly. While the fiscal problems of the early 1990s were exacerbated by the 1992 bank crisis, the final breakdown of full employment has more deep-seated origins. Both bourgeois and social democratic governments of the last twenty years have departed from the tradition of political independence in favour of the more liberal public policies that prevail within the EU.

Political reasons for reformism limiting itself

To return to Marshall's theme of how citizenship provides cohesion where class generates division, I have argued elsewhere[7] that the blue-collar union confederation, LO,[8] lost its 1975–83 campaign to institute economic democracy primarily because it insisted that wage-earners rather than all citizens elect representatives to manage collective investment funds. LO insisted that the citizenry of an economic democracy be comprised of wage-earners rather than all national citizens because it failed to see past a political paradox rather than because it capitulated to the power or inexorable development of global capitalism.

Briefly, LO proposed and campaigned for a remarkably concrete scheme to implement a radical transition from capitalism to economic democracy (Meidner, Hedberg and Fond 1978; Matthews 1989; Higgins 1992). In 1976, LO proposed a scheme in which profitable corporations would be compelled to issue special shares to collectively controlled and democratically accountable wage-earners' investment funds. These share issues would ensure that a certain amount of venture capital would go into long-term projects and thus maintain full employment. They would also render superfluous the extreme wealth of entrepreneurs who can afford to risk their money in uncertain enterprises. Within 25–75 years wage-earners would, collectively, own majority holdings in the largest most profitable corporations. These radical proposals provoked a storm of extraordinarily heated criticism. SAP subsequently sought to moderate LO's proposals, abandoning share issues in favour of a levy on profits and wages. This would raise capital and be placed in a stock exchange that would remain viable. In 1983, the SAP government legislated a greatly watered down version of the investment funds.

The LO unions are affiliated with SAP, and LO has long been a powerful actor in Swedish politics. Its initial proposal to socialise ownership and control over the most successful corporations was therefore taken most seriously. The 'funds' were a central issue at the 1976, 1979 and 1982 elections. Defeat of LO's campaign for wage-earners' investment funds was, however, never inevitable or destined to happen. It demonstrates neither the harsh imperatives of revolution nor the treacherous contingencies of parliamentary reformism. The most interesting lessons about LO's defeat are to be found in analysing a political paradox. Only the most powerful of collective actors that have triumphed in past struggles and have shaped current rules of conflict, have any prospect of becoming agents of radical change. Only actors such as SAP or LO can pursue objectives so radical as to entail constituting a whole new arena of conflict.[9] Economic democracy necessarily challenges conventional boundaries between the parliamentary and electoral arena of liberal democratic politics and the industrial arena of capitalist economics. At the same time, the most successful and powerful of actors are least likely to abandon the arena of past triumphs in favour of founding an entirely new arena.

The history of SAP and LO arguably shows that a powerful collective actor can only become an agent of radical change if it formulates substantive and open-ended objectives (on this point see Higgins 1985b, 1988). These objectives must *both* mobilise internal support to overcome opposition from other actors *and*, subsequently, allow dispersal of that support and the opposition in order to allow new institutions, practices and actors to establish themselves in the new arena of conflict. LO's wage-earners' investment funds scheme did mobilise strong support among union officials and SAP's active members. But neither the original nor the later versions of the scheme fully emphasised the moral value of democracy, in which all national citizens are entitled to an equal say on crucial aspects of their working life. This meant that wage-earners' funds could neither mobilise wide support nor overcome intense opposition to the prospect of 'union bosses' running both the Government and industry. Consequently, the next Bourgeois Government in 1991 abolished SAP legislation instituting so-called wage-earners' funds in 1983.

A chief shortcoming of LO's scheme lay in the insistence that the funds be democratically accountable to an electorate of wage-earners only, which excluded students, the retired, home-makers, invalids, professionals and small business people, and of course employers and managers. LO's economists argued that a wage-earner only electorate would ensure a degree of economic efficiency, measured primarily in terms of the maintenance of full employment. An all-national citizens' electorate would introduce the contradictory interests of consumers, ecological sustainability and all manner of issues external to workplaces proper. In this insistence upon a wage-earner electorate, we can see that unionists hoped to reproduce themselves and their organisation within the new arena of economic democracy. On the other hand, some SAP leaders' preference for an all-citizens' electorate derived from a hope that SAP might reproduce itself in the new arena that might displace Parliament. These paradoxes might have been surmounted only by emphasising the moral importance of democracy as something worthwhile for its own sake. The citizen of an economic democracy would need to be much more actively involved in both debates and implementing decisions than the voter who chooses one or other party at parliamentary elections every few years.

With such a long and proud history of major political triumphs it would be wrong to conclude that Sweden's social democratic labour movement has now, finally, become more like ordinary parties and unions elsewhere. SAP may have abandoned its tradition of cultural independence and political struggle, but the LO unions have not. The large public sector union for blue-collar workers, for instance, has in recent years led a vigorous campaign against the liberal direction of SAP's current public policies. Whether they return home to care for the young, sick and old or they remain at work in the public sector and attempt to do more caring for lower budget outlays, it will be women who come to carry much of the burden of the SAP's shift towards economic liberalism. The future vitality of the Swedish unions and the exceptionality of the Swedish labour movement may well rest not so much on the way class complicates the relationship between citizenship and democracy as on the way in which gender complicates that relationship (Higgins 1996). In any case, the question of whether capitalism sets limits on welfare reforms remains open-ended and controversial. This very open-endedness cannot be encapsulated in any, necessarily simplified, 'Swedish model' of linear progress and rational harmony.

Notes

1 *Socialdemokratiska arbetarpartiet*, the Social Democratic Workers' Party.
2 For commentary on this speech in Swedish see Fredriksson, Strand and Södersten (1970), Isaksson (1985, 1990), and Hedborg and Meidner (1984).
3 My translation of an extract from the full text in Hansson (1928: 3). See Korpi (1978: 85) for a longer extract, translated by D. Saingbury.
4 *Sozialdemokratische Partei Deutschlands*.
5 Usually, wages and labour market policies feature in a 'Swedish model' but I have chosen other policies in order to illustrate how aspects of social citizenship were achieved against opposition, which then links to later arguments about political setback.
6 The best studies of Swedish unionisation compared to the rest of world are in Swedish. See Kjellberg (1980, 1997).
7 In my PhD thesis, A. Vandenberg, 'Social democracy and wage-earners' funds in Sweden', Macquarie University, Australia 1999.
8 *Landsorganisationen i Sverige*.
9 On this point, see Harding (1992) for an excellent discussion of democracy and efficiency in the early years of the Soviet Union.

References

Anderson, Perry (1962) 'Sweden: Mr Crosland's Dreamland, part one', *New Left Review*, no. 7 (Jan./Feb.): 4–12.
——(1963) 'Sweden: Mr Crosland's Dreamland, part two', *New Left Review*, no. 9 (May/June): 34–45.
Bosworth, Barry and Rivlin, Alice (eds) (1987) *The Swedish Economy*, Washington, DC: The Brookings Institute.
Castles, Francis (1987) 'Australia and Sweden: the Politics of Economic Vulnerability', *Thesis Eleven*, no. 16: 112–21.
Childs, Marquis (1936) *Sweden: The Middle Way*, New Haven, CT: Yale University Press.

Clement, W. and Mahon, R. (eds) (1994) *Swedish Social Democracy: A Model in Transition*, Toronto: Canadian Scholars' Press.

Crosland, Anthony (1956) *The Future of Socialism*, London: Cape.

Dow, Geoff (1993) 'What do we know about social democracy?', *Economic and Industrial Democracy*, vol. 14: 11–48.

Esping-Andersen, Gøsta (1985) *Politics Against Markets: The Social Democratic Road to Power*, Princeton, NJ: Princeton University Press.

Fredriksson, G., Strand, D. and Södersten, B. (1970) *Per-Albin-linjen*, Stockholm: Pan/Norstedts.

Fulcher, James (1991) *Labour Movements, Employers, and the State: Conflict and Co-operation in Britain and Sweden*, Oxford: Clarendon Press.

——(1994) 'The Social Democratic Model in Sweden: Termination or Restoration', *Political Quarterly*: 203–13.

Hansson, Per-Albin (1928) *Per Albin om Folkhemmet, Per Albin Hanssons tal om folkhemmet–medborgarhemmet i riksdagens remissdebatt 1928*, Stockholm: Metodica Press.

Harding, Neil (1992) 'The Marxist-Leninist Detour', in J. Dunn (ed.), *Democracy*, Cambridge: Cambridge University Press.

Heclo, Hugh (1974) *Modern Social Politics in Britain and Sweden; From Relief to Income Maintenance*, New Haven, CT: Yale University Press.

Hedborg, Anna and Meidner, Rudolf (1984) *Folkhemsmodellen*, Stockholm: Rabén och Sjögren.

Higgins, Winton (1985a) 'Political Unionism and the Corporatism Thesis', *Economic and Industrial Democracy*, vol. 6, no. 3: 349–81.

——(1985b) 'Unemployment and the Labour Movement's Breakthrough in Sweden', in Jill Roe (ed.), *Unemployment – Are there Lessons from History?*, Sydney: Hale & Iremonger.

——(1988) 'Swedish Social Democracy and the New Democratic Socialism', in Dianne Sainsbury (ed.), *Democracy, State, and Justice*, Stockholm: Almqvist & Wiksell.

——(1992) 'Swedish Wage-Earner Funds: The Problematic Relationship Between Economic Efficiency and Popular Power', in Jane Marceau (ed.), *Reworking the World; Organisations, Technologies, and Cultures in Comparative Perspective*, Berlin, New York: Walter de Gruyter.

——(1996) 'The Swedish Municipal Workers' Union – A Study in the New Political Unionism', *Economic and Industrial Democracy*, vol. 17: 167–97.

Isaksson, Anders (1985) *Per Albin, I. Vägen mot folkhemmet*, Stockholm: Wahlström och Widstrand.

——(1990) *Per Albin, II. Revolutionären*, Stockholm: Wahlström och Widstrand.

Israel, Joachim (1978) 'Swedish Socialism and Big Business', *Acta Sociologica*, vol. 21, no. 4: 341–53.

Kjellberg, Anders (1980) *Facklig organisering i tolv länder*, Lund: Arkiv förlag.

——(1997) *Fackliga organisationer och medlemmar i dagens Sverige*, Lund: Arkiv förlag.

Korpi, Walter (1978) *The Working Class in Welfare Capitalism: Work, Unions and Politics in Sweden*, London: Routledge & Kegan Paul.

——(1983) *The Democratic Class Struggle*, London: Routledge & Kegan Paul.

Lachman, Desmond, Bennet, Adam, Green, John H., Hageman, Robert and Ramanaswamy, Ramana (1995) *Challenges to the Swedish Welfare State*, Occasional Paper 130, Washington, DC: International Monetary Fund.

Lewin, Leif (1985) *Ideology and Strategy, a Century of Swedish Politics*, Cambridge: Cambridge University Press.

Martin, Andrew (1984) 'Trade Unions in Sweden: Strategic Responses to Change and Crisis', in Peter Gourevitch *et al.* (eds), *Unions and Economic Crises*, London: George Allen & Unwin.

Marshall, Thomas H. (1950) *Citizenship and Social Class*, Cambridge: Cambridge University Press.

Matthews, John (1989) 'The Democratisation of Capital', *Economic and Industrial Democracy*, vol. 10: 165–93.

Meidner, R., Hedborg, A. and Fond, G. (1978) *Employee Investment Funds: An Approach to Collective Capital Formation*, London: George Allen & Unwin.

Misgeld, Klaus; Molin, Karl and Åmark, Klas (eds) (1992) *Creating Social Democracy: A Century of the Social Democratic Labor Party in Sweden*, Pennsylvania: Penn State Press.

Olsen, Gregg (1994) 'Labour Mobilisation and the Strength of Capital: The Rise and Stall of Economic Democracy in Sweden', in Clement and Mahon (1994).

Pontusson, Jonas (1984) 'Behind and Beyond Social Democracy in Sweden', *New Left Review*, no. 143: 69–96.

——(1987) 'Radicalisation and Retreat in Swedish Social Democracy', *New Left Review*, no. 165 (Sept.–Oct.): 5–33.

——(1992a) 'At the End of the Third Road: Swedish Social Democracy in Crisis', *Politics and Society*, vol. 20, no. 3 (Sept.): 305–32.

——(1992b) *The Limits of Social Democracy: Investment Politics in Sweden*, Ithaca, NY: Cornell University Press.

Rothstein, Bo (1990) 'Marxism, Insitutional Analysis, and Working-Class Power: the Swedish Case', *Politics and Society*, vol. 16, no. 3: 317–45.

Ryner, Magnus (1994) 'Economic Policy in the 1980s: 'The Third Way': the Swedish Model and the Transition from Fordism to Post-Fordism', in Clement and Mahon (1994).

Swenson, Peter (1989) *Fair Shares: Unions, Pay and Politics in Sweden and West Germany*, Ithaca, NY: Cornell University Press.

Stråth, Bo (1998) *Mellan två fonder: LO och den svenska modellen*, Uddevalla: Atlas.

Tilton, Timothy (1990) *The Political Theory of Swedish Social Democracy: Through the Welfare State to Socialism*, Oxford: Clarendon Press.

Therborn, Göran (1985) 'The Coming of Swedish Social Democracy', *Estratto Da 'Annali' Della Fondazione Giangiacomo Feltrinelli 1983/1984*, Milan: Fondazione Giangiacomo Feltrinelli.

——(1986) *Why Some Peoples are more Unemployed than Others*, London: Verso Books.

——(1992) 'A Unique Chapter in the History of Democracy: the Social Democrats in Sweden', in Misgeld, Molin and Åmark (eds) (1992).

Turner, Bryan (1986) *Citizenship and Capitalism: The Debate Over Reformism*, London: Allen & Unwin.

Vandenberg, A. (1990) 'Uncommon Drama in the Swedish Riksdag', *Australian Society*, vol. 9, no. 4 (April): 33–4.

——(1991) 'Sweden Sour', *Australian Left Review*, November: 6.

Wallerstein, M. (1989) 'Union Organization in Advanced Industrial Democracies', *American Political Science Review*, vol. 83, no. 2 (June): 481–502.

12 RUSSIA: WITHDRAWAL TO THE PRIVATE SPHERE

Derek Verrall

This chapter about post-communist Russia draws on both political analyses of the role of parties and sociological analyses of the absence of any sense of trust and civility among strangers within a larger community. Referring to Macpherson's argument (also noted in Chapter 1), Verrall argues that Russia's political parties cannot effectively mediate between the government and the citizens. In his criticism of Marshall, Turner has argued that any theory of citizenship needs to account for the way it developed from the bottom up, as in the USA and France, or from the top down, as in the UK and Germany. The democracy 'from above' that has been imposed on Russians has, however, little foundation in either elites' commitment to the rule of law or in any popular sense of civility towards anyone outside one's own family or neighbourhood ethnic group.

It is misleading to think that the collapse of the communist era in the former Soviet Union heralded a transition from communism to liberal democracy or free market capitalism. It is clear that Russia has thrown off the trappings of a totalitarian state. The dominant ideology, the centralised state structures (set up and run by the Communist Party which controlled the repressive state apparatus of police, army and the courts), and all significant political institutions in society comprehensively collapsed along with the centralised command economy that the Communist Party administered. The Russian state has also lost its contiguous empire and seen itself eclipsed as a global superpower in all respects save the important field of nuclear weapons. Yet it is not obvious where Russia is headed. While its leaders speak the language of market capitalism, and of government by the rule of law and liberal democracy, Russia is none the less characterised by 'strong personalised rule, weak representative institutions, ineffective courts, criminalised parties, wide social divisions and [a] passive citizenry' (White 1997: 440). After seven decades of communist rule, Russia lacks an integrated civil society.

The political leadership is predominantly former members of the Communist Party of the Soviet Union (CPSU). They learned their methods of ruling, political mores and ways of relating to the wider public during their struggles for influence within the CPSU. Yeltsin himself had been a party member for 30 years and a member of the CPSU Politburo, the party's highest policy-making body. A recent study suggests that about 75 per cent of Yeltsin's top leadership and over 80 per cent of the leading officials in the Russian regions were former members of the communist *nomenklatura* (Kryshtanovskaya and White 1996).

Economic shock therapy, administered by economic reformers close to President Yeltsin in the context of strong international pressures exerted by the major capitalist states and institutions such as the International Monetary Fund (IMF), has had the immediate impact of dramatically worsening people's material conditions. This has forced people to get by without government in a process which is at once both satisfying, in that it promises to put the repressions and waste of the past behind them, and disturbing, in that it is difficult to survive in the resulting wreckage (Rose 1994). The identifiable centres of decision-making, dominated by external pressures and distrusted by an overwhelming majority of citizens are, in important respects, inaccessible to citizens. Their subsequent disquiet has been managed by the political leadership through a combination of populism, fear of the past, and the promise of a shining future following the introduction of reforms.

Peter Reddaway has pointed to a resulting 'many layered feeling of moral and spiritual injury', the loss of bearings and sense of self and society, the bewilderment and frustrations engendered by the widening divisions in society, and the pervasive feelings of insecurity (1993: 30) which have led to a widespread sense of identity crisis. This crisis has been exploited by extreme nationalists and the neo-communists who have sought to blame Yeltsin for the disintegration of the USSR, the decline of Russia's greatness on a global scale, and the ensuing social and economic collapse. It has also led almost everyone to turn increasingly to their family and other connections based on kinship or ethnic groups for solutions to the pressing problems of making do on an everyday basis (Rose 1994).

'Democracy' and 'citizenship' in contemporary Russia

Throughout most of their history the Russian people have been subjects of the Tsar or the Communist Party rather than rights-bearing citizens participating in the processes of politics. They have been a people to whom politics has been done rather than a community of citizens who, to some extent, do politics either as individuals or through voluntary associations.[1] Although the previous regime had to take the interests of important social groupings into account, there was no formalised institutional base for this process beyond the CPSU after the rise of the Bolsheviks. The CPSU regime fell when it could no longer accommodate the political interests of emerging groups or give them sufficient stake in the continuity of the regime. In the absence of the rule of law and an independent judiciary, any state-granted rights to welfare, housing or education could be terminated in individual cases. Under Stalin the absence of law meant that even the right to life could be arbitrarily eliminated by the regime.

Russian people now have the right to choose their leaders through relatively fair competitive elections, and they can read a diversity of newspapers and enjoy a range of civil rights previously denied them, but there are limitations on their democracy. The legislature has little control over the executive, political parties are weak, the judiciary and the rule of law are aspirations rather than realities. The elimination of bourgeois attitudes under the Bolsheviks eroded the development of characteristics such as tolerance, self-organisation and self-help which underlay the growth of civil society in what were to become the European liberal democracies after the Second World War. Assuming Russia follows a European pattern, the formation of a middle class will have to accompany or follow the development of civil society in Russia (Miller 1992: 143).

It is important to remember these qualifications before too readily accepting the Schumpeterian (1947) view that Russia has become a democracy because there are competitive elections between alterna-

tive leaders of the government. The personalised nature of the political process, the weakness of civil society, the weakness of state institutions, and the absence of organised mass-membership political
parties distinguish contemporary Russian politics. In the current
context, it is difficult to foresee any development of 'A free society
[which], acting through the press and elected representatives, restrains
the state, while the law restrains both' (Ignatieff 1995: 129).

Civil society

The concept of civil society encompasses a wide variety of social institutions, associations, clubs, groups, unions, religious organisations and
interest groups which stand between the state and the individual. It
has been defined as 'those structures and processes through which
individuals and groups interact [relatively] autonomously of the
command structures of the state in pursuit of their particular concerns' (Rigby 1992: 14). As such, civil society is distinct from both the
state and society but constantly interacts with both. It seeks to resist
the excessive constraints imposed by a fragmented society on the one
hand and excessive regulation by the state's command structures on
the other. Civil society remains distinct from the command structures
of the state but is in a close symbiotic relationship with the political
order more generally. As Robert Putnam (1993: 152–62) has argued,
civil society is where individuals learn the important civic virtues of
trust, reciprocity and mutuality which both constitute and preserve
liberal democracy and the development of a free, efficient and honest
market economy. However, it is not the existence of groups *per se* that
is important. If groups of people are to found a civil society then the
groups should be characterised by openness, overlapping member-
ships, voluntarism, and democratic internal organisational structures.
As a necessary but not sufficient condition for the emergence of
liberal democracy, civil society has evolved through a long process of
organisational development in specific historical contexts, which give
it unique characteristics in each country.

The informal associations that emerged in the last years of the communist regime[2] played little part in the collapse of the CPSU and the
eventual disintegration of the USSR. Neither have they provided the
means for citizens' participation in the emergent post-communist
regimes, or provided building blocks for the construction of a limited

range of political parties. Instead there has been a marked withdrawal from political action, highlighted by declining participation rates in elections since 1990, and a withdrawal of support from all political institutions (Rose 1994: 26; White 1997: 437–8). In the economic circumstances facing the majority of the population, closed familial groups and highly privatised operations in the 'alegal' cash economy are a means of achieving some degree of economic security.

The weakness of both civil society and the institutons of state has resulted in the rise of 'mafia capitalism'. Former members of the communist *nomenklatura* have been the chief beneficiaries of this process. Their connections with the state-subsidised sector, relevant government officials and parliamentary representatives (many of whom are directors of state-owned farms, factories and other institutions) have given them a position of strategic dominance in the privatised and deregulated economy. The redistribution of property and resources that followed the collapse of the previous system suggests the state is unable to check the concentration of economic power within closed circles of elites who are concerned primarily with the welfare of their own members and exhibit loyalties confined to their immediate group. The professional associations of managers, entrepreneurs and regional leaders dominate the economy and extract monopoly privilege from it. They sell goods abroad without paying taxes and bribe their way through customs. Local 'mafias' develop close relationships with the local military, police and courts. Under such circumstances it has been estimated that Moscow receives only 35–40 per cent of the taxes for which it budgets (Rahr 1992: 15).

Contemporary Russian society has been marked by the emergence of a vast array of parochial, sectarian and fundamentalist movements. Thus the emergence of civil society is hampered by a society riddled with actual and potential sources of intolerance, extremism, sectarianism, populism, traditionalism, ethnicity and patriarchy. Non-elite organisations are frequently based on extended family and kinship connections or closed neighbourhood groupings based on ethnicity. Such groups, where they involve the provision of goods and services such as food, home repairs, the exchange of favours or the provision of a telephone connection, studiously avoid regulation and taxation. This is understandable, given the collapse of the Russian economy, where inflation has wiped out people's savings, workers and pensioners receive their incomes infrequently, and widespread poverty is a visible fact of life, but it is counter productive for the development of civil society and the rule of law. It is unlikely to lead to the evolution of trust, reciprocity and mutuality beyond the group, or to generalised conceptions of human respect, the common good or freedom which transcend ethnic and familial boundaries and are the hallmarks of a developed civil society. Rather it suggests isolated groupings deriving much of their cohesion from the need to ward off threats from outsiders, be they state officials or other competitor groupings; such cohesion may lead to inter-communal tensions and sporadic outbreaks of violence.

President Yeltsin's 'revolution from above'

President Yeltsin did not seek to build broad-based social support for the economic reform process, the major dynamic for which has been pressure from external institutions. Perhaps such support would have been impossible to gain, but the consequence has been that the effect of popular domestic political involvement in, and support for, the key issue of post-communist policy has been marginalised and all political institutions are regarded with high levels of distrust. Yeltsin chose to rely on highly personalised authoritarian populism. He merged his own undoubted prestige, as the man who led the final overthrow of the Communist Party, with personalised influence over the electronic media, and a fear of the alternatives. These alternatives, represented by the ultra-nationalist Zhirinovsky and the neo-communist Zuganov, won the support of sizeable minorities in the Presidential election of June 1996 but they have been unable to win a majority of the voters in various local election campaigns. Zhirinovsky's and Zuganov's impressive showing at elections for the legislature in December 1995 suggests that voters have sought to use the groupings they represent as a check on presidential power and as a way of voicing disapproval of government policy.

In government, President Yeltsin relied on a narrow, closed and individually dispensable group of advisers who rose and fell in influence primarily as a result of domestic power struggles within the leadership and the President's desire to maintain the support of Western liberal democracies. Thus most of Yeltsin's liberal supporters had been sacrificed by the end of 1992, most noticeably reform economist Yegor Gaidar and key adviser Gennardy Burbulis. (See Kovalev 1996 for a letter of resignation from one of the remainder of this group.)

Similarly, the electoral alliance of convenience, between the President and General Lebed following the first round of the 1996 presidential election, collapsed within six months of Yeltsin's victory.

The introduction of a written constitution conferred dominance upon the executive after the upheavals between the presidency, the legislature and the Constitutional Court which resulted in the shelling of the legislative buildings and the dismissal of the Court in September 1993. However, the new institutional order has not established clearly defined responsibilities for different branches of government and levels of power. The tendency to rule by presidential decree in the face of a hostile Parliament has avoided the need to establish procedures to reconcile conflicts between the legislature and the executive.

Prior to the forced dismissal of his parliamentary opponents many conflicts and inconsistencies between decrees and legislative acts were taken to the Constitutional Court, involving the Court in direct political conflict. Its rulings were openly criticised by those who considered themselves to have lost on specific issues and the Court was derided as a 'nest of vipers' by members of the presidential entourage.

The attempt to impose economic reform via a 'revolution from above' is unlikely to succeed in Russia (Johnson 1994). The central government has little control over the regions, making it unlikely that Russia can emulate those Asian states that have successfully modernised their economies under the guidance of a strong centralised state. Regional leaders, overwhelmingly former members of the *nomenklatura*, attempt to run an apparatus of government in the old style but at the same time they jealously guard their newly-won autonomy. They usually pursue personally beneficial regional policies of economic development, and ignore central government decrees and resolutions. Such tendencies further strengthen regional sentiments and lead to fragmentation. There is a widespread refusal to collect and send revenue to Moscow. Complaints that regional laws are inconsistent with laws from the centre are met with the demand that the centre brings its laws into line with the regions and that officials appointed by the President to ensure compliance with the centre's laws be recalled.

Within its own sphere, the central government has not displayed any sense of cohesion or collective responsibility. President Yeltsin was reluctant to give strong and consistent support to his ministers when the reform policies associated with them proved unpopular.

Rather, Yeltsin adopted a position of being 'above the fray of politics' in order to distance himself as much as possible from ministers in difficulty. The President's long bouts of incapacity, due to recurrent health problems, were marked by a constant jockeying for position among potential successors and public disunity on important issues such as the Chechen peace process.

Absence of stable political parties

Since the overthrow of the Communist Party, Russian leaders have not sought to form a system of stable broad-based political parties. Political parties in liberal democracies play a major role in organising political activity. They channel participation and, in theory at least, provide a means of making participation effective by offering a choice of programmes and candidates in election campaigns. They give some direction to public policy and maintain a pattern of interaction with major elements in the wider society. They have been instrumental in providing for the involvement of people *in* their government while maintaining the rigorous separation of the people *from* their government [Chapter 3 above also discusses this point]. Parties, in performing this dual role, have enabled the reconciliation of political equality inherent in the democratic tradition with the economic inequality generated under capitalism by distancing the political elite from their mass support base. This distance enables leaders to make the necessary compromises between the opposing interests which are a feature of decision-making whichever party is in power and irrespective of its support base (Macpherson 1977: 64–9).

The absence of stable political parties, which exacerbates the contradiction between political equality and economic inequality, will be extremely difficult to resolve while the strains imposed by sectional, religious and ethnic cleavages militate against the emergence of a stable social order on the basis of which such parties could be formed. Moreover the process of economic reform, the prominence of the profit motive, the spread of market relations and the growing emphasis on individual activity and closed groups weakens those elements of civil society which many hoped would be strengthened following the demise of the CPSU (Offe 1991: 875–6).

The proliferating parties, with the exception of the re-formed Communist Party of the Russian Federation (CPRF), are based on prominent figures within the political elite. The leaders are significant in attracting groupings within the legislature and in giving the wider population a personality to support. Hence most political groupings are identified by their leader's name rather than an articulated programme, a broad ideology or an identifiable support base in the wider community: former Prime Minister Chernomyrdin was Our Home is Russia, Yavlinsky is Yabloko, Zhirinovsky is the ultra-nationalist Liberal Democratic Party of Russia. Parties have little internal cohesion, organisational structure or means of communication, and they lack organised grass-roots support bases. Loyalties within parties remain at the ethnic and regional level rather than relating to a party leader, platform or broad social category. Political conflict in Russia has not been institutionalised but rather remains confined to an elite revolving around the president. Conflict is highly personalised which makes compromise more difficult and the cost of losing much higher.

The CPRF rose in the wake of the 1992 ruling by the Constitutional Court that communists were free to begin parties on the local and regional level. By mid-1996 the CPRF had an estimated 560000 members which, while small compared to the 20 million members of the old CPSU, far exceeded the size of any other party. The party has its own publication, *Zavtra* (*Tomorrow*), a monthly which features bold headlines and stories which attack and lampoon Yeltsin and predict an apocalyptic future for Russia under its present leadership (Remnick 1996). Compared with other parties it has a degree of organisational structure. Despite its size and organisational ability the CPRF has been unable to counter the fears of a return to the past. The liberal freedoms of speech, association and religion, and the removal of many of the cultural controls (a legacy of Gorbachev's *glasnost*), are regarded as important gains not to be surrendered.

There is also widespread antipathy among the broader public for the very concept of party. Partly this is a product of their past experience which links party with corruption and insider politics. Reports of recent opinion polls indicate that 40 per cent of Russians believe that political parties have no relevance for ordinary people and that over half those polled thought that the new parties were based on greed for power. Disdain for political parties is matched by distrust of all other political and social institutions, a falling participation rate in presidential and parliamentary elections and a general withdrawal from politics (White 1997: 436–8).

President Yeltsin did not formally align himself with any specific party, claiming to be 'above politics'. Failure to form his own party in the immediate aftermath of the defeat of the coup plotters in 1991 and to call a parliamentary election in late 1991, which his supporters would have won handsomely given his huge popularity at the time, has had serious consequences for the emergence of a party system and for political developments in Russia. Yeltsin could have rid himself of an increasingly hostile and unpopular legislature. Subsequently Yeltsin refused to back any political party strongly. However, by the 1995 parliamentary election his personal popularity appeared to have eroded.

The liberal reform intelligentsia and the emerging class of property owners are deeply divided by personality clashes and interests. Two of Russia's major economic reformers, Yegor Gaidar and Grigor Yavlinsky, appear to be so deeply divided by personal antagonism that co-operation between them seems impossible. The politics of jockeying for personal influence, power and access to the President make it more difficult to compromise and negotiate on the policy differences within the reform programme. Yavlinsky was unable to come to an accommodation with Yeltsin in the 1996 Presidential election despite the fact that both shared a common interest in defeating Zhirinovsky and Zuganov.

The failure to form stable political parties can partly be attributed to the lack of acceptance or understanding, at either an elite or popular level, of concepts such as compromise and negotiation essential to conflict resolution. The political elite continues to be drawn overwhelmingly from amongst those who learned their methods of ruling, skills and mores in the ranks of the CPSU where compromise was seen as a temporary expedient to be overturned when circumstances permitted and competition was for position and access to the ear of the powerful. The political power holders, in the regions as well as the centre, are tough-minded dealers who have been sufficiently flexible to adapt to the emergence of the new 'democratic' institutions and keep them weak.

The failure to establish the rule of law

Despite official claims that Russia is now a society based on the rule of law, those in power continue to evade the law when it is in their interests to do so. The fragility of the rule of law is most obvious in the individual's contact with officialdom, where the 'blat' system of the Soviet era has continued much as before (see Attard 1997: ch. 2). The blat system is an economy of informal favours and understandings, not necessarily involving money, by which people sought access to jobs, education, goods and services in short supply. In the late 1980s, as food shortages become apparent, blat dominated the informal economy and became widespread through out society; previously it had operated primarily amongst the nomenklatura. Today, widespread corruption and influence peddling mean that it is impossible to do business honestly in Russia. There is no stable law of contract, on the basis of which business arrangements can proceed with certainty. Connections are crucial to find a way through the complexity of bureaucracy and inconsistent laws and regulations at the various levels of government.

There has been a turbulent relationship between the President and the Russian Constitutional Court since the collapse of the Soviet Union culminated in the dismissal of the Court and its chairman at the same time as the President asserted his superiority over the legislature. Whenever the President has been unable to get his way in the various cases before the Court, he or his supporters have denounced the Court itself. The idea of a judiciary independent of both the legislature and the executive, judging cases on their legal merits, remains remote from Russian experience and shows little sign of establishing itself or being accepted by the political elite or general population as a necessary element of the political process.

Future developments

The Russian state would appear too fragmented to allow for the restoration of a highly centralised authoritarian regime. The regions and various ethnic groupings have sought to exploit the current weakness of the centre. However, they are themselves too fragmented to mount a co-ordinated and sustained opposition to the centre and arrive at a new stable division of power.

The fragmentation of society into relatively closed insular groups, unable to develop relationships based on trust and reciprocity, or to deal with their conflicts with a degree of civility, suggests major difficulties for the development of civil society. Since the collapse of the communist order, Russians have experienced the development of a wide range of groups and associations and the enjoyment of personal freedoms and civil liberties (Kenny 1997).[3] These voluntary associations have developed as a means through which people seek to advance their specific individual interests and concerns in the context of a major erosion of their material circumstances. Many of these groups seek to evade the law in the desperate struggle for a degree of economic advantage and security. As such they appear to be unlikely components in the development of civil society and democracy in Russia.

Citizenship, civil society and democracy are achievements which governments may help or hinder by their actions but which are essentially created by people acting in open public forums in a civil manner. Civil society draws its strength from widely shared beliefs and attitudes concerning the relations of individuals as citizens, and between the community of citizens and the state. The development of civil society and democracy involves the development of capacities for the peaceful resolution of conflicts, the setting of the outer limits for dissent and deviance, and determining modes and styles for the pursuit of particular interests. In all these respects, Russia falls short of the conditions required for the emergence of a pluralist form of democracy. At best it seems destined to experience an extended period of formal democracy, characterised by regular elections in which dominant personalities compete for the votes of a passive electorate overwhelmingly preoccupied with the immediate struggles of getting by on a daily basis (Lewis 1997). The post-communist period has seen a wholly understandable retreat into the private sphere.

Notes

1 For an account of the vestiges of civil society which existed under the communist regime see Rigby (1992).
2 Rigby (1992: 21) estimates that there were at least 60 000 unofficial clubs and associations which operated in the open by the end of 1988. Perhaps a quarter of these were concerned with public issues.
3 A major research project, currently being conducted through Deakin University's Centre for Citizenship and Human Rights involving Australian and Russian academics, is exploring the development of voluntary welfare

associations in Russia and comparing this with the role of such organisations in Australia and Sweden. Such research will not only tell us much about the development of civil society in Russia but may lead to the development and transfer of skills, values and attitudes appropriate to an emerging civil society. For a brief report of this research which is more optimistic than my account see Kenny (1997).

References

Attard, M. (1997) *Russia: Which Way Paradise?* Sydney: Doubleday.

Ignatieff, M. (1995) 'On civil society; why Eastern Europe's revolutions could succeed', *Foreign Affairs*, vol. 74, no. 2 (March /April): 128–36.

Johnson, J. (1994) 'Should Russia adopt the Chinese model of economic reform?', *Communist and Post-Communist Studie*, vol. 27, no. 1: 59–75.

Kenny, S. (1997) 'The emergence of non-governmental organisations in post-communist societies. The road to active citizenship?', *Forum*, no. 11: 2–3, 5.

Kovalev, S. (1996) 'A letter of resignation, 23rd Jan 1996', trans. C. Fitzpatrick, *New York Review of Books*, vol. 43, no. 3: 29–30.

Kryshtanovskaya, O. and White, S. (1996) 'From Soviet nomenklatura to Russian elite', *Europe-Asia Studies*, vol. 43, no. 5: 711–33.

Lewis, P. (1997) 'Political participation in post-communist democracies' in D. Potter *et al.*, *Democratisation*, Cambridge: Polity Press: 443–65.

Macpherson, C.B. (1977) *The Life and Times of Liberal Democracy*, Oxford: Oxford University Press: 64–9.

Matlock, J. (1996) 'The Russian prospect', *New York Review of Books*, vol. 43, no. 3: 43–7.

Miller, R.F. (1992) 'Concluding essay' in R.F. Miller (ed.), *The Developments of Civil Society in Communist Systems*, Sydney: Allen & Unwin: 130–47.

Offe, C. (1991) 'Capitalism by democratic design? Democratic theory facing the triple transition in east–centre Europe, *Social Research*, vol. 58, no. 4: 865–92.

Putnam, R. (1993) *Making Democracy Work: Civic Traditions in Modern Italy*, Princeton, NJ: Princeton University Press.

Rahr, A. (1992) 'A Russian paradox: democrats support emergency powers', *Radio Free Europe/Radio Liberty Research Report*, vol. 1, no. 48 (December).

Reddaway, P. (1993) 'Russia on the brink?', *New York Review of Books*, vol. 40, no. 3: 30–5.

Remnick, D. (1996) 'Hammer, sickle and book', *New York Review of Books*, vol. 63, no. 9 (23 May): 45–51.

Rigby, T.H. (1992) 'The USSR: End of a long dark night?', in Miller (1992): 11–23.

Rose, R. (1994) 'Rethinking civil society; Post-communism and the problem of trust', *Journal of Democracy*, vol. 5, no. 3: 18–30.

Schumpeter, J.A. (1947) *Capitalism, Socialism and Democracy*, London: Allen & Unwin: p. 269–73.

Shevtsova, L. (1995) 'Russia's post-communist politics: revolution or continuity?', in G. Lapidus (ed.), *The New Russia: Troubled Transformation*, Boulder, CO: Westview Press: 5–37.

White, S. (1993) 'Post-communist politics: towards democratic pluralism?, in S. White, R. di Leo and O. Cappelli (eds), *The Soviet Transition: From Gorbachev to Yeltsin*, London: Frank Cass: pp. 18–32.

——(1997) 'Russia's troubled transition', in D. Potter *et al.* (eds), *Democratisation*, Cambridge: Polity Press: 421–42.

13 Democracy and Difference in American Social and Political Thought

Vince Marotta

In the exchange between Michael Sandel and Richard Rorty discussed in Chapter 1, each of them drew their own interpretations of John Dewey's thought to support contrary views about philosophy and politics. In this chapter, Marotta's position avoids either Sandel's or Rorty's interpretation of Dewey. His criticisms of Dewey are much more like Hindess's criticisms of the misleading choice between realist and participatory models of democracy. Yet Marotta points out that postmodern accounts of democracy often have some hidden element of the universalism or essentialism that they criticise in mainstream arguments about democracy. This chapter concludes by endorsing Bauman's argument for recognition of the ambivalence of any ethical relationship. The conclusion has some similarities to Anna Yeatman's argument in favour of recognising a very general sense of violence between the subject and the other. It also has similarities to the argument of Chapter 1 in favour of making contest rather than consensus the essence of democracy and citizenship.

In 1911 the American black sociologist W. E. B. Du Bois wrote, 'whether at last the Negro will gain full recognition as a man, or be utterly crushed by prejudice and superior numbers, is the present Negro problem' (Du Bois 1980: 111). Events in America in the 1990s have done little to dispel the concern raised by Du Bois. In fact, the 1990s have been a decade where the issue of race has once again literally exploded on to the American public agenda. In 1991, with the public telecasting of a video depicting a black man – Rodney King – being brutally attacked by members of the Los Angeles police force, the 'colour problem' violently and tragically re-emerged. For some public commentators, the incident was a reaffirmation of the violent oppression that particular sections of the black community still endure. On the other hand, more conservative observers maintained that this was an issue concerning police brutality, and race had little to do with it. The riots in Los Angeles, which followed the acquittal of the four white police officers, clearly highlighted the fact that racial issues, both between whites and blacks, and between African-Americans and Asian-Americans, were still unresolved. As coverage and discussion of the Los Angeles riots began to recede into the back pages of the major newspapers, the O. J. Simpson case brought the race issue back to the front pages. The O. J. Simpson case, according to a CBS poll, expressed the division between blacks and whites. As the O. J. Simpson trial began, the poll found that 64 per cent of whites polled believed he was guilty, while 12 per cent of blacks thought he was probably guilty, but 59 per cent thought he was innocent. Finally, according to one commentator (Jacoby 1996), the Million Man March, organised by the leader of Nation of Islam, Louis Farrakhan, reflected the alienation and anger felt by the 'black community'.

In addition to these incidents, the debate about affirmative action policies and 'political correctness' has further problematised the relationship between the different races. Affirmative action policies have been associated with the proactive pursuit of civil rights, which protect group rights over individual rights. These policies, according to their critics, emphasise equality of outcome rather than opportunity and focus on group rights at the expense of individual rights.

The Rodney King incident, the Los Angeles riots, the Million Man March and debates about affirmative action and political correctness have resulted in an intense public debate in America over the goal of a multicultural society and its relationship to democracy and citizenship. These issues have become the focal points around which questions surrounding racial identity, democracy and multiculturalism have been publicly debated. For example, for some observers the verbal and physical violence against blacks has highlighted the fact that formal citizenship rights for blacks have not been translated into equal respect for all. Institutionalised racism, moreover, is said to be particularly apparent in the legal system. These incidents have also led to reflections on the type of society that America is and should become. In a multicultural society such as the USA, what type of relationship should exist between democratic citizenship and maintaining one's group identity? The public concern in America with race, identity and democracy has also been reflected in the scholarly literature on multiculturalism and democracy. This literature examines whether the discourse on identity can be reconciled with a democratic regime.

The discourse about identity, at least at a theoretical level, cannot be confined to the past three decades because these philosophical and religious questions of self-identity have been prevalent since the European religious wars of the 1500s and 1600s. But what makes this discourse distinctively modern is that since the mid-1700s identity has been perceived as problematic and contingent. As this discourse of modern identity has become more prominent, an intellectual debate has emerged in Western societies regarding the relationship between democracy and culture. Within the scholarly literature, two positions have emerged. One contends that the demands for the recognition and maintenance of specific cultural identities have resulted in 'undemocratic' processes. Those who advocate group rights based on particular social and cultural identities express the second position. They conclude that their demands are consistent with liberal democratic principles. In order to address the theoretical and conceptual relationship between identity, difference and democracy and the underlying differences between these two positions, this chapter initially examines deliberative and 'postmodern' accounts of democracy. The chapter concludes by considering an ethical democratic polity where the relationship between the self and the other is premised on being responsible for, and maintaining the autonomy of, those who are socially and culturally different.

Deliberative democracy and the other

This section considers past and present accounts of deliberative democracy and the ways in which they deal with cultural pluralism or difference. In other words, how do these democratic models understand the relationship between self and other, especially when this other is culturally and racially different? Some deliberative democrats move beyond questions of procedure or calls for equal representation and take up issues concerning the fairness of the terms of the debate, while others are more concerned with how participation in the public sphere fosters particular democratic values and norms.

In American social thought, John Dewey was one of the earliest social theorists who advocated a democratic polity based on public communication and debate. By listening to and debating with others, one will be exposed to different ideas and values; this, according to Dewey, will make individuals more open and thus more likely to change their perceived opinions. In this way, Dewey believes that 'participation in democracy not only demands but fosters a particular sort of personality, one whose public proposals are deliberated and presented as subject to public scrutiny' (Festenstein 1997: 88). The limitations of Dewey's participatory democracy are highlighted in his *Ethics of Democracy* (1997). For Dewey, in order to participate in public communication and debate, one needs to have a particular 'personality' and this 'personality', as the following discussion will demonstrate, excludes difference.

Dewey critically examines the major differences between an ethical dimension of democracy and the 'quantitative or numerical dimension' (Dewey 1997: 184). Dewey's notion of democracy emphasises the underlying universal quality of the human condition rather than difference in the condition of groups of particular people. This is expressed through his critique of classical liberalism. Dewey is critical of atomistic liberalism because its version of democracy is premised on what was later described as possessive individualism and negative freedom. Atomistic liberalism views society as a social contract where 'men are mere individuals, without any social relations until they form a contract' (Dewey 1997: 184); as a consequence, individuals, in their natural state, are perceived as non-social units. The social contract theorists, maintains Dewey, assume that some artifice must be theorised to constitute individuals into political theory (Dewey 1997: 186). In contrast, Dewey's notion of democracy begins from a different premise because democracy, as a social and political idea, is a living entity: an 'organism'.

[T]he non-social individual is an abstraction arrived at by imagining what man would be if all his human qualities were taken away. Society, as a real whole, is the normal order and the mass as an aggregate of isolated units is the fiction.

> If this be the case, and if democracy be a form of society, it not only does have, but must have, a common will; for it is this unity of will which makes it an organism. (Dewey 1997: 187)

The individual and society are organically inter-related and democracy tends to reflect this harmonious relationship where the common will, and hence democracy, resides in the personality of the citizens. As a metaphysical proposition, Dewey associates democracy with a state of oneness. Like Plato before him, Dewey argues that the self-realisation of the individual can only occur through society and the state (Dewey 1997: 197). It is incorrect, asserts Dewey, to perceive democracy as only a form of government: rule by the many. Democracy, concludes Dewey, 'is a form of government only because it is a form of moral and spiritual association' (Dewey 1997: 196). Dewey has an ontological conception of democracy. To be a democrat is to be a person who belongs to a society. Democracy and individuality refer to an ethical and spiritual state. However, if individuals cannot be socially and spiritually separated from the political society which constitutes them, then those who do not contribute to the establishment of the 'common will' will be marginalised.

> [There] are individuals who are not organs of the common will, who are outside of the political society in which they live, and are, in effect, aliens to that which should be their commonwealth. Not participating in the formation or expression of the common will, they do not embody it in themselves, Having no share in society, society has none in them. (Dewey 1997: 193)

'Aliens' are those individuals who have not participated in the ethical and spiritual formation of society. It follows from this that one cannot participate in public communication and debate if one's 'personality' or identity does not reside within the society in which one lives. Consequently, Dewey's conception of democracy potentially excludes immigrants, African-Americans and indigenous people because their self-identity seems to be at odds with the collective identity of the host society. These groups, because their personalities have been formed by a different common will, cannot be included. Thus, Dewey's 'common will', and the democratic ethos underlying it, does not embrace the cultural or racial other because difference is inimical to his organic view of democracy.

The tension between democracy and difference is further highlighted in Dewey's conception of equality. Equality is not an arithmetic, but an ethical concept (Dewey 1997: 201). This ethical conception of equality is manifested in his highly abstract notion of 'personality'. Personality is 'indifferent to all distinctions which divide men from men . . . and there is no trace by which one personality may be distinguished from another so as to be set above or below'. Democracy 'is a form of society in which every man . . . has a chance to become a person' (Dewey 1997: 201) and it fosters an individualism which emphasises freedom, responsibility and initiative towards ethical ideals; it does not encourage the individualism of greed or self-centredness. Unlike an aristocratic system, democracy allows individuals to find a place of their own in the social organism. None the less, this personality or individuality can only come to fruition through an 'objective form in society' (Dewey 1997: 199). Dewey's conception of democracy leaves little scope for tolerating, let alone encouraging, difference within the social organism because the personality which underpins Dewey's democracy produces a sameness in 'the human condition' rather than reveals differences in human conditions.

In America today, these theoretical and conceptual tensions between difference and deliberative democracy have reappeared in the contemporary writings of Jean Bethke Elshtain (1993), Sheldon Wolin (1993) and Amy Gutman (Gutman and Thompson 1993; Gutman 1995). These political philosophers assert that there are inherent problems in trying to reconcile America's multiculturalism with democracy. Elshtain's, Wolin's and Gutman's views of democracy tend to look askance at both multicultural advocacy of group rights and philosophical argument in favour of cultural relativism. The type of multiculturalism that these scholars reject is sometimes referred to as 'radical multiculturalism' or 'critical multiculturalism' (Chicago Cultural Studies Group 1994). Recent debates in the USA over affirmative action and 'political correctness' suggest that there is an inherent tension between a radical multiculturalism and a particular form of democracy and citizenship. Multiculturalism in the USA is usually associated with the intellectual, social and political ideas of non-Western cultures, in particular African, Hispanic and indigenous cultures, and it is contrasted with a 'Western' or 'Eurocentric' cultural hegemony. This opposition has been reflected in debate over the curriculum taught at universities and colleges. The controversy has been between those who want a 'multicultural curriculum' (Kanpol and McLaren 1995; Tamir 1995; Peters 1996) and those who argue that there is no reason to dismiss the Western Canon (David 1987; Bloom 1994; Orwin 1996).

Responding to advocates of radical multiculturalism in the USA, Elshtain contends that the promotion of a racial and cultural identity can be detrimental to democracy. She intimates that the relationship between radical multiculturalism, democracy and citizenship is problematic. Elshtain is critical of the radical multicultural agenda because she believes that it advocates separatism and leads to policies that favour certain groups over others. She also has reservations about those in the higher education system in America who want to throw away a core curriculum based on Western texts in favour of a multicultural curriculum. Elshtain's criticism of the 'multicultural curriculum' does not mean that she finds multicultural texts intellectually unworthy; rather, her criticism is directed towards those who assume that the Western Canon has little of value in it. She maintains that a multiculturalism that promotes separatism in the USA works against a recognition of commonality.

Elshtain concludes that to the extent to which 'citizens begin to retribalise into ethnic or other "fixed-identity groups", democracy falters' (1993: 75), while Wolin observes that it is the 'illusion of internal unity within each difference', which multiculturalism fosters, that results in anti-democratic tendencies (1993: 477). These remarks strike at the very heart of identity politics and radical multiculturalism. They imply that a radical multicultural society may not be conducive to a democratic politics. What does Elshtain, in particular, mean by democracy here? How can affirming an African-American identity put democracy at risk? What has happened to the concept of democracy when the affirmation of one's cultural and social identity undermines it?

Although Elshtain supports liberal democracies because they allow civil, religious and political liberties, she is critical about their procedures. She observes that representative government based on majority rule has the potential to result in authoritarianism (1993: 28). Instead, she argues that for the USA to have an *authentic* democracy, and here she echoes Dewey's ideas, it needs to adopt a less empirical and more normative conception. Democracy, observes Elshtain, is a type of social interaction. Democracy here overlaps with a notion of citizenship. It is 'an ethos, a spirit, a way of responding, a way of conducting oneself every day' (Elstain 1993: 91). The democratic ethos, unlike the radical multicultural ethos, promotes mingling across boundaries of class, gender, ethnicity and race. It provides a common thread running through various social and cultural groups. What is implied in Elshtain's argument is that to be an American citizen is to be able to find a common bond with others that over-rides particular identities. Reminiscent of the sentiments expressed by Dewey, Elshtain implies that universalism is more conducive to citizenship and democracy than particularism. The presupposition underlying Elshtain's argument is the binary opposition in liberalism between the public and private sphere. This dichotomy assumes that in the public sphere only universal rights are legitimate and only individual rights are legally protected, whereas it is in the private sphere that group identities should be expressed. If we accept Elshtain's view, then the radical multicultural ethos tends to be incompatible with citizenship and democracy. Elshtain has a communitarian view of politics and citizenship that wants to revive the civic republican conception of citizenship as the key identity that over-rides all others. She refers (1993: 88) to a 'democratic social covenant' which is premised on the belief that in a civil society, a society separate from the institutions of the state, there will be citizens who are people of goodwill. These are people who want the opportunity to work together as citizens rather than be members of racial, class or ethnic groups. Consequently, a multicultural society, which supports the maintenance of social and cultural boundaries between people, is less conducive to a civil society where these boundaries are transcended.

Moreover, the radical multiculturalist agenda, if we accept Elshtain's view, is the reason why civic culture and democracy is faltering in the USA. But can this, on its own, explain the crises within democracy and citizenship in America? This view ignores the fact that with the globalisation of financial markets, states have less capacity to control their own economies and combat rising inflation and high unemployment. The crises of governability and the new economic arrangement, argues one social scientist, are also leading to fragmentation and civil discord (Jusdanis 1996: 108). Threats to Elshtain's democratic ethos may have more to do with economic globalisation than radical multiculturalism.

Contrary to Elshtain's position, deliberative democracy is not, in itself, inimical to difference. In Gutman's critique of procedural and constitutional democracies, she argues that they neglect the importance of moral conflict and that deliberation should be part of the democratic process (1995: 109). As an alternative, Gutman and

Thompson (1993) put forward a 'deliberative universalism' which provides scope for different social and cultural voices to be expressed. They maintain that our 'moral understanding of many-sided issues, like legalizing abortion, is furthered by discussions with people with whom we respectfully disagree especially when these people have cultural identities different from our own' (1993: 203). This deliberative universalistic democracy, like Dewey's ethical democracy, fosters mutual understanding because 'deliberation can help citizens better understand the moral seriousness of the views they oppose' and, as a consequence, one is better able to co-operate with those who hold different views. In addition, deliberative universalism may bring previously excluded voices into politics. This type of democracy is universalistic because debate and conflict over moral disagreements should occur within transcultural universal principles such as respect for human life, liberty and opportunity (1993: 206). Although Gutman and Thompson's deliberative democracy seems to provide more political and social space for difference, this difference is not one that the advocates of radical multiculturalism favour. In their concluding remarks, Gutman and Thompson make it very clear that 'deliberative democracy' is not conducive to 'cultural polarisation' (1993: 206). So difference is accepted and encouraged as long it upholds certain universal principles.

Postmodern democracy and difference

The preceding discussion has demonstrated the ways in which the relationship between democracy and difference or multiculturalism, for some scholars, is problematic. However, with the view that political life in the USA has become increasingly 'postmodernised', 'decentred', and 'fragmented', and that a unitary and unified public sphere is something of a myth, the emphasis now has been on how 'particularities not only matter, [but] they are the stuff of which political thought is made' (Kauffman 1990: 10). This 'postmodern stance' has questioned and problematised the 'foundationalist' principles underlying the deliberative view of democracy. Postmodern discourse theorists question the foundation of existing democratic theory in rationality and suggest that a plural democracy should recognise and foster differences which are both rational and emotional. Recent work on democracy takes a less 'essentialist' view of the human condition and thus is more sensitive to the ways in which democracy and difference are intrinsically interconnected. These new discursive dimensions of democracy have been expressed through the ideas of 'radical', 'communicative', 'multicultural' and 'postmodern' democracy. This section examines the ideas of an early American political philosopher who conceived democracy and difference as synonymous and then delineates recent attempts to reconcile democracy and difference.

In the USA, the social and political philosopher, Horace Kallen was one of the first scholars to explicitly address the possibilities of reconciling democracy and difference without dissolving difference under universal principles. In several essays on 'Americanism' written in the 1920s, Kallen (1970) examined the relationship between democracy and cultural pluralism. He stated that democracy involves 'not the elimination of differences, but the perfection and conservation of difference . . . It involves a give and take between radically different types, and a mutual understanding' (1970: 61). Unlike the 'American citizens of British stock' who are troubled by difference, Kallen (1970: 115) argues that a 'true' democracy acknowledges and fosters difference. He maintains that ethnic groups should be allowed to form their own schools, associations and organisations. In addition, Kallen contends that it is only by encouraging difference that the dangers of 'like-mindedness', so prevalent in the USA, can be halted (1970: 101). Kallen favours an Americanism and democracy that is cosmopolitan. To be an American, according to Kallen, would be similar to being a citizen of the world (1970: 64); this cosmopolitan would emphasise working harmoniously with other cultures, rather than enforcing a union or common culture (1970: 18–19). It is only by adopting this cosmopolitan, democratic identity that the distinction between the universal and particular can be blurred and mutual understanding can be encouraged. The process of mutual understanding, unlike Gutman's and Dewey's, respects the radical otherness of other people and thus does not try to suppress them under the umbrella of universal principles. For Kallen, ethnic and religious differences are the centre of an individual's identity and emotional life, and any political system that suppresses this is morally unacceptable.

Like Dewey, democracy for Kallen is a cultural phenomenon where spirituality rather than possessive individualism is fostered. According to Kallen, the type of 'Americanism' that exists in the USA cultivates standardisation, levelling, commodification and mass education.

As a consequence, the cultural groups of immigrants, rather than enriching and contributing to a spiritual and cultural state, become 'mere cogs in the industrial machine' (1970: 95). It is difference or cultural pluralism that will allow democracy to thrive and become the basis for a dynamic social and political society. Kallen maintains that the true deliberative and ethical nature of democracy can only be constituted when difference is acknowledged, tolerated and supported. None the less, there have been suggestions that Kallen overemphasises culture to the detriment of politics because cultural pluralists, such as Kallen, argue that spiritual life is located in culture rather than politics (Walzer 1990). This tends to be at odds with the more republican view adopted by Elshtain and Gutman that places politics and civic virtue above culture.

Other scholars, such as Iris Marion Young (1996), Manning Marable (1995) and Fred Dallmayr (1996) reinforce Kallen's position that democracy and difference are intrinsically interconnected. Young illustrates this through her notion of a 'communicative democracy' which will allow social and cultural groups to more effectively participate in the body politic. Young is critical of those, such as Gutman, who advocate a deliberative democracy because they assume that 'bracketing political and economic power' makes speakers equal (Young 1996: 122). This denies or ignores the ways in which social power is premised on the assumption that the way people speak and understand are similar. On the contrary, this can only be true, for Young, if we eliminate their cultural and social differences. Young maintains that 'deliberative democracy tends to assume that deliberation is both culturally neutral and universal' (1996: 123). Young's communicative democracy is apparently more sensitive to group difference and allows space for those differences to be expressed in the political system. Communicative democracy does not erase these social and cultural boundaries because, rather than inhibiting democracy, they can enhance it (1996: 127). Young perceives difference in social position and identity perspective as a resource for public debate rather than a hindrance to it. Difference allows democracy to flourish and heterogeneity, rather than homogeneity, is the basis for Young's conception of communicative democracy.

Marable's notion of 'multicultural democracy' also favours an intergroup dialogue which not only allows African-Americans to converse with other cultural groups, but also suggests that a 'non-racist democracy' needs to 'recognise class commonalties and joint social-justice interests of all groups' (1995: 201). On the other hand, Dallmayr maintains that 'democratic multiculturalism' refers to the extension of individual rights to group or collective rights. This grants a degree of autonomy and self-government to ethnic groups and leads to the formation of policies that involve consensual interaction between group leaders in multi-ethnic societies. It would also involve a parliamentary system based on bi-cameralism or multicameralism (1996: 289). The normative argument that a democratic ethos should be based on heterogeneity reappears in Chantal Mouffe's concept of 'radical democracy' (1992). For Mouffe, there is no final or universal conception of democracy. There are different competing interpretations of equality, liberty and the 'common good', and therefore different views of citizenship. Mouffe concludes that this relativist position means that it is impossible to fully achieve democracy and she argues that her conception of a radical-democratic project is different from other forms of 'postmodern' politics that emphasise heterogeneity, dissemination and incommensurability. These alternative versions of 'postmodern' politics tend to lead 'to a complete *indifferentiation* and *indifference*' (1992: 13) towards cultural and racial groups.

Though there are some clear similarities between these scholars, there are also important internal differences. In Kallen's and Young's version of democracy there is an implication that all types of differences should be acceptable in a democratic polity, whereas Mouffe argues that a criterion should exist which decides which differences are admissible and which are not. There is an apparent paradox here. How does Mouffe reconcile the fact that a radical democracy can only exist when there is a recognition and articulation of the multiplicity of social logics with the assertion that this 'multiplicity' has to be qualified? There is also a conceptual confusion here because multiplicity tends to imply the expansion, not the reduction, of differences. In addition, Mouffe's 'criterion', which becomes the basis for judging the value of particular differences, is under-theorised. Mouffe never clearly and concisely articulates its parameters. Who sets up the criteria on limiting differences? How do we define 'just' and 'fair' differences? Overall, though Mouffe argues that a universal and definitive definition is not possible in a society which is pluralistic and fragmented, there seems to be a detached, objective point by which one can judge which differences are compatible with a 'radical democracy' and which are not. There may be no universal definition of democracy, but Mouffe implies that there is a universal, ahistorical criterion that can judge appropriate and inappropriate differences. This universalistic tendency reappears in Marable's notion of multi-cultural democracy because he seeks to locate (class) commonalties underlying racial and cultural differences. Moreover, Dallmayr (1996: 291) speaks of 'lateral universalism' where universal principles are found within, rather than outside the local and particular identities. Although recent attempts to reformulate the relationship between democracy and difference seem to be less essentialist and foundationalist, an implicit 'strategic essentialism', or what others have called a double gesture (Anderson 1992), still exists. This 'strategic essentialism' simultaneously supports a theoretical anti-humanism and a political humanism. These 'postmodern' accounts of democracy deconstruct common values and the human condition but also advocate transcultural principles such as justice, liberty and equality.

Democracy as an ethical relationship

By way of conclusion, I want to put forward an ethical view of democracy and compare it to how postmodern and deliberative accounts theorise the relationship between democracy and difference. Work by the social theorist Zygmunt Bauman may help us explore the kind of ethics that could be the basis for a democratic polity. The relationship between the self and other which exists under Dewey's, Elshtain's and Gutman's account of democracy is where the identity and autonomy of the other is either suppressed or superficially acknowledged. Bauman argues that 'responsibility is the essential, primary and fundamental structure of subjectivity' (1989: 183). It is only by being responsible for the other that we constitute ourselves as ethical subjects. It is only by 'being-for' the other that the uniqueness of the other is protected, whereas when the self is 'being-with' the other then the meeting is fragmentary and precarious and, according to Bauman, it is the 'meeting of incomplete and deficient selves' (Bauman 1995: 50). The relationship between self and other under Dewey's and Elshtain's account of democracy tends to deny the uniqueness of the social, racial and cultural other because democracy works towards commonality rather than heterogeneity. While Gutman's position does provide space for difference, this is based on a relationship that is 'with' rather than 'for' the other. Postmodern accounts of democracy come closer to Bauman's conception of an ethical relationship because there is a tendency to perceive the other as a unique and autonomous individual. None the less, these postmodern accounts tend to under-emphasise the ambivalent nature of the ethical relationship between self and other. As Bauman concludes, any relationship that is ethical is fraught with ambivalence. To act ethically is characterised by ambivalence because to be responsible for another may lead to domination or paternalism that undermines the autonomy of the other, while tolerance can lead to indifference. Bauman argues that 'no act, no matter how noble and unselfish and beneficial for some, can be truly insured against hurting those who find themselves, inadvertently, on its receiving end' (1989: 181). It is this ambivalent character underlying the relationship between democracy and difference that the postmodern accounts seem to minimise when they implicitly adopt a strategic essentialism. In other words, although they are critical of unifying and foundationalist approaches to democratic theory, they cannot jettison all certainty about an essence or a foundation. This aversion to ambivalence is exemplified in Mouffe's criterion and Dallmayr's lateral universalism. Democracy, as the postmodern accounts have demonstrated, is intrinsically connected to diversity and difference, but one needs to be aware that this relationship is fraught with contingency. Accounts of democracy in American social and political thought have tended to shun this contingency. This may say less about the strength or weakness of the theoretical and conceptual framework that these theorists embrace, and more about the need for order and structure in human affairs.

References

Anderson, A. (1992) 'Cryptonormativism and Double Gestures: The Politics of Post-structuralism', *Cultural Critique*, no. 2: 63–95.

Bauman, Z. (1989) *Modernity and the Holocaust*, Cambridge: Polity Press.

——(1995) *Life in Fragments: Essays in Postmodern Morality*, Oxford: Basil Blackwell.

Bloom, H. (1994) *The Western Canon: The Books and School of Ages*, New York: Harcourt Brace.

Chicago Cultural Studies Group (1994) 'Critical Multiculturalism', in David Theo Goldberg (ed.), *Multiculturalism: A Critical Reader*, Oxford: Basil Blackwell: 114–39.

Dallmayr, F. (1996) 'Democracy and Multiculturalism', in Seyla Benhabib (ed.), *Democracy and Difference: Contesting the Boundaries of the Political*, Princeton, NJ: Princeton University Press: 278–90.

David, A. (1987) *The Closing of the American Mind*, New York: Simon & Schuster.

Dewey, J. (1997 [1888]) 'The Ethics of Democracy', in Louis Menand (ed.), *Pragmatism: A Reader*, New York: Vintage Books: 182–204.

Du Bois, W.E.B (1980 [1911]) 'The Negro Race in the United States of America', in *W.E.B Du Bois: On Sociology and the Black Community*, edited with an introduction by D.S. Green and E.D. Driver, Chicago: The University of Chicago Press: 85–111.

Elshtain, J.B. (1993) 'Democracy and the Politics of Difference', in *Democracy on Trial*, Ontario: Concord.

Festenstein, M. (1997) *Pragmatism and Political Theory*, Cambridge: Polity Press.

Gutman, A. (1995) 'The Challenge of Multiculturalism in Political Ethics', *Philosophy and Public Affairs*, vol. 22, no. 3: 171–206.

Gutman, A. and Thompson, D. (1993) 'Moral Disagreement in a Democracy', *Social Philosophy and Policy*, vol. 12, no. 1: 87–110.

Jacoby, T. (1996) 'Divided we stand: the Million Man March and the culture that made it possible', ⟨http://www.dlcppi.org/tnd/9607/cover3.htm⟩ 10 September 1998.

Jusdanis, G. (1996) 'Can Multiculturalism Disunite America', *Thesis Eleven*, no. 44: 100–10.

Kallen, H.M. (1970 [1924]) *Culture and Democracy in the United States*, New York: Arno Press.

Kanpol, B. and McLaren, P. (eds) (1995) *Critical Multiculturalism: Uncommon Voices in a Common Struggle*, Connecticut: Bergin & Garvey.

Kauffman, L.A. (1990) 'Democracy in a Postmodern World', *Social Policy*, vol. 2, no. 2: 6–11.

Kinder, D.R. and Sanders, L.M. (1996) *Divided by Color: Racial Politics and Democratic Ideals*, Chicago: The University of Chicago Press.

Marable, M. (1992) 'Race, Identity, and Political Culture', in Gina Dent (ed.), *Black Popular Culture*, Seattle: Bay Press: 292–301.

—— (1995) 'Beyond Racial Identity Politics: Toward a Liberation Theory for Multicultural Democracy', in *Beyond Black and White: Transforming African-American Politics*, London: Verso: 185–202.

Mouffe, C. (1992) 'Democratic Citizenship and the Political Community', in C. Mouffe (ed.) *Dimensions of Radical Democracy: Pluralism, Citizenship, Community*, New York: Verso: 225–39.

Orwin, C. (1996) 'All quite on the post-Western Front?', *The Public Interest*, no. 123: 3–21.

Peters, M. (1996) *Poststructuralism, Politics and Education*, Connecticut: Bergin & Garvey.

Quillian, L. (1996) 'Group Threat and Regional Change in Attitudes toward African-Americans', *American Journal of Sociology*, vol. 102, no. 3: 816–60.

Tamir, Y. (ed.) (1995) *Democratic Education in a Multicultural State*, Oxford: Basil Blackwell.

Traub, J. (1994) 'Can Separate be Equal', *Harper's Magazine*, vol. 288, no. 1729: 34–47.

Walzer, M. (1990) 'What does it mean to be an "American"?', *Social Research*, vol. 57, no. 3: 591–614.

Wolin, S. (1993) 'Democracy, Difference and Re-cognition', *Political Theory*, vol. 21, no. 3: 464–83.

Young, I.M. (1996) 'Communication and the Other: Beyond Deliberative Democracy', in Seyla Benhabib (ed.), *Democracy and Difference: Contesting the Boundaries of the Political*, Princeton, NJ: Princeton University Press: 120–36.

14 SOUTH AFRICA: DEMOCRACY AND CITIZENSHIP IN A PLURAL SOCIETY

David Dorward

In this study of South Africa, David Dorward draws on socio-economic analyses of race and class but it is primarily a historical analysis of how the institutions of apartheid arose during the first half of the twentieth century and fell during the 1980s. His study suggests an interesting comparison against the decline during the 1950s and 1960s of European imperialism in Africa and racist institutions in the USA, as well as the collapse of communism in Eastern Europe in the 1980s. A primary conclusion is that it is a mistake to essentialise tribal or ethnic groups in the country, and it is important to recognise the international historical and economic position of black labour heavily exploited by white citizens in South Africa.

South Africa is a society deeply divided along lines of class, race and ethnicity. While such cleavages are not unusual, South Africa provides a stark example of the institutionalisation of racial divisions and the limitations of a concept of citizenship that can exclude the vast majority of the population from the democratic processes. Europeans have never been more than 15 per cent of the population, and yet for most of South Africa's history they have enjoyed a monopoly of citizenship.

In a state where exclusion and differing entitlements have been rooted in race and 'ethnicity', students of South African history and politics need to be sensitive to the construction of ethnic consciousness. The pitfall is to essentialise 'tribal' and 'ethnic' categories, such as Zulu and Afrikaner. The shallow historical depth of 'Afrikaner' self-identity and the fluidity of definitions are important to an appreciation of the ethnic politics of plural South Africa. That the National Party was able to win the 1994 post-apartheid election in the Western Cape Province on the basis of 'Coloured' political support needs to be explained, as does the power and influence of Gatsha Buthelezi's tribally-based Inkatha Freedom Party.

To understand the origins, justifications and ongoing legacy of apartheid, it is necessary to delve beyond the popular imagery of discrimination imposed by an Afrikaner-dominated National Party government. While the National Party, which ruled South Africa from 1948 to 1994, was responsible for apartheid, it built upon a legacy of racist legislation and popular convictions amongst the White minority electorate, as well as wider ideas and events that shaped South African attitudes and political culture.

The historical background of apartheid

The genesis of racism and segregation can be traced back to the era of the Dutch East India Company. Shortly after the Dutch settled the Cape in 1652, the first governor had a thorn hedge planted to separate the area of Christian 'civilisation' from that of the indigenous African Khoisan peoples. The introduction of slave labour from Dutch Indonesia and East Africa encouraged an association of limited political rights, 'heathen', non-European and manual labour versus European and Christian citizenship. Within the settled world of the colonised, Dutch Burghers were citizens and slaves were not, while beyond the frontier were the African 'savages'.

As in any slave society, sexual exploitation of female slaves led to mixed-race offspring, the so-called 'Cape Coloured'. To the extent that such individuals obtained their freedom, became baptised Dutch Reformed Christians and went into a trade, limited numbers were able to secure recognition as citizens or 'freeburghers' with legal and voting rights that could be passed on to their children.

As the population of the Cape grew, white settlers began to push out beyond the hedge, towards an ever-expanding frontier. The saga of frontier hardship, adventure and 'taming' of the landscape became the basis of subsequent colonial mythology and claims to ownership. Yet on the frontier race relations were often ambiguous. Trekboers (or migratory Dutch hunter-herdsmen), together with their families, servants and slaves, both warred against and formed alliances with Africans. Relations with African women gave rise to the so-called 'Bastaard' communities. There were instances of 'Coloured' offspring being integrated into Afrikaner frontier society, but 'Bastaards' and Free Blacks were precariously located between Whites and Africans. By the beginning of the nineteenth century a set of social conventions had evolved, defining 'community' by notions of race and culture.

At the end of the Napoleonic Wars, the Cape Colony passed under British rule. In an attempt to secure a loyal foothold on this strategic landfall on the sea route to India and the East, Britain encouraged British settlement. The result was a struggle for political-economic hegemony between British settlers and capital, on the one hand, and Boer frontier society on the other, portrayed by British liberal historians as that between Boer racist intransigence and British 'enlightenment' colonialism. Realities were more complex. The British colonisers, even the missionary defenders of Africans, were no less imbued with convictions of racial superiority and civilisation to the exclusion of non-Europeans from consideration as 'citizens'. Africans were at best 'protected persons' under a system of benign paternalism. However, British colonial racism was increasingly justified in more subtle terms of pseudo-scientific racism.

For most of the nineteenth century, South Africa was a British provisioning station on the route to India, complicated by costly frontier wars with African states over the control of agriculturally marginal territory. All that was changed with the discovery of first diamonds and then gold. Britain was on the gold standard and the Boer frontier Republic of South Africa (commonly known as Transvaal) rapidly became the world's major supplier of gold. The Anglo-Boer War of 1899–1902 was a power struggle between Britain and the Afrikaner frontier states over control of the mineral rich regions of South Africa.

In the aftermath of the war, many impoverished Afrikaner farmers migrated to the cities and found themselves in direct competition with Africans for employment and perceived hostility from the British. Afrikaner response took the form of an assertive cultural nationalism, led by theologically conservative Dutch Reformed Church pastors, many of them influenced by a leading Dutch Calvinist theologian and politician, Abraham Kuyper (1837–1920).[1] Within the South African socio-political context, Kuyper's teaching of the Divine origins of church, state and *volk*, each with its own function and disposition, provided a powerful and irreducible justification for separation of Calvinist from others, White from Black, Afrikaans-speakers from other peoples. However, the Afrikaner community was far from united.

British accommodation towards Afrikaner leaders who were prepared to enter into a political accord rapidly led to self-government under Afrikaner control, while protecting British economic and strategic interests. The Act of Union of 1910, the founding constitution of the South African state, entrenched White power. Non-Whites were all but excluded from the franchise. Only in Cape Province was a small minority of non-Whites allowed to vote, on the basis of restrictive property qualifications. Even in the Cape, only Whites could be elected to Parliament. The vast majority of non-Whites was entirely excluded from citizenship. British justifications for segregation were based on pseudo-scientific racism rather than Afrikaner Calvinist Christian-Nationalist theology, though the outcome was much the same.

British colonialism defined African 'citizenship' in tribal terms. The African polity found expression through the institution of chieftaincy, an autocratic system in accord with European colonial rule. However, chiefs were not sovereign; they could be removed on order of the governor. Africans were not 'citizens' but 'subjects', governed by administrative regulations through their chiefs. Even Africans working in the Johannesburg goldmines were, in theory, under the authority of some chief in a distant tribal reserve. Africans, however well educated, culturally adjusted or economically integrated, were excluded from citizenship on the grounds that Western institutions were culturally alien to them.

To the extent that tribal chieftaincies were the only avenue for African protest and entitlement, particularly in the rural areas, they acquired 'legitimacy'. Chieftaincies were not simply subordinate political entities; they often constituted enclosed and semi-autonomous civil societies, with distinct tribal laws, language and culture. The so-called 'homelands' established parochial interests that demanded accommodation within the wider political arena.

At a deeper level, South African racism had an economic dimension. Segregation on cultural grounds was a guise for inequalities in the provision of services: education, health, housing, wages, and so forth. State resources, drawn largely from African workers' productivity, were channelled into the White minority electorate. Moreover, under pressure from White working-class voters and the corporate sector, successive South African governments instituted laws to protect White workers from African competition while maintaining low African wages. The Native Labour Regulation Act of 1911 made it a criminal offence for Black workers to strike. The Mines and Works Amendment Act of 1926, the so-called 'Colour Bar' Act, reserved skilled jobs for Whites and Coloureds.

The 1913 Native Lands Act set aside 15 per cent of South Africa as 'native reserves', entrenching White dominance of the agricultural sector by restricting African land ownership. Reserves become overcrowded labour reservoirs for the powerful mining industry. At the end of the apartheid era, Whites owned 85 per cent of the land and 95 per cent of the wealth of South Africa, while Blacks did most of the labour.

The rise of the apartheid regime

With the election of the National Party government in 1948, apartheid gave systematic expression to hitherto *ad hoc* laws and regulations. Racial classification was legally defined and non-Whites were formally excluded from any notion of citizenship. Racial inter-marriage was made a criminal offence. All amenities, schools, hospitals, transportation, and even residential areas, were segregated.

Apartheid sought to maintain an African under-class of workers, who lacked the skills to effectively challenge White hegemony. In 1954, Dr Henrik Verwoerd, then Minister of Native Affairs, stated: 'There is no place for him [The Bantu] in the European community above the level of certain forms of labour . . . What is the use of teaching a Bantu child mathematics when it cannot use it in practice? That is absurd. Education must train people in accordance with their opportunities in life' (South African Senate, 7 June 1954). Under the Population Registration Act of 1950, everyone in South Africa was classified as White, Coloured or Native, while non-Whites were compelled to carry racial identity passes. The Group Areas Act, No. 41 of

1950, defined where individuals could live and own property. Those who lived or owned property in an area designated as belonging to a different race were forced to move. Some 3 548 900 people, over-whelmingly non-Whites, were 'removed' from their homes between 1960 and 1983 (Platzky and Walker 1985: 11).

Under the system of influx control, intended to restrict non-Euro-peans in the urban areas to those needed for employment, it was an offence to be in a place designated for another Group without a valid reason. In 1984 alone, 238 894 arrests were made for pass offences.

The influence of Abraham Kuyper on citizenship and sovereignty was reflected in the statement of the Minister for Bantu Administra-tion, M. D. C. de Wet Nel, in 1959:

> The philosophy of life of the settled white population of South Africa, both English-speaking and Afrikaans-speaking in regard to the colour or racial problem . . . rests on three main basic principles . . . the first is that God has given a divine task and calling to every People in the world, which dare not be destroyed or denied by anyone. The second is that every People in the world, of whatever race or colour, just like every individual, has an inherent right to live and to develop. Every People is entitled to the right of self-preservation. In the third place, it is our deep conviction that the personal and national ideals of every individual and of every ethnic group can best be developed within their own national community. Only then will the other groups feel that they are not being endangered . . . The Zulu is proud to be a Zulu and the Xhosa proud to be a Xhosa . . . If the white man is entitled to separate national existence, what right have we to deny that these Peoples have a right to it also? (M. D. C. de Wet Nel, *South African Parliament, Hansard*, 18 May 1959)

The formal exclusion of Africans from the South African body politic was promulgated through a series of laws: the Bantu Authorities Act of 1950 entrenched the system of Bantu Authorities based on so-called 'tribal custom'; the Promotion of Bantu Self-Government Bill in 1959 transformed the native 'reserves' into 'homelands'; the Bantu Home-lands Citizenship Act of 1970 made Africans 'citizens' of their 'home-lands' and not South Africa; and the Bantu Homelands Constitution Act of 1971, which turned Transkei, Bophtutswana, Venda and Ciskei into nominally 'independent' countries in 1976, 1977, 1978 and 1981, respectively. By these laws Africans ceased to be South Africans.

As in many Western states, prevention of communism was used to suppress democratic opposition and restrict the rights of citizens. The Suppression of Communism Act of 1950 defined a communist as any person who 'advocated, advised, defended or encouraged the achievement of any of the objects of communism' and communism as 'any doctrine or scheme . . . which aims to bring about any political, industrial, social or economic change within the Union [of South Africa] by unlawful acts or omissions . . . [or which] aims at the encouragement of hostility between European and non-European races of the Republic'. The Unlawful Organisations Act of 1960 allowed the government to ban any organisation. All members of a banned organisation were barred from any activities similar to those of the banned organisation. The assets of a banned organisation could be seized by the state. Other laws authorised detention without trial, even indefinite detention without trial in cases where a person was suspected of 'terrorist' offences. The definition of 'terrorism', like that of 'communism', was wide-ranging.

Opposition to apartheid

Despite repeated government attempts to stifle debate, the nature of the state, civil society and citizenship remained contested issues.

In response to the apartheid laws, the African National Congress (ANC) organised the Defiance Campaign in 1952, aimed at breaking the government's resolve through mass disobedience. Over 2500 resisters were arrested in September alone, while most of the campaign's leaders were charged under the Suppression of Communism Act. Opposition to apartheid was widespread, but many were uncertain what various opposition groups stood for. In 1955, ANC, the South African Indian Congress, the communist-inspired South African Congress of Democrats and the South African Coloured People's Congress held a 'Congress of the People' at Kliptown, a township near Johannesburg. Though the meeting was eventually broken up by the police, the 'Freedom Charter' that resulted from the meeting affirmed the rights of all South Africans to common citizenship and equality before the law.

Not all Black activists agreed with multiracialism. African nationalism was sweeping the continent. In 1959 Black nationalists broke from the ANC to form the Pan Africanist Congress (PAC). Its leader, Robert Sobukwe, was eventually imprisoned with Nelson Mandela and other ANC leaders on Robbin Island. While the PAC failed to establish a strong organisation, its ideology of 'Africa for Africans' remained influential.

The other enduring influence on Black political thinking was the Black Consciousness Movement, associated with Steve Biko. In 1967, Biko was elected a delegate to the annual conference of the National Union of South African Students, a predominantly white student institution. Rhodes University, where the conference was held, refused to allow mixed-race student accommodation and meals. In response, Biko formed an all-Black South African Students' Organisation in 1969. He promoted esteem and self-motivation amongst the marginalised and disempowered Black majority. He was banned in 1973. He died in police custody in 1977 (a commentary on the South African regimes' fear of the power of ideas).

South African White liberals sought a compromise position between apartheid White-exclusivist articulations of 'citizenship', a European concept of civil society, and African demands for majority rule. The Progressive Party, hailed by the Western media during the 1970s and 1980s as the voice of reason in South Africa, advocated a gradual extension of non-White franchise based on educational and cultural qualifications. Their cautious approach to citizenship and enfranchisement, evocative of nineteenth-century British debates, failed to become an effective force in South African politics.

Opposition to apartheid also found expression, albeit limited and often self-seeking, from Gatsha Buthelezi, Chief Minister of Kwazulu from 1972. He founded the Zulu *Inkatha yeNkululeko yeSizwe* (Freedom of the Nation) Movement in the mid-1970s, but steadfastly refused 'independence' for the impoverished territory. While far from consistent in ideology or in issues of democracy and citizenship, Buthelezi gradually moved towards a form of 'consociationalism'. He advocated government by a coalition of leaders representing elements of a pluralist society, recognising divisions based on race, religion, ethnic and cultural differences. Minority interests, political representation and access to the spoils of power would be protected through a federal system based on 'concurrent' majority principle or veto by factional leaders, who would enjoy a high degree of local autonomy.

The fall of the apartheid regime

The beginning of the end for the apartheid regime was arguably 1984, when increased government taxes and charges sparked popular protests. Around 7000 police and troops were sent into the townships to arrest 'ringleaders'. They were confronted by students behind barricades of burning buses and tyres, who fought back with stones. It was the beginning of a sustained urban revolt, thousands of black casualties and mounting international opposition to apartheid.

International sanctions and mounting unrest within South Africa brought increasing pressures on the National Party government of P. W. Botha. In 1983, the South African Constitution Act granted a measure of non-European participation in the government by creating three houses of Parliament: a 178-member White House of Assembly elected by White voters; an 85-seat 'Coloured' House of Representatives members elected by 'Coloureds'; and a 45-member Asian House of Delegates elected by Asian voters. In matters affecting more than one group, decisions were by a majority in a joint session, effectively entrenching a White veto. Africans were not represented, the administration of Black affairs being vested in the State President, who could declare a 'State of Emergency' and rule the nation by decree.

The new constitution proved an inadequate response. In 1989, F. W. de Klerk succeeded the ailing P. W. Botha as President. He instituted a process of reform that rapidly took on an irreversible dynamic of its own. The State of Emergency and detention without trial were rescinded. Restrictions on the ANC, PAC and South African Communist Party, along with over 30 other organisations, were lifted. Nelson Mandela and other political prisoners were released. It marked the beginning of a tortuous process leading to the first non-racial elections in 1994 and the formation of the Government of National Unity.

Shortly after his release from prison, Nelson Mandela reaffirmed the ANC's non-racial policy on citizenship:

> The ANC offers a home to all who subscribe to the principles of a free, democratic, non-racial and united South Africa. We are committed to building a single nation in our country. Our nation will include blacks and whites, Zulus and Afrikaners, and speakers of every other language . . . This is the challenge we face today . . . Our call is, 'One nation, one country'. We must be one people across the whole of South Africa! (Mandela 1990: 222–8)

Progressive Whites, represented by the Democratic Party, wanted guarantees. While accepting universal franchise in principle, Dr Denis

Worrall, formerly South African Ambassador to Australia and leading Democrat, summarised White progressive reservations regarding democracy:

> in a deeply divided society such as ours, it is in no one's interest if 49 per cent of the votes count for nothing and 50 per cent plus one takes everything. In such a society, mechanisms need to be instituted that provide for minority interests and for checks and balances against majoritarian excesses. The mechanisms we envisage . . . include a federal system of government (which brings government as close to the people as possible), a proportional representation voting system (which guarantees representation to minority parties), an independent judiciary and an entrenched bill of rights. (Denis Worrall, *South African Foundation Review*, August 1989: 5)

White Conservatives called for the creation of a separate white 'Boerstaat' or White homeland. In the Western Cape, the National Party appealed to Coloured fears of domination by the Black majority by playing upon their shared language and the Dutch Reformed Church.

A post-apartheid regime

The post-apartheid transitional Government of National Unity was a product of protracted negotiations and political compromises, fraught with potential pitfalls. South Africa was divided into nine provinces, each with a popularly elected government. The National Assembly consisted of 400 members, half elected nationally on the basis of universal adult franchise, half elected on a proportional basis reflecting provincial election results. There was a 90-person Senate, with equal representation from each province based on proportional party representation in the province. At the last moment before the election, an ill-defined advisory House of Chiefs was announced.

Considerable power was vested in the Executive President, who appointed the Cabinet. However, under the Government of National Unity, the Cabinet included members of the ANC, the South African Communist Party, the National Party and Buthelezi's Inkatha Freedom Party. Two ill-defined Deputy Executive Presidents were also appointed, representing the two parties that had secured 10 per cent of the national vote: F. W. De Klerk of the National Party, and Thabo Mbeki of the ANC.

The National Assembly and Senate, sitting in joint session, constituted the Constitutional Assembly, charged with drafting the final post-apartheid constitution. However, it was constrained by political realities. The powers of state and central government were deliberately left vague, and provincial authorities proved reluctant to surrender advantage to the central government, even in the case of ANC-controlled provincial governments. An independent Constitutional Court, was empowered to rule on the validity of any law according to a set of basic rights.

The ANC won an overwhelming victory in South Africa's first nonracial election in 1994, Nelson Mandela being elected President. Yet the newly elected African majority government, dedicated to social reform and greater equity, was confronted with the power of the South African corporate sector. Less than a dozen interlocking corporate conglomerates dominated the South African economy. Like other pressure groups, the South African corporate sector sought to influence government policies. The combined might of such transnational corporations, with financial power and global networks rivalling the nation-state, raises important issues regarding the constraints on constitutional development and soveriegnty.

All too often South Africa is presented in the simplistic terms of a white versus black paradigm, which ignores the historic tensions between English and Afrikaner, between capital and labour, between White and Black labour, as well as tensions over various differences between and within non-European societies. These numerous cleavages mean that the extent to which any sort of civil society can be said to exist in South Africa today remains problematic.

The 1996 Constitution, a new dispensation

In 1996 the new draft constitution was adopted. It was a complex and detailed document that not only addressed the structure of government and powers inherent in various offices and institutions, but also sought to redress the inequities of the past and provide a framework for the future. Regarding citizenship, it stated: 'There is a common South African citizenship. All citizens are equally entitled to the rights, privileges and benefits of citizenship; and equally subject to the duties and responsibilities of citizenship.' The Constitution also includes an elaborately written Bill of Rights which:

enshrines the rights of all people in our country to affirm the democratic values of human dignity, equality and freedom ... [and enjoins the state to] ... respect, protect and fulfil the rights in the Bill of Rights [which] ... applies to all laws and binds the legislature, the executive, the judiciary and all organs of state.

Among the long list of Rights detailed, that of Equality stands out as particularly relevant:

Everyone is equal before the law and has the right to equal protection and benefit of the law. Equality includes the full and equal enjoyment of all rights and freedoms ... [Neither the state nor the individual can] ... unfairly discriminate directly or indirectly against anyone on one or more grounds, including race, gender, sex, pregnancy, marital status, ethnic or social origin, colour, sexual orientation, age, disability, religion, conscious, belief, culture, language and birth.

No Bill of Rights, no Constitution, can guarantee rights and freedoms. They must be constantly defended and upheld if they are to remain more than hollow phrases. Nevertheless, the 1996 South African Constitution with its provision for democracy based on universal suffrage is a radical departure from the restrictive and discriminatory political systems that have prevailed in South Africa during the previous 350 years of European hegemony. While such instruments cannot legislate civil society into existence with common shared values, they do lay the foundations for its evolution.

Note

1   Kuyper was a leading figure in the neo-Calvinist revival. He wrote over 200 books; he was Prime Minister of Holland from 1901 to 1905 and Professor of Theology at the Free University of Amsterdam.

References

Benson, Mary (1994) *Nelson Mandela; The Man and the Movement*, Harmondsworth: Penguin.
Cobbett, William and Cohen, Robin (eds) (1988) *Popular Struggles in South Africa*, London: James Currey.
Davenport, T.R.H. (1994) *South Africa: A Modern History*, 4th edn, London: Macmillan.

Denoon, Donald and Nyeko, Balam (1986) *Southern Africa since 1800*, London: Longman.

Lodge, T. (1983) *Black Politics in South Africa since 1945*, London: Longman.

Mandela, Nelson (1990) *The Struggle is My Life*, London: International Defence and Aid Fund.

Mermelstein, David (ed.)(1987) *The Anti-Apartheid Reader: South Africa and the Struggle against White Racist Rule*, New York, Grove Weidenfeld.

Mugubane, Bernard Makhosezwe (1979) *The Political Economy of Race and Class in South Africa*, New York: Monthly Review Press.

Omer-Cooper, J.D. (1988) *History of Southern Africa*, London: James Currey.

Platzky, Laurine and Walker, Cherry (1985) *The Surplus People: Forced Removals in South Africa*, Johannesburg: Ravan Press.

15 The Gendering of 'Citizenship' in Australia

Jennifer Curtin

This study of Australia looks at how Australian feminists resisted the way 'worker-citizen' excluded women first by means of a mother-citizen during the 1920s and 1930s, and then by way of gendering the worker as women entered the workforce in greater numbers during the 1960s and 1970s. Feminist criticisms of liberal citizenship are part of the background for this study but it has also drawn on Turner's use of Marshall's late argument about the hyphenated society. Curtin concludes that in Australia the practices of mother-citizenship had a racist aspect that excluded Aboriginal women but gendered worker-citizenship can potentially reinforce current attempts to include wider social groups into a fuller sense of political citizenship.

Citizenship in Australia was not mentioned explicitly in law until 1948 when the Nationality and Citizenship Act was passed. Up until this time, to be Australian was to be a British subject. Yet despite this lack of explicit reference to citizenship in legislation or the Constitution, over time various conceptions of citizenship have been deployed within the political arena with a view to drawing boundaries between those who are included and excluded. In taking the vote as a narrow measure of citizen status, it is apparent that until 1902 women were excluded (although in South Australia and Western Australia women had been granted the vote before the turn of the century). Aboriginal people were not granted the right to vote until 1962, and prior to 1948 women who married 'aliens' forfeited their right to vote. When thinking about citizenship in broader terms, it becomes apparent that the notion has been constructed and reconstructed within the political arena with particular images of the citizen being privileged over others (Johnson 1996: 25), which has in turn resulted in differential access to economic and social rights.

Much of what is written on citizenship is normative. It highlights the type of citizenship needed and debates how the concept might be reinvented to better include the diversity evident within nation-states. This chapter does not focus on that normative discussion but rather discusses the 'particularity' of notions of citizenship when deployed within specific historical and political contexts. While citizenship and issues of multiculturalism are 'hot topics' at present, challenges and contests to the dominant portrayal of what it means to be a citizen in Australia have occurred throughout this century. The aim of many of these contests has been to make citizenship more inclusive but, as this chapter reveals, this has not always been the case. In an effort to understand the way in which these portrayals have constructed and favoured specific types of citizenship status, definitions are denoted in hyphenated form: citizen-worker, citizen-mother, political-citizen. This study concludes by drawing out what these gendered contests mean for traditional citizenship models.

Citizen-worker

Irving suggests that around the turn of the century when women were fighting for female suffrage, notions of citizenship, in an informal sense, appeared to focus on an ideal of 'community standing and contribution, the demonstration of both respectability and selflessness' (Irving 1996: 45). However, in addition to this emphasis on social and community service as characteristic of citizenship was an emphasis on the (male) citizen-worker. Indeed, the concepts of the people and the working classes were often confused and melded in political discourse (Davidson 1997: 53). Working-class ideology in Australia incorporated an ethos of mateship that focused on egalitarian principles, solidarity and fellowship. It arose first from the hardship of outback bush life but was picked up in the 1880s by trade unions of unskilled and semiskilled miners, shearers and waterside workers (Archer 1992: 381–2). Various feminist writers have highlighted how this explicitly masculine form of mateship enhanced the exclusion of women from any sense of belonging within trade unions and the Labor Party (Lake 1986; Sawer and Simms 1993; Pocock 1995; Curtin 1999).

This notion of the (male) citizen-worker was privileged by a variety of state policies. A unique feature of the labour relations environment in Australia was the extent to which government sought to regulate the system. Conciliation and arbitration dominated Australian industrial relations from the turn of the century until recently and, in the process, evolved into a comprehensive method of state determination of wages and conditions (Macintyre and Mitchell 1989: 18).

In terms of wage determination, the most famous ruling of the Court of Arbitration was the Harvester Judgment of 1907, whereby the court ruled that a fair wage ought to be based on need and not on either profit or the market value of labour. The minimum wage was set as the amount by which a (male) worker could support his dependent wife and three children in frugal comfort (Macintyre 1985: 55). This decision was underpinned by the assumption that tariffs and restricted immigration provided employers with enough protection to pay wages according to need. In this way, the arbitration system provided male workers with a family wage but, in the process, the position of women was officially rendered different from that of men and women's exclusion from the paid labour force was officially reinforced (Bryson 1995: 49).

Those women who did work were concentrated in factory and domestic work and this occupational segregation was aggravated by the activities of male unionists who fought successfully to exclude cheaper female labour from the better paid male crafts. There is debate as to whether this exclusion by male unionists can be attributed to sexism, with men defending their privileges against women, or class, in that workers were protecting themselves against employers' attempts to erode male wages (see Frances 1991). Whatever the motivation, the result was that women who wanted to unionise were forced to do so separately. In 1882, the first women's union, the Victorian Tailoresses Union, was created and, after 1890, more women's unions were established.

Few of these unions survived into the twentieth century and those that did were gradually subsumed into unions encompassing both male and female workers. Ryan and Prendergast (1982: 268) argue that the arbitration system stifled the continued development of women's unions. Registered unions gained the sole right to represent employees in their particular industry or occupation and women usually lacked the precise coverage of a distinct occupational or industry group required by the labour courts. In addition (in New South Wales, for example), domestic workers were excluded as an occupation eligible for registration, thus prohibiting union representation in this area of work where women dominated (Ryan and Prendergast 1982: 268). In this sense, women's right to work and the right to organise were curtailed by the dominant perception of worker as male.

The dominant cultural ethos of these early years was not one of *laissez-faire* individualism or rampant revolution but of 'labourism'. Collectivist 'new liberal' ideas had encouraged the state to play a central role in assisting and empowering its citizens (Macintyre 1989: 11) and the working class saw the state as a key actor in managing the economy in a way that protected and even benefited wage-earners. This labourist philosophy underpinned the development of Australia's welfare state with the primary premise being wage security rather than social security. Castles (1985: 102) coined the phrase 'wage-earners' welfare state' to best describe the way in which the principle of a living wage set the foundation for social policy development in Australia. Just as wages were set according to need, welfare provision was based on need and the existence of a (male) wage-earner's entitlements.

By focusing on wage-earners as the basis for entitlements, Australia's citizenship rights were more industrial than social (Castles 1985; Beilharz 1993). Yet even after the notion of needs-based wage increases was replaced in the 1930s, when industrial tribunals sought to link wage increase to economic indicators based on the ability to pay, the notion of the citizen-worker remained a gendered one. A male basic wage, of which women were only entitled to 75 per cent, was maintained for many years and there was considerable resistance by industrial courts, employers and trade unions to the implementation of the International Labour Organisation Convention on equal pay (ILO No. 100).

While it is apparent that the industrial citizenship tradition of Australian labourism has recently been challenged by the deregulation of the economy and labour relations, the masculine conception of industrial citizenship has been challenged before. Indeed, a variety of feminist alternative conceptions of citizenship have flourished throughout the twentieth century, initially focusing on the citizen-mother and later, as women's labour force participation increased, on gendering the citizen-worker.

Citizen-mother

Lake argues that enfranchisement meant much more to women than being granted the right to vote. Instead women conceived their new citizenship status as providing economic independence and 'deliverance from masculine conjugal authority' (Lake 1994: 25). Marriage for women was seen to undermine their status as individual citizens. Indeed, prior to 1948, women who married non-British subjects forfeited their own nationality and citizenship status (including their right to vote). Early feminists maintained that recognising women as autonomous individuals meant breaking down the single category of wife/mother. They argued that in their roles as mothers, women were providing services to the state rather than services to their husbands. Thus women were not seeking to challenge the institution of marriage as such but rather to undermine the dependence of wives on their husbands. In policy terms, this contest over women's status as citizen-mothers was played out first in the fight for a maternity allowance and was invoked again in an effort to have the state provide an income to women independent of men's family wage. The latter proved unsuccessful (Lake 1994).

In this way, early feminists were not openly challenging the conception of the citizen-worker[1] as masculine but, as Pettman argues, sought instead to introduce a conception of the citizen-mother as equal to, but different from, the citizen-worker (Pettman 1996). In doing so, women took as the basis of their claims those assumptions which underpinned men's status as citizen-workers; in particular, the right to sell their labour and be economically independent. However, by focusing on motherhood, women did not undermine male dominance in the paid labour force.

Neither did the conception of citizen-mother undermine the dominant ideal of a White Australia. White women were allocated an important role in the national population project as mothers, and payment of the maternity allowance was thought to be as much about protecting mothers as citizens as ensuring that children, the next generation of Australian citizens, would receive 'proper attention' (Lake

1993: 379). However, by pursuing this particular conception of the citizen-mother as 'mothers of the race', feminist arguments effectively excluded Aboriginal women.

Aboriginal women were not seen as mothers of the race but as the 'biological means for either maintaining or "breeding out" the race' (Brock 1995: 135). Assimilation policies allowed for Aboriginal children to be taken away from their mothers in an effort to 'rescue' children and absorb Aboriginal culture (Brock 1995: 136). Furthermore, while White women were seeking conjugal autonomy, the conjugal rights of Aboriginal women were regulated by the states (until the 1967 referendum which gave the federal government concurrent powers). The existence of segregated dormitories and Aboriginal reserves aimed to control sexual relations between Aboriginal women and both White and Aboriginal men (Brock 1995: 135). Many states adopted legislation which prohibited inter-racial sexual relations and which gave the states control over Aboriginal choice of marriage partners (Markus 1995: 248). Thus while White women were seeking to transfer their dependence on husbands to a 'contract' as mothers with the state, no such opportunity existed for Aboriginal women.

The number of women in the labour force has increased considerably over the last 20 years, supplementing women's status as mothers with that of paid worker. Nevertheless, Pateman argues that motherhood and citizenship remain 'intimately linked' (Pateman 1992: 29). In recent years, there has been some discussion by feminists as to how notions of citizenship might better address the political significance of sexual difference, as it is manifest through motherhood. This perspective emphasises the need to value maternalism and draw it more decisively into the political arena. In response, others have argued that feminists should not reduce women's identity to that of mother, since focusing on the maternal reinforces the divide between public and private (see Pateman 1992). Thus tensions still exist in terms of how best to reconceptualise citizenship in a way which takes account of the issue of motherhood.

Gendering the citizen-worker

The depression of the late 1920s and 1930s brought with it increasing unemployment and the definition of women as mothers was used to justify attempts to comprehensively exclude women from the paid workforce. In response, feminist conceptions of a more inclusive citizenship shifted away from ideas of 'citizen-mother' and towards the campaign for women's right to work (Lake 1993: 392).

While the fight for women's full inclusion into the paid labour force and the right to equal pay was taken up vigorously by women in the 1930s, it was not until the 1960s that any real gains were made. In 1959 the New South Wales Teachers Federation won their claim to equal pay, but further claims were thwarted by the introduction of legislation by the New South Wales Government which effectively stifled claims for work of equal value (Ryan and Conlon 1989). In 1967, a 'total wage' concept replaced the previous wage-setting process, and this transition undermined the family wage concept and opened the way for equal wages to be paid to men and women. In 1969, the Commonwealth Arbitration Commission decided to support equal pay for similar work, but it was not until the second decision was handed down in 1972 that any substantial gains were made in closing the gender-wage gap.

In terms of labour force participation, married women were, until 1967, not allowed to remain in the public service and, in 1977, the Arbitration Commission finally ruled that dismissal of women on the grounds of marital status equated to sex discrimination. Furthermore, it was only after considerable lobbying from women trade unionists during the 1970s that the Australian Council of Trade Unions (ACTU) dropped its policy of trying to ensure that women were not forced to work, affirming instead the right to work for anyone who chose to do so (Hargreaves 1982: 9, 63).

Despite the fact that between 1973 and 1995, women's labour force participation rates increased from 47 per cent to 65 per cent (OECD 1996), discarding the legally and politically entrenched view of women as temporary and secondary citizen-workers has not been easy. Full employment implicitly meant male full employment in full-time employment. Trade unions were hesitant to accept part-time work as legitimate and so many women who undertook such work as a means of juggling economic and family responsibilities were ignored as potential recruits.

During the 1960s and 1970s, it took considerable effort on a number of fronts by women from a variety of organisations to alter such perceptions. Women lobbied politicians, unionists and political parties to have their demands met, often employing overtly feminist discourses to do so. Paid maternity leave for public servants, increases to childcare funding and feminists entering the bureaucracy were but a few of the outcomes of such action (Sawer and Simms 1993; Curthoys 1994: 16–17). During the 1980s, this bureaucratic presence resulted in a range of feminist-inspired legal reforms in regard to sex discrimination and affirmative action (Sullivan 1994; Curtin and Sawer 1996).

Within the trade union movement, groups such as the Women's Action Commission, the Women's Trade Union Commission and the various Working Women's Centres sought to alter the explicitly masculine identity of the citizen-worker. Numerous conferences and meetings led to the production of objectives and guidelines for the trade union movement to address the needs of working women (Booth and Rubenstein 1990: 124–6). A Working Women's Charter was published, which was then adopted by the ACTU Congress in 1977. Following the adoption of the Charter, the ACTU Women's Committee was established to ensure the goals of the Charter are implemented.

Much of women's struggle against exclusion within the trade union movement has led them to argue for inclusion in a gender-specific manner, embracing the notion of a 'woman's interest' as a means of having their 'needs' met. Strategies of separate organising were first expressed early this century with the formation of women's trade unions and are now apparent with the increasing number of women's committees, conferences, networks and officers. This mode of organising has been crucial in providing women with their own form of solidarity within the union movement. It has also led to the politicisation of concerns of explicit interest to women, which have then reached the union movement's policy agenda. The issues of sexual harassment, parental leave and equal pay have begun to gain currency in the mainstream industrial arena. In this sense, some progress has been made in gendering the conception of the citizen-worker (Curtin 1999).

Gendering the political-citizen

Citizenship in a liberal democracy such as Australia brings with it the right to vote, to free speech, free association and freedom of movement. Advocates of 'social citizenship' argue that provision of adequate social and economic rights are also requirements to practise as autonomous political citizens. Either way, each citizen is supposedly free from conditions that might act as a constraint on the capacity to participate in their own voice, in the process of political decision-making. Indeed, J. S. Mill argued that every citizen not only ought to have a voice in the exercise of government, but at least occasionally ought to take part in government 'by the personal discharge of some public function, local or general' (J. S. Mill in James, 1992: 64).

However, in the Australian context, at the time of federation and the drafting of the Constitution there were only founding fathers. All delegates to the constitutional conventions were men and while some women and Aboriginals in a few states could vote for delegates, no women or Aboriginal people were elected as delegates. As a result, the involvement of the 'citizens' of the soon-to-be Commonwealth of Australia was severely limited. With this has come an assumption that Australia's political institutions were designed in a way that reflected ethnocentric and patriarchal views about who could participate and what constituted legitimate politics (Irving 1996).

Despite gaining the right to vote and stand for Parliament in 1902, women did not have much success as federal candidates in the early part of the century. It was not until 1943 that the first women were elected to the Commonwealth Parliament. By the 1996 election, this number had increased to 46 (21 per cent). However, despite this increase, Labor Party women in particular have continued to focus on the need for more women in Parliament and, to this end, have had the party adopt a rule change to ensure women gain 35 per cent representation in winnable seats by the year 2002.

With the approach of the centenary of the federation of Australia and the issue of Australia becoming a republic, citizen involvement in remaking Australia's democracy has received considerable attention. Labor Prime Minister Paul Keating in 1995 expressed a desire to provide women with equal opportunity, equal representation and equal rights in the new republic (Irving 1996: 37). The Liberal-National Party Coalition Government also sought to involve the people through the staging of a People's Convention in February 1998, whereby citizens and politicians came together to debate and discuss the possible design of a republican Australia.

Arguably this forum presented women, Aboriginal people and other minority groups who were previously excluded from voicing their views with an opportunity to demand representation in a process of considerable constitutional importance which was integral to a further redefinition of the dominant conceptions of citizenship. In attendance at the Convention were 152 delegates, half of whom were elected (by proportional representation) and the other half appointed. Of the 76 appointed, 40 were politicians and the other 36 were non-parliamentary delegates chosen by the Government. Liberal Prime Minister John Howard maintained that these appointments would ensure that groups which 'might not otherwise be properly represented, for example Aboriginal and Torres Strait Islanders, are able to participate' (Howard 1997). Howard also noted that the appointments would reflect a proper balance between men and women.

In an effort to secure this 'proper' balance, the Women's Electoral Lobby argued in their submission to the Constitutional Convention (Election) Bill 1997 that each group standing for election should be made to alternate men and women nominees on their ticket. While this demand was not included in the final Act, several tickets, including the two major groups, the Australian Republican Movement and Australians for a Constitutional Monarchy, did alternate men and women. As a result, women made up 38 per cent of the elected delegates (and were almost half of the 36 non-Parliament appointed positions). By making political representation in state or federal Parliament a condition for the remaining 40 positions, the gender imbalance amongst premiers and opposition leaders at state level, and in both major parties federally, contributed to the under-representation of women as parliamentary delegates.

Women's groups also sought to enhance women's participation in the political debates around the republic and issues of citizenship by organising a Women's Constitutional Convention that immediately preceded the People's Convention. The two-day Convention aimed to promote both the education of women and the representation of women's interests with respect to Australia's shift to a republic. The outcomes focused not only on the republic and a new head of state, but also on broader concerns regarding a bill of rights, electoral reform, and civic education. It has since been argued that women's mobilisation around issues of political citizenship have indeed had an impact on the mainstream debate about constitutional reform (Sawer 1998; Women's Constitutional Convention Secretariat 1998). The extent to which this participation leads to women gaining equal and permanent status as political citizens remains to be seen.

Conclusion

Both political and popular understandings of the concept of citizenship and what constitutes citizenship rights have changed significantly over time. Challenges have also been made to theories of citizenship which assume there can exist a homogeneous citizenry and that universal citizenship rights can iron out the inequalities created by the market place. Turner, in Chapter 2, highlights the difficulties these assumptions pose, considering that cultural and ethnic diversity is now a prominent feature of modern society. While he does not refer to gender in his examination, feminists elsewhere have provided comprehensive critiques of these models (see O'Connor 1993; Voet 1994; Orloff 1996). This chapter, in reviewing the gendered contests around dominant notions of citizenship in Australia, indicates that differences between men and women, and between women themselves, complicate the search for an all-inclusive universal citizenship.

While women have belonged as citizens of the Australian nation-state since gaining the right to vote in 1902, women themselves have sought to extend the conception of an inclusive citizenship beyond this formal right to vote. By first focusing on the rights of citizen-mothers, women argued that their difference from men be acknowledged. However, while such claims were made by early feminists on behalf of all women, the way in which these claims were framed was necessarily selective and therefore exclusive of some interests, particularly those of Aboriginal women. As the political context changed, feminists themselves reformulated their strategies for inclusion, seeking equality as workers. More recently, feminists have concentrated on including women in the male-dominated institutions of citizenship, with demands for equal representation in the 1998 People's Convention, and staging a separate women's convention, thereby seeking to further transform the gendered nature of the political in Australia.

What is apparent in all of this is that the way in which demands for the reconceptualisation of citizenship are framed very much depends on the particular historical context. It is also clear that while there may be an ongoing search for an all-inclusive citizenship, the very diversity of perspectives and identities mobilised within the political arena suggests that the idea of a universal perspective is both a myth and undesirable. Universal citizenship ignores and obscures the requirement that all experiences, needs and perspectives be heard and respected (Young 1989). Finally, while alternative, including feminist, arguments have challenged conventional, ethnocentric and masculine conceptions of citizenship over time, these alternatives must also continue to avoid the entrenchment and privileging of a particular identity (Johnson 1996).

Note

1   Neither, as Pettman (1996) and Pateman (1992) note, did they challenge the notion of the citizen-soldier.

References

Archer, Robin (1992) 'The Unexpected Emergence of Australian Corporatism', in Jukka Pekkarinen, Matti Pohjola and Bob Rowthorn (eds), *Social Corporatism: A Superior Economic System?*, Oxford: Clarendon Press: 377–417.

Beilharz, Peter (1993) 'Republicanism and Citizenship', in Wayne Hudson and David Carter (eds), *The Republicanism Debate*, Sydney: UNSW Press: 109–117.

Booth, Anna and Linda Rubenstein (1990) 'Women in Trade Unions in Australia', in Sophie Watson (ed.), *Playing the State*, Sydney: Allen & Unwin: 121–35.

Brock, Peggy (1995) 'Aboriginal Families and the law in the era of assimilation and segregation, 1890s–1950s', in Diane Kirkby (ed.), *Sex, Power and Justice: Historical Perspectives of Law in Australia*, Melbourne: Oxford University Press: 133–49.

Bryson, Lois (1995) 'Two welfare states: One for women, one for men', in Anne Edwards and Susan Margarey (eds), *Women in a Restructuring Australia*, St Leonards: Allen & Unwin: 60–76.

Castles, Francis G. (1985) *The Working Class and Welfare*, Sydney: Allen & Unwin.

Curthoys, Ann (1994) 'Australian Feminism since 1970', in Norma Grieve and Ailsa Burns (eds), *Australian Women: Contemporary Feminist Thought*, Melbourne: Oxford University Press: 14–28.

Curtin, Jennifer (1999) *Women in Trade Unions: A Comparative Perspective*, Aldershot: Ashgate.

Curtin, Jennifer and Marian Sawer (1996) 'Gender Equity in the Shrinking State: Women and the Great Experiment', in Francis G. Castles, Rolf Gerritsen and Jack Vowles (eds), *The Great Experiment: Labour Parties and Public Policy Transformation in Australia and New Zealand,* St Leonard's: Allen & Unwin: 149–69.

Davidson, Alastair (1997) *From Subject to Citizen*, Melbourne: Cambridge University Press.

Frances, Raelene (1991) 'Marginal Matters: Gender, Skill, Unions and the Commonwealth Arbitration Court – A Case Study of the Australian Printing

Industry, 1925–1937', in Raelene Frances and Bruce Scates (eds), *Women, Work and the Labour Movement in Australia and Aotearoa/New Zealand*, Sydney: Australian Society for the Study of Labour History: 17–29.

Hargreaves, Kaye (1982) *Women at Work*, Ringwood: Penguin.

Howard, John (1997) Second Reading of the Constitutional Convention (Election) Bill, 26 March.

Irving, Helen (1996) 'Equal Opportunity, Equal Representation and Equal Rights?: What Republicanism Offers to Australian Women', *Australian Journal of Political Science*, vol. 31, no. 1: 37–50.

James, Susan (1992) 'The Good-Enough Citizen: citizenship and independence', in Gisela Bock and Susan James (eds), *Beyond Equality and Difference: Citizenship, Feminist Politics and Female Subjectivity*, London: Routledge.

Johnson, Carol (1996) 'Shaping the Future: Women, Citizenship and Australian Political Discourse', in Barbara Sullivan and Gillian Whitehouse (eds), *Gender, Politics and Citizenship in the 1990s*, Sydney: UNSW Press: 25–43.

Lake, Marilyn (1986) 'Socialism and Manhood: the Case of William Lane', *Labour History*, vol. 50: 54–62.

——(1993) 'A Revolution in the Family: The Challenge and Contradiction of Maternal Citizenship', in Seth Koven and Sonya Michel (eds), *Mothers of a New World,* London: Routledge: 372–95.

——(1994) 'Personality, Individuality, Nationality: Feminist Conceptions of Citizenship, 1902–1940', *Australian Feminist Studies*, vol. 19 (Autumn): 25–38.

Macintyre, Stuart (1985) *Winners and Losers: The Pursuit of Social Justice in Australian History*, Sydney: Allen & Unwin.

——(1989) *The Labour Experiment*, Melbourne: McPhee Gribble Publishers.

Macintyre, Stuart and Richard Mitchell (1989) 'Introduction', in Stuart Macintyre and Richard Mitchell (eds), *Foundations of Arbitration: The Origins and Effects of State Compulsory Arbitration 1890–1914*, Melbourne: Oxford University Press: 1–24.

Markus, Andrew (1995) 'Legislating White Australia, 1900–1970', in Diane Kirkby (ed.), *Sex, Power and Justice: Historical Perspectives of Law in Australia*, Melbourne: Oxford University Press: 237–51.

O'Connor, Julia (1993) 'Gender, class and citizenship in the comparative analysis of welfare state regimes: theoretical and methodological issues', *British Journal of Sociology*, 44, 3: 502–18.

OECD (1996) *Employment Outlook*, Paris: OECD.

Orloff, Ann Shola (1996) 'Gendering the Analysis of Welfare States', in B. Sullivan and G. Whitehouse (eds), *Gender, Politics and Citizenship in the 1990s*, Sydney: UNSW Press: 81–99.

Pateman, Carole (1992) 'Equality, difference, subordination: the politics of motherhood and women's citizenship', in Gisela Bock and Susan James (eds), *Beyond Equality and Difference: Citizenship, Feminist Politics and Female Subjectivity*, London: Routledge: 17–31.

Pettman, Jan Jindy (1996) 'Second-class Citizens? Nationalism, Identity and Difference in Australia', in Barbara Sullivan and Gillian Whitehouse (eds), *Gender, Politics and Citizenship in the 1990s*, Sydney: UNSW Press: 2–24.

Pocock, Barbara (1995) 'Women in Unions: What Progress in South Australia?', *Journal of Industrial Relations,* vol. 37, no. 1: 3–23.

Ryan, Edna and Anne Conlon (1989) *Gentle Invaders*, 2nd edn, Ringwood: Penguin.

Ryan, Edna and Helen Prendergast (1982) 'Unions are for Women Too!', in Kathryn Cole (ed.), *Power, Conflict and Control in Australian Trade Unions*, Melbourne: Pelican Books: 261–78.

Sawer, Marian (1998) 'Engendering Constitutional Debate', *Alternative Law Journal*, vol. 23, no. 2, (April): 78–81.

Sawer, Marian and Marian Simms (1993) *A Woman's Place*, 2nd edn, Sydney: Allen & Unwin.

Sullivan, Barbara (1994) 'Contemporary Australian Feminism: A Critical Review', in Geoff Stokes (ed.), *Australian Political Ideas*, Kensington: University of New South Wales Press: 152–67.

Voet, Rian (1994) 'Women as Citizens: A Feminist Debate', Australian Feminist Studies, vol. 19 (Autumn): 61–77.

Women's Constitutional Convention Secretariat (1998) 'Sinclair Welcomes Outcomes', *Media Release*, 3 February.

Young, Iris Marion (1989) 'Polity and Group Difference: A Critique of the Ideal of Universal Citizenship', *Ethics*, vol. 99, no. 2: 250–74.

16 THE DIMENSIONS OF CITIZENSHIP IN MODERN JAPAN: GENDER, CLASS, ETHNICITY AND SEXUALITY

Vera Mackie

In this chapter, Vera Mackie argues that there are unspoken expectations about citizenship in Japan which implicitly privilege a middle-class, white-collar and male citizen. People marginalised by a failure to meet these expectations include women and various indigenous, outcaste and immigrant groups. Their marginalisation presents a stark contrast to an extraordinarily liberal constitution. Mackie's study of Japan resembles the studies in Chapters 10 and 15 of gender in the UK and in Australia, and it also resembles the study in Chapter 13 of multiculturalism and ethnic difference in the USA.

The popular and academic interest in issues of citizenship is an international one. In Europe, the political upheavals following the fall of the former communist regimes have refocused attention on the possibilities and limitations of liberalism, while the development of the European Union has placed citizenship in a transnational context [as we have seen in Chapters 8, 9, 10 and 11]. In Australia, much of the interest in citizenship has been stimulated by the Republican movement and the impetus to reframe the Australian constitution. These perspectives can also be brought to bear on Japan, where models of citizenship implicitly privilege the male, white-collar 'citizen in a suit', and marginalise the indigenous Ainu, outcaste Burakumin, second- and third-generation Korean and Taiwanese residents, and newer immigrants from South and Southeast Asia. In the United States [as we have seen in Chapter 13] and Australia, multicultural-ism is the subject of intense debate. In Japan, too, older and newer waves of immigration mean that issues of difference must be dealt with in the public sphere. In several countries, feminist political inter-ventions have forced a rethinking of the assumptions behind suppos-edly gender-neutral models of citizenship [as we have seen in Chapters 10 and 15]. In Japan, as in the other capitalist liberal democ-racies, the model of the citizen is based on being part of a nuclear family unit based upon a heterosexual couple, further marginalising those who do not fit the heterosexual norm.

In Japan, too, there has been recent interest in questions of citizenship, as globalisation and the internationalisation of labour markets mean that people of various cultural and linguistic back-grounds now co-exist within the boundaries of the Japanese nation-state. The apparent newness of this problem may, however, be seen to be illusory. Since the late nineteenth century Japan has had to deal with various kinds of difference: the incorporation of the peoples of the Ryûkyû islands and the non-Japanese residents of the Ogasawara islands; the management of the colonies of Korea and Taiwan in the early twentieth century; the use of (often enforced) Korean and Chinese labour in Japan during the Second World War; and the accom-modation of over 700000 Korean and over 200000 Chinese residents in the post-war period (Morris-Suzuki 1998).

Citizenship may be discussed in the context of the legal and insti-tutional structures that determine who has the right to participate in the political systems of voting and elected governments. Such a context includes the duties that are linked with these rights: the lia-bility for taxation, or the requirement that men perform military service. From this point of view, Japan has one of the most liberal con-stitutions in the post-war world, guaranteeing rights to work, choice of domicile, choice of religion, freedom of assembly and association, and freedom from discrimination on the grounds of sex, race, status or religion (Constitution of Japan 1947, in Tanaka and Smith 1976). These legal structures do not, however, exhaust discourse on citizenship. More recent ways of looking at citizenship have considered less tangible aspects of political participation: the familial structures which mediate relationships between individual and state; the ideologies which relegate women to the domestic sphere; the sexual division of labour in the home which determines the different ways in which women and men participate in waged labour; the privileging of the heterosexual nuclear family in work practices and social policy, and what I will refer to below as the 'sexual subtext' of citizenship. Another aspect of citizenship in this broader sense involves the possibility of participating in public discourse on political issues.

When we think of a Japanese citizen, who do we think of? Is it one of the group of men in business suits who graced the outside cover of the catalogue of a recent photographic exhibition called *The Japanese People* (Japan Foundation 1996)? The besuited male, working long hours at an office several hours away from his family, may be thought of as the model worker and citizen. Indeed, the 'salaryman' embodies one aspect of post-war Japanese national identity (Kondo 1997: 157–86). He also provides the model for Members of Parliament and the bureaucracy, and is valorised in television dramas and a genre of novel known as the 'salaryman' novel. These men, whom I refer to as the 'citizens in suits', are also the major addressees of public policy. Men gain legitimacy as citizens through participation in paid labour; while public policy, the taxation system, the welfare system and working conditions are organised for the needs of a heterosexual male at the head of a nuclear family. His private needs are taken care of by a woman confined to the domestic sphere, while his sexual needs are addressed in the commodified entertainment sector (Fraser 1987, 1989; Allison 1994, 1996).

What does this model of citizenship mean for women in contemporary Japan? There are, of course, some women who can conform to some aspects of this masculine model of citizenship. There are some heroic women in the public eye who have achieved an important public political role, such as Doi Takako, leader of the Social Democratic Party of Japan, Ichikawa Fusae, fomer suffragist and one of the most popular members of the Upper House until her death in the 1980s, or Katô Shidzue, campaigner for birth control and family planning, and another popular member of the Upper House for much of the post-war period.

For most women, however, the sexual division of labour in the home ensures that they enter the public sphere of waged work and political participation on different terms from their male partners. This is reflected in the different working patterns of men and women. Elite men tend to stay in one position, gradually achieving seniority in wages and status. Women, on the other hand, tend to work in their twenties, retire on childbirth, and return to part-time work in their forties. This results in the familiar 'M-shaped' labour curve for women, whereby participation rates peak in the mid-twenties and late forties, with a trough of low participation in the thirties.

Responsibility for domestic labour makes it difficult for most married women to engage in full-time waged labour, and this also shapes the possibilities for political activism. In parliamentary politics, women still comprise only 6 per cent of the combined total of both houses. Female parliamentarians interviewed by political scientist Iwai Tomoaki complained of a 'double burden' similar to that suffered by other working women (1993: 112). In another case which high-lighted the masculinism of parliamentary culture, a Socialist member of the Tokyo Metropolitan government, Mitsui Mariko, caused a stir when she resigned from her position claiming sexual harassment by her male socialist colleagues (Mitsui 1994).

Given the difficulty of conforming to masculine models of citizen-ship, some women have created new models of political activism. Without rejecting their responsibilities for childcare and domestic labour, they engage in part-time activism, focusing on issues in their local communities. One model is provided by the members of the Seikatsu Club (Lifestyle Club), a consumers' co-operative which has moved into activism in local government. Another model is provided by the women who founded a co-operative restaurant with the title 'Apron', achieving a sense of autonomy through bringing their 'domestic' skills into the market sphere (Ling and Matsuno 1992: 60–2; Iwao 1993: 246–60). Should we see these 'part-time citizens' as conservatives who sustain the status quo by reinforcing gendered spheres of activity, or as radicals who are creating new forms of citi-zenship and community (see Nakamatsu 1995)? Other women have acted as pressure groups in campaigns for equal opportunity legisla-tion, for retention of labour legislation which addresses the needs of working women, and against attempts to restrict access to abortion (Mackie 1996).

Consideration of the gendered patterns of participation in waged work, domestic work and political activity alerts us to what Nancy Fraser has called the 'masculine subtext' of citizenship. Citizens, however, are also constructed according to classed and ethnicised identities, and may belong to other sub-cultural groupings. Minority groups within Japan include the indigenous Ainu people, the Burakumin outcaste group, the descendants of the Korean and Taiwanese immigrants of the colonial period (Upham 1994: 325–46), and the newer groups of labour immigrants from South-East Asia, South Asia, West Asia and Latin America (Sellek 1994: 169–201).

While the post-war Japanese Constitution, as we have seen, explicitly prohibits discrimination on the grounds of race, creed, sex, status or family origin, this is not systematically supported by Equal Opportunity legislation or Affirmative Action programmes. The Equal Employment Opportunity Act of 1985 (effective 1986) only refers to sexual discrimination in employment, and is supported by specific legislation directed at working women.[1] There is no legal proscription of homosexual behaviour, but the privileging of heterosexual family forms acts to marginalise lesbians, gay men and others who attempt to survive outside the family system. The Special Measures Law, applicable to the outcaste community, is mainly directed at welfare measures and improvement of the physical environment of outcaste areas. Resident Koreans and Chinese have protested about the requirement to carry 'Alien Registration Cards' bearing photographs and fingerprints (after the enactment of the Alien Registration Law of 1947),[2] their exclusion, until recently, from public service positions, and the gap between their liability for taxation and their lack of political representation. Arguments have been made for extending local government voting rights to long-term residents, although this had not yet been implemented at the time of writing.

There are, however, newer groups of immigrant workers – often illegal immigrants – who seem to be beyond the pale of discourses of citizenship. Who are these immigrant workers? Those skilled workers, often from European backgrounds, who are working in Japan legally are usually taken care of under the label of *kokusaika*, or internationalization. However, there are also numbers of workers from less prosperous Asian countries, of varying degrees of legality, from students and trainees engaging in part-time work to those workers who enter on tourist visas and over-stay while engaging in various kinds of work. There are also interesting gendered patterns, with particular regions providing different proportions of male or female workers, and quite distinctive employment patterns for male and female immigrants (Miyajima and Kajita 1996: 1–3).

There is an implicit privileging of mental labour over physical labour encoded in immigration policy: a mind-body split whereby intellectual, white-collar work is given recognition, but not manual and physical labour, and certainly not sexual labour. While male workers in construction and manufacturing are often discussed in terms of labour policy, the women who come to work in the entertainment industry are discussed in terms of morality and policing (Mackie and Taylor 1994). So far, the Japanese Department of Immigration has failed to permit immigration for the purpose of engaging in unskilled labour. There are, however, several major loopholes. Students may engage in limited part-time work. Some workers enter the country as 'trainees', although it is doubtful how much 'training' they actually receive. Women often enter the country as 'entertainers', but may end up in the prostitution industry. A special category for those of Japanese ancestry has brought immigrants from Japanese communities in Latin America to Japan as manufacturing process workers.[3] These workers often bring families, and thus local government and education authorities have been faced with issues of multiculturalism and linguistic diversity.

As a result of the official prohibition on importing 'unskilled' labour, it is illegal to import labour for the purpose of domestic work, although anecdotal evidence suggests that some families are finding ways to employ overseas maids. Japan is thus relatively distinctive in not importing large numbers of domestic workers.[4] It seems, rather, that the overwhelming majority of women entering the country from South-East Asia are working in some part of the entertainment industry, and popular cultural representations of such workers reflect their sexualised identity (Mackie 1998).

If we look at legal workers by residence status, we see that 'entertainers' are the largest single status. While entertainers enter Japan under a legal visa category, this status often masks employment in hostess bars or massage parlours. If we look at illegal workers by employment category, male workers are overwhelmingly employed in construction and factory labour: jobs described as 'dirty, difficult, and dangerous'. The largest single category for illegal immigrant women is bar hostess, followed by factory work, prostitution, dishwashing and waitressing. The largest suppliers of immigrant workers by nationality are: Malaysia, South Korea, Thailand, China and the Philippines. Illegal immigrants from Thailand and the Philippines are mainly female, while immigrants from Bangladesh, Sri Lanka and Pakistan are overwelmingly male.

In order to consider these patterns, we must consider first of all the economic conditions prevailing in Japan in the mid to late 1980s. The rising numbers of illegal immigrant workers reflect the rapid growth of the Japanese economy in the mid to late 1980s, and the rapid appreciation of the yen from 1985, meaning that Japanese wage levels were significantly higher than other countries in the region. The economic situation in those countries which dispatch emigrant workers to Japan is also relevant. The high proportion of women from Thailand and the Philippines suggests a connection between particular constructions of gender and ethnicity in the Japanese context, but also suggests particular features of the contemporary situation in Thailand and the Philippines, where agrarian transformation and industrialisation have led to gendered patterns of labour migration, first of all from rural to urban areas and then to overseas destinations as remittance workers or in marriage migration.

We can also see interesting patterns developing over time. The year 1988 seems to provide a turning point, with significant increases in total numbers of illegal immigrant workers, changes in the proportion of male and female workers (with males outnumbering females for the first time), and illegal immigrants entering from a wider range of countries. Until around 1988, the majority of illegal immigrant workers were women, so that that these women formed the vanguard of the present influx of workers from overseas. I would argue, however, that it is only when large numbers of male workers started to enter the country as unskilled workers that this was seen as a labour issue. One commentator reveals this attitude in a book on Japan's 'guest workers'. Aside from statistics on relative proportions of male and female workers according to nationality, visa status and employment category, he pays little attention to the issues surrounding female immigrant workers. He goes on to propose a training scheme for those workers in the construction and manufacturing industry, but has no concrete proposals for those industries which employ large numbers of women (Shimada 1994). For male illegal immigrants, their engagement in what is seen as productive labour means that there is a space for discussion of their situation, and even space to consider granting them a limited form of citizenship, perhaps as 'guest workers'.

From around the time when the proportion of male workers

reached 40 per cent, and absolute numbers of both male and female workers started to increase rapidly, newspaper articles increasingly focused on the illegal immigrants as a problem for economic and labour market policy. One strand of this commentary is voyeuristic, describing the living conditions, their wages and working conditions in fine detail, drawing attention to the co-existence of disparate groups of people in local communities. Another strand of reporting concentrates on foreign residents and their collisions with the criminal justice system, in cases related to visa problems, theft, assault or the forging of telephone cards in a desperate attempt to keep in touch with relatives in their home countries.

Such articles also, however, fulfil the function of addressing the popular interest in the co-existence of disparate groups of people within the boundaries of the Japanese nation-state; highlighting the exploitation of illegal foreign workers, and stimulating public discussion on the management of difference within Japan. Given the sensationalised image of these immigrant workers, there have been two major responses to the issue: as a matter for policing, and as a matter of morality. The government and bureaucracy have seen the issue as one of policing. The immigration department is interested in preventing such workers from entering the country, while the police and judiciary are interested in the regulation of the sex industry.

Private organisations have tended to see the issue in welfare terms, setting up refuges for immigrant women. Some women's groups have been interested in exploring the unequal relationships between Japan and other Asian countries, and the factors which bring young Thai and Filipino women to Japan to work in jobs which usually have some sexual element. Lawyers' associations have helped by defending those immigrant workers who have come into contact with the legal system. Unfortunately it is often only in their collisions with the legal system that the words of immigrant workers are heard.

The mainstream union movement has demonstrated little interest in such workers, but the new community unions which have sprung up since the mid-1980s have paid more attention to the problems of illegal immigrant workers. They attempt to bring together all of those groups who have been marginalised by the mainstream union movement and political processes. The union movement has only been interested in those workers who fit standard categories of permanent full-time employees, while mainstream parliamentary politics is only concerned with those who come under the category of citizen. Several groups fall outside the category of citizen. Long-term Korean and Chinese residents lack the rights of citizenship, but have the recognisable category of permanent resident. Recent moves to extend limited voting rights in local assemblies to permanent residents suggest that they have attained a limited degree of legitimacy.

While economic rationalist arguments may be made for the recognition of immigrant workers in manufacturing and construction, another group of workers remains beyond the pale of discourses of citizenship. These are the women from Thailand and the Philippines who engage in entertainment, waitressing and prostitution. Like their male counterparts, they are subject to voyeuristic attention, with an added element of sexualisation. While male workers' jobs are physically dirty, these women bear the stigma of sexualised labour. Like their male counterparts, they engage in work with long hours and difficult working conditions, with the added dangers of violence and sexually transmitted disease.

Many community organisations connect with immigrant workers in attempts to provide welfare services. In this context, the relationship between state (including local government) and community organisations is interesting. In many cases the state may be seen to be subcontracting services to community organisations. What does this suggest about the state's duty to look after members of a national community (or does responsibility stop with those who are not citizens)? Technically, immigrant workers have no citizenship rights. Some community groups are attempting to find new ways of conceiving citizenship, in ways which recognise the contributions of these workers to a community, in order to listen to them as participants with legitimate voices. Organisations which perform advocacy for immigrant workers attempt to see immigrant workers primarily as *workers* rather than as illegal immigrants.

The rationale of some of the community unions, on the other hand, is to emphasise membership of a local community. Some of the new 'Community Unions', which mobilise those workers marginalised by the mainstream union movement (handicapped workers, part-timers, temporary workers, women) have also shown an interest in the situation of illegal immigrant workers. This suggests that they see an alliance with such workers as being in the interests of the Japanese working class as a whole. The alliances forged by the members of the new community unions provide an implicit critique of mainstream understandings of the dynamics of gender and class relations in Japan.

Commentators in Japan are currently engaged in a debate on how political discourse can be expanded to include those excluded from mainstream discourses of politics and citizenship, whether they be long-term foreign residents, illegal immigrant workers in the construction industry, or illegal immigrant workers in the entertainment industry. While there are spaces for speaking about these workers, in terms of policing, morality and welfare activities, there are few spaces or positions from which these workers can speak back to the Japanese community. Such commentators are attempting to bring discussion of immigrant workers into the mainstream of political discussion, not simply as the objects of more or less benevolent policy initiatives, but as participants in a dialogue (see Miyajima and Kajita 1996). Their perspectives could be brought together with recent theorisations of citizenship which advocate that we abandon 'the rigidity and fixedness of a formal constitutional and statutory notion of citizenship' in favour of a 'fluid conception of a national community which coheres around mutually recognised needs even as it sustains difference' (Gill 1998: 34).

Elizabeth Grosz and other feminist commentators have argued that women and subordinate groups 'embody' all of those elements which are marginalised from masculine models of citizenship (1994). The illegal immigrant woman worker from South-East Asia, in a marginalised and sexualised occupation, may be seen as the antithesis of the archetypal male besuited citizen: female rather than male, non-Japanese rather than Japanese, engaged in physical labour rather than mental labour, sexualised rather than abstracted. One way to consider citizenship is through a focus on these archetypical male citizens. Another way to consider citizenship is through a focus on the marginalised others, their marginality highlighting the limits of discourses of citizenship, and the exclusions built into the model of the citizen as a male, heterosexual, white-collar worker. It is this figure who is also interpellated as the desiring customer of the sexualised entertainment industry (Allison 1994, 1996). By considering his relationship with various sexualised others in contemporary Japan, we can see the sexual subtext of his claims to citizenship. We can also use these features (male: female; Japanese: non-Japanese; physical: mental; active: passive) to consider the positioning of other figures at different points on the discursive spectrum of citizenship.

The Japanese working-class male may in many cases share the patriarchal privileges of the middle-class white-collar worker. But, at times, his engagement in manual labour may align him more closely with the male and female immigrant workers. While the working-class male may be celebrated in some cultural forms, it is the besuited white-collar worker who is seen as archetypal. The Japanese female citizen is different in that there is an expectation that she will engage in reproduction and domestic labour. She also, however, may be sexualised in ways similar to the female immigrant other. The male immigrant worker shares the stigma of engaging in physical labour, and may sometimes be racialised in similar ways to the female immigrant worker. However, for male immigrant workers, their engagement in what is seen as productive labour means that there is a space for discussion of their situation, and even space to consider granting them a limited form of citizenship as 'guest workers'.

In this chapter I have focused on different groups in Japan which provide ways of thinking about citizenship in contemporary Japan. Japanese men and women are protected by a liberal constitution which guarantees political rights, rights to freedom of assembly and association, and the right to bargain for acceptable working conditions. However, an examination of the patterns of participation in work and politics reveals that men's and women's activities in the public sphere are shaped by discourses of masculinity and femininity, and the interaction between the domestic and public spheres. Citizenship in Japan, as in other countries, has a gendered subtext and a sexual subtext. If we shift attention to the most marginal groups in contemporary Japan, we can see the limits of discourses of citizenship. Despite their residence and participation in local communities, there are few spaces for the discussion of issues relevant to illegal immigrant workers. A focus on attempts to deal with this issue is instructive for an understanding of the politics of citizenship and democracy in contemporary Japan.

Notes

1   Article 14 of the Constitution of 1947 encodes liberal principles of equality: 'All of the people are equal under the law and there shall be no discrimination in political, economic or social relations because of race, creed, sex, social status or family origin.' The Labour Standards Law (*Rôdô Kijun Hô*) of 1947 is somewhat more specific. It stated the principle of 'equal pay for equal work' (Article 4) and also included provision for maternity leave (Article 65), nursing leave (Article 66), and menstruation leave (Article 67). Provisions which

prevented women from engaging in dangerous occupations (Article 63) and excessive overtime or night work (Article 62) were the subject of controversy at the time of the introduction of the Equal Opportunity Act (Mackie 1995).

2   All overseas residents in Japan who are there for more than 90 days must be registered in their local government area and carry an Alien Registration Card (*Gaikokujin Tôroku Sho*), which bears a photograph and fingerprints, at all times. The law on alien registration was revised in 1993, so that permanent residents are no longer required to be fingerprinted.

3   In 1990, the Immigration Control Act was modified to allow third generation descendants of Japanese emigrants to enter Japan for up to three years, in a long-term resident category with no restriction on engaging in employment. While in some ways the Japanese ethnicity of such immigrants was probably expected to cut down on problems of difference, in fact local communities must deal with contact between groups with different social and cultural expectations, while schools are addressing the necessity of multilingual and multicultural education for the children of these families.

4   Diplomatic personnel may employ domestic workers or chauffeurs who speak English. This allows for them to employ overseas workers, often from the Philippines. While such workers have a legitimate visa status, they do not come under the purview of the Labour Standards Law. The Labour Standards Law is the legislation which regulates the working conditions of regular workers, but does not apply to domestic workers.

References

Allison, Anne (1994) *Nightwork: Sexuality, Pleasure and Masculinity in a Tokyo Hostess Club*, Chicago: Chicago University Press.

——(1996) *Permitted and Prohibited Desires: Mothers, Comics, and Censorship in Japan*, Boulder, CO: Westview Press.

Fraser, Nancy (1987) 'What's Critical about Critical Theory? The Case of Habermas and Gender', in Seyla Benhabib and Drucilla Cornell (eds), *Feminism as Critique*, Cambridge: Polity Press.

——(1989) 'Women, Welfare and the Politics of Need Interpretation', in *Unruly Practices: Power, Discourse and Gender in Contemporary Social Theory*, Cambridge: Polity Press.

Gill, Judith (1998) 'Revisioning Citizenship: Feminist Concerns and Republican Sentiments', in Chilla Bulbeck *et al.* (eds), *Proceedings of the Australian Women's Studies Association Seventh Conference*, Adelaide: University of South Australia.

Iwai, Tomoaki (1993) '"The Madonna Boom": Women in the Japanese Diet', *Journal of Japanese Studies*, vol. 19, no. 1: 103–20.

Iwao, Sumiko (1993) *The Japanese Woman: Traditional Image and Changing Reality*, Cambridge, MA: Harvard University Press.

Japan Foundation (1996) *The Japanese People*, Tokyo: Japan Foundation.

Kondo, Dorinne (1997) *About Face: Performing Race in Fashion and Theatre*, London: Routledge.

Ling, Yuriko and Matsuno, Azusa (1992) 'Women's Struggle for Empowerment in Japan', in Jill M. Bystydzienski (ed.), *Women Transforming Politics: Worldwide Strategies for Empowerment*, Bloomington: Indiana University Press.

Mackie, Vera (1995) 'Equal Opportunity and Gender Identity', in Johann Arnasson and Yoshio Sugimoto (eds), *Japanese Encounters with Postmodernity*, London: Kegan Paul International.

——(1996) 'Feminist Critiques of Modern Japanese Politics', in Monica Threlfall (ed.), *Mapping the Women's Movement*, London: Verso.

——(1998) '"Japayuki Cinderella Girl": Containing the Immigrant Other', *Japanese Studies*, vol. 18, no 1 (May): 45–63.

Mackie, Vera and Taylor, Veronica (1994) 'Ethnicity on Trial: Foreign Workers in Japan', paper presented at the Conference on Identities, Ethnicities and Nationalities, La Trobe University, July 1994.

Mitsui, Mariko (1994) *Seku Hara Hyakutôban*, Tokyo: Shûeisha.

Miyajima, Takashi and Kajita, Takamichi (eds) (1996) *Gaikokujin Rôdôsha Kara Shimin e*, Tokyo: Yûhikaku.

Morris-Suzuki, Tessa (1998) *Re-Inventing Japan: Time, Space, Nation*, New York: M.E. Sharpe.

Nakamatsu, Tomoko (1995) '"Part-Timers" in the Public Sphere: Married Women, Part-Time Work and Activism', in Vera Mackie (ed.), *Feminism and the State in Modern Japan*, Melbourne: Japanese Studies Centre.

Sellek, Yoko (1994) 'Illegal Foreign Migrant Workers in Japan: Change and Challenge in Japanese Society', in J.M. Brown and R. Foot (eds), *Migration: The Asian Experience*, London: Macmillan: 169–201.

Shimada, Haruo (1994) *Japan's "Guest Workers": Issues and Public Policies*, Tokyo: University of Tokyo Press.

Tanaka, Hideo and Smith, Malcolm (eds) (1976) *The Japanese Legal System*, Tokyo: University of Tokyo.

Upham, Frank K. (1994) 'Unplaced Persons and Movements for Place', in Andrew Gordon (ed.), *Postwar Japan as History*, Berkeley, CA: University of California: 325–46.

17 ISSUES CONCERNING DEMOCRACY AND CITIZENSHIP IN INDONESIA

Greg Barton

In this chapter, Greg Barton reflects on wider implications of the dramatic economic and political developments that took place in Indonesia during 1997–9. Against the expectations of most observers, the worst of the economic and political crises were over by November 1999, with the surprising election of Abdurrahman Wahid and Megawati Sokarnoputri as the President and Vice-President. Parties in Indonesia have well-organised connections to religious followings and can express the interests of their followers in political arenas. At the same time, the mediatory tasks of political parties in Indonesia are especially difficult because of severe ethnic, religious and regional tensions. Indonesia will need to shift rapidly to a federal system in order to avoid the dangers of 'Balkanisation' in what has long been a highly centralised nation state.

The end of the authoritarian Soeharto regime was widely anticipated, but few expected the political change that began in 1998 to be so rapid. This chapter was finished in November 1999, in the midst of rapid change. It is bound to have been overtaken by events in some areas. Consequently, it sets out to review the major issues concerned with the development of democracy in Indonesia and to lay a foundation for further reading.

1998: the Indonesian economy hits the wall

When speculating about future developments in Indonesian politics we do well to remember that the cataclysmic events of May 1998, culminating in the resignation of Soeharto after 32 years in power, were precipitated by a regional economic crisis of massive proportions that only ten months earlier was totally unanticipated. The trickle that became the flood that washed away three decades of masterfully consolidated, elaborately centralised, military-backed and economically successful authoritarian government in Indonesia began with the floating of the Thai baht in July 1997. A crisis of confidence about the level of indebtedness of Thai business, corruption and the unproductive nature of much investment saw the newly floated currency sink with astonishing rapidity as nervous investors pumped capital out of the country. Neighbouring economies were rapidly caught up in Thailand's economic woes as the flight of capital broadened in the wake of increasing nervousness about the region. Suddenly the buzz word was 'contagion'. South-East Asia was in the grip of an epidemic.

At first, it appeared as if Indonesia's robust economy might prove immune. Not only was its stock market booming, its fundamentals were thought to be sound, with a broadly balanced budget, modest current account deficit (around 3.5 per cent of GDP), inflation below 10 per cent and declining, and decades of growth at around 7 or 8 per cent. Sadly, once Indonesia had fallen ill it rapidly became very ill indeed. On 14 August, the central bank succumbed to the inevitable and floated the currency which, like most neighbouring currencies, had previously been effectively pegged to the US dollar. The rupiah weakened, then slid and finally collapsed, moving from Rp2500 to the US dollar in August to 4000 in late October, before plummeting beyond 10 000 in early January 1998.

Once the collapse had begun, Indonesia's crisis was compounded at every turn. Not only did foreign capital flee the archipelago, but so too did billions of dollars of local capital. Already for some years the focus of rioting by the frustrated poor, the minority ethnic Chinese population (Indonesia's favourite scapegoats) began to feel increasingly nervous. Many of the wealthiest Chinese left the country, at least for the short term, resulting in a disastrous flight of badly needed human and financial capital.

It is likely that it will not be until at least 2002 that the economy returns to sound health, and even then, much depends on the course of national politics. In the meantime, the outlook for Indonesia is very grim indeed. The world's fourth largest nation entered the final year of the twentieth century with 80 million people, or roughly 40 per cent of its population, living below the (already very modest) poverty line, inflation running at around 70 per cent, and annual 'growth' in the region of minus 15 per cent. Two years earlier, those figures stood at 10 per cent below the poverty line, 7 per cent growth and 10 per cent inflation. Whatever else happens in Indonesian politics, until at least 2002 one of the central issues will be economic recovery.

Up until late 1997, poverty declined enormously under the authoritarian regime of Soeharto. It came down from 60 per cent below the poverty line in 1965. Average per capita calorie intake increased by 50 per cent, infant mortality rates were halved, and 85 per cent of the population received basic schooling as compared to 50 per cent in 1965. It is a sad irony that just as Indonesia seemed set to experience genuine democracy for the first time since the mid-1950s, with the potential for the greatest period of openness and respect for human rights in over four decades, its biggest challenge has come to lie in meeting basic needs.

Soeharto's denouement

If one good thing can be said to have come out of the economic crisis of the late 1990s it is that it saw a complete erosion in confidence in Soeharto. It was this collapse of credibility that led to senior government and military figures finally siding with students' and other activists' demands for Soeharto to step down.

Soeharto had arguably been in decline since the death of his wife and his close confidant, Tien, in April 1996. Thereafter the behaviour of the ageing president and master tactician had become increasingly erratic. In mid-1996, he engineered the ousting of Megawati Soekarnoputri (daughter of the late Sukarno, Indonesia's first president) as the popular leader of the PDI.[1] He then ordered the brutal storming of the central Jakarta PDI headquarters occupied by Megawati loyalists. The immediate consequence was that Jakarta experienced its worst riots in decades as community anger boiled over. From that time on the nation has experienced years of sporadic rioting and community protest, much of it apparently engineered.

April and May 1998 saw the President facing increasingly outspoken protests from civil society groups, in particular university students backed up by some senior academics. Incremental price rises, the failure of the rupiah to recover, and the collapse of the banking sector, were interpreted as signs that Indonesia's economic recovery was dependent on the sort of political reform that had occurred elsewhere in the region.

Nation-building and the legacy of history

Indonesia is a nation riddled by profound paradoxes that are far from easily understood. One of the founding paradoxes of modern Indonesia is that it is simultaneously home to ancient cultures and is a newly created modern nation. In certain respects, it is very much a product of the twentieth century and indeed of the second half of twentieth century. Unlike China, or even to some extent India, the notion of a state, nation or kingdom by the name of Indonesia that in any way approximates what we know by the name of Indonesia today is very recent. There was no sense in which the whole archipelago could be spoken of as being a single entity. Neither was there any one language that spanned the region, giving a sense of common identity. The Javanese, who today are the single biggest ethnic group in Indonesia, were in recent centuries not much inclined to maritime trade or to travel beyond the island of Java. This they left largely to the Malays and other ethnic groups such as the Bugis from Sulawesi, and consequently the language of the Javanese was not widely used. In fact the archipelago was home to hundreds of separate languages. Nevertheless, over time, in part because of the trade activities of the Malays, Malay became a kind of lingua franca, a trade language. In the late nineteenth century it was adopted by the colonial administration and several decades later taken up by the incipient nationalist movement. Only in the early twentieth century did a clear sense of national identity begin to coalesce, and in large measure this was only possible because of the emergence of a national language.

It is not surprising that one of the first goals of the new Indonesian Government was to work towards the formation of a strong sense of Indonesian identity. The Government set out to build a nation around this identity, after first declaring independence in 1945, fighting the Dutch for four years, and then finally achieving independence in 1949.

Communalism

The problem of communalism was one of the reasons that Indonesian democracy, such as it was during the 1950s, steadily disintegrated, and was finally replaced in 1957 by something that Sukarno styled 'guided democracy'. Communalism was not the only reason that the Indonesian democracy can be said to have failed in the 1950s but it was certainly one of the main forces working against robust democratic government. Separatist revolts, regional instability and a series of faction-riddled parliaments prompted Sukarno to declare that he would move to a state of emergency, invoking the short and vague revolutionary constitution of August 1945. Revolts in Southern Sulawesi and in West Sumatra in 1958, where regional forces sought, if not independence, then at least greater autonomy from Jakarta and Java, served to strengthen Sukarno's hand in the face of apparent national disintegration. Given this history, it is not surprising that one of the chief obsessions of the New Order government of President Soeharto was the maintenance of Indonesian unity.

An important complication in the plural nature of communalism within modern Indonesia is the diversity of religious affiliations. Around 87 per cent of Indonesians are Muslims but they have commonly divided into *abangan* Muslims and *santri* Muslims. The former are said to be only nominally Muslim, in the extent to which they carry out religious practices, while the latter are orthodox in their observance of religious practices. But the terminology is somewhat complex and disputed. Moreover, the *santri* population of Muslims can be further divided into Modernists and Traditionalists. There are a number of organisations that represent these different sections of Muslim society. The various ethnic groups that contribute to the Muslim community also have their own cultural preferences and styles reflected in their expressions of Islam. Apart from these Muslim communities, there is also a significant Hindu community, mostly concentrated in Bali, and small but very significant Christian communities. Indonesians generally make an important distinction between Catholic and Protestant Christians. Around 6 per cent of the total population are Protestants and 3 per cent are Catholics. In certain regions, however, such as Northern Sumatra and Eastern Indonesia, the Christian proportion of the population is very much higher. Many Christians are ethnic Chinese who comprise around 4 per cent of the population. Small numbers of the ethnic Chinese are also followers of Taoism, Confucianism and Buddhism. Further to this variety, the indigenous people of Kalimantan, West Papua, and even some of the more remote areas of Java and Sumatra, have their own unique religions which can be loosely described as animist.

Within this fractured diversity of loyalties and beliefs, the period 1950 to 1957 saw a remarkably rapid turnover of coalition parliaments. On average, governments lasted less than 12 months until they broke up due to one or more of their coalition partners disagreeing on some issue. To some extent this is not surprising given that the first general elections, and in many ways Indonesia's only free and open general elections, prior to 1999, were not held until 1955. It is unfortunate that even the general elections of 1955 brought no stable system of coalition multiparty government. The primary reason coalition governments of the 1950s, even after the 1955 election, were so unstable was that the parties were almost entirely defined along communal lines. The 'big four' parties were Nahdlatul Ulama (NU), which represented the traditionalist *santri* Muslims living mostly in Java, Madura and Javanese-settled outer islands; the Muslim Modernist Party of Masyumi; the Nationalist Party (PNI); and the Indonesian Communist Party (PKI). Together, these four parties, representing four distinct communal alliances and groupings, won about 80 per cent of votes in the 1955 election. The remaining 20 per cent went to a group of small parties representing particular communities.

Currently, there is great concern that the communalism demonstrated in the 1950s will reappear in a post-Soeharto Indonesia. This communalism led in the first instance to Masyumi backing regional separatist movements, particularly the West Sumatra and South Sulawesi bids for autonomy in 1958. More importantly, however, it saw a growing tension between the PKI on the one hand and Masyumi and NU, the two major Islamic parties on the other hand, and between the Communist Party and the Indonesian Armed Forces (or ABRI). This tension increased to the point where 1964 was described (famously, in a film and Christopher Koch's earlier book) as 'The Year of Living Dangerously'. By the mid-1960s, Indonesian society had become extremely polarised. Following the flashpoint of 1965, this tension flared up with horrible violence. Hundreds of thousands of people were killed, mostly in vigilante and hand-to-hand confrontations. So traumatic and awful was that period of Indonesian history that throughout the Soeharto era it remained a taboo topic for discussion and was seldom referred to in open discourse. Nevertheless, it undoubtedly remains one of the chief reasons why Indonesians of all political colours are wary of a return to inter-communal tension and rivalry.

Despite its troubled and eventful nature, or indeed perhaps partly because of it, one of the great achievements of the Sukarno period was the development of a strong sense of Indonesianness, and a sense of being one nation. To a large extent this was the product of having to fight the Japanese and allied forces following their return to Indonesia. The ultimate victory over Dutch colonialism was by no means solely obtained by military force. The guerilla tactics of the Revolutionary Army, effective though they were, were not sufficient to repel the Dutch. The ultimate achievement of independence came very much because of international pressure but, nevertheless, it reflected the great resilience and spiritual commitment shown by the Revolutionary forces. Consequently, the revolutionary struggle, however much it has been romanticised and exaggerated, has had an enormously positive effect in creating an sense of unity amongst Indonesians of various ethnic and religious backgrounds. Most Indonesians now regard themselves as belonging to one great modern nation that is as unified as its components are diverse. Greatly helping this sense of Indonesianness has been the relatively high level of inter-marriage, not only between different ethnic groups but also between different religious groups. This highlights one of the distinctive cultural features of modern Indonesian society. There is a general disposition towards tolerance and a strong desire for harmony. This desire for tolerance and harmony is a hallmark of Javanese culture but it has also become a central aspect of the various cultures of all Indonesians and modern Indonesian culture. To some extent, these cultural preferences are formulated in the Indonesian doctrine of state, the 'Pancasila.'

Pancasila

The word Pancasila derives from Sanskrit and literally means the 'five principles' or 'five sila'. These five principles are (1) belief in one supreme God, (2) well adjusted and civilised humanity, (3) national unity, (4) democracy led by the inner wisdom of unity arising out of deliberations among representatives, and (5) social justice for the whole of the Indonesian people. Pancasila was first formulated in 1945 in the lead-up to the declaration of independence. It is said to be based on traditional 'Indonesian' cultural values. Despite its relative antiquity, in the modern state little reference was made to 'Pancasila' during the Old Order regime. Instead this doctrine has been championed by the New Order, often as a way of justifying or checking criticism of various political innovations and policy measures.

Pancasila was formulated at the time when the leading members of the elite responsible for setting up the basic institutions of independent Indonesia were arguing about the pros and cons of various models of state. In particular many Muslim leaders argued that Indonesia should in some way be an Islamic state even if the Islamic law, the Syari'ah, was not instituted as government legislated law in the sense that it is in, say, Pakistan, Saudi Arabia or Iran at the present time. They argued that in some way state legislation should acknowledge that Indonesia is an Islamic state. Latterday Malaysia provides a good example of what many wanted. Whilst Malaysia is not an Islamic state Islam is the official state religion of Malaysia and of all ethnic Malays. As a consequence, Islam, and the religious obligations incumbent upon all Muslims, are legislated in Malaysia in a way that is largely unparalleled in Indonesia. Other Islamic leaders in Indonesia, and certainly many other nationalist leaders, argued strongly against this. To make Islam, as it were, the official doctrine of state, or at least the source of the doctrine of the state, would, they argued, lead to inter-sectarian tension and communal rivalries that would be an unhealthy development for a young nation. Pancasila, then, was initially formulated as an alternative doctrine of state that was catholic and ecumenical in tone. Pancasila is sufficiently broad and general that it excludes no one, atheists aside, and importantly it presents level grounds for everyone before the state whether they were Muslim or Christian, Hindu or Buddhist.

Dwi fungsi and TNI

Another important term that was much used during the Soeharto New Order period, but met nowhere near as much universal acceptance as Pancasila, is the term Dwi Fungsi. This term literally means dual function and refers to the armed forces' two roles in modern Indonesian life. It was formulated, or at least applied, early in the Soeharto period. The first function of the Armed Forces (now TNI, previously ABRI) was defence of the nation from both external and internal threats and the maintenance of stability and order. The second function was to ensure the smooth running of Indonesian society through active involvement in political life and civil administration. This second function was very much in evidence in the first decade of the New Order. Typically the heads of most major government agencies, departments, bureaucracies, businesses and so on were military officers. In time, as the Indonesian economy developed, and as a new generation of better educated younger Indonesians came through, these ABRI figures were gradually replaced by civilians for the most part. ABRI retained a number of strategic posts, however. Governors of provinces, other rural bureaucrats and certain senior government positions are occupied by either serving or retired military officers.

Of course many people argue against Dwi Fungsi, or at least argue for its diminution, on the basis that Indonesia can never have a healthy, democratic system of government so long as the military is actively involved. There is plenty of available evidence to support this argument. Some of the strongest evidence comes from cases where the military has been closely involved in civil governance and policing. This was most clearly to be seen in East Timor, West Papua and Aceh where the relatively benign, or at least stable, conditions of law and order and justice for ordinary citizens that mostly prevailed elsewhere in modern Indonesia were completely distorted. Young dissidents were constantly in danger of their lives, and of torture, and had no basis for feeling any sense of trust towards the armed presence in the territory.

Indonesia's new century: challenges to democracy

Much to the surprise of his critics, including the international community, Habibie performed much better as interim president than had been expected. He instituted a series of significant political reforms. No doubt Habibie was partly driven by the belief that he might rehabilitate the government party, Golkar, sufficiently well for it to form a coalition government after the June 1999 elections, and in turn be elected President by Parliament in October 1999. Habibie's, and Golkar's, shortcoming is association with the corruption and nepotism of the Soeharto era. Golkar's great strength, however, is its long established, well-organised and well-funded national political machine. For various reasons, Golkar has been able to retain the support of a large number of experienced highly skilled technocrats, something that has proved difficult for the other major parties.

PKB (Partai Kebangkitan Bangsa, or the National Awakening Party), closely associated with the 35 million strong traditional Islamic organisation of NU, benefits from its strong grass-roots support base through the *pesantren* (traditional Islamic boarding schools) system and stands as the party of choice for traditionalist Muslims, who are generally rurally based and poor.

PDI-P is a natural coalition partner for the PKB.[2] Since 1995, PDI-P's Megawati has shown a keen interest in working with NU chairman Abdurrahman Wahid, and generally there is an easy relationship between the supporters of PKB and PDI-P. Like PKB, PDI-P draws on the support of the *rakyat* (the common people), and shares a common nationalist outlook with PKB.

Of the three major non-Golkar parties, PAN (Partai Amanat Nasional), led by Amien Rais and closely associated with Muhammadiyah, has proved the most sophisticated in developing policy positions. One of PAN's great strengths, the charismatic leadership of Amien Rais, has also proved to be one of its greatest liabilities. Despite the clearly inclusionary policy position adopted by PAN, many people remain wary of Amien on account of his performance over many years as a Modernist Muslim leader who is prone to resort to sectarian rhetoric. Reinforcing this impression is his long friendship with members of the reactionary Islamist organisations Dewan Dakwah and KISDI, most of whom became involved with PBB (Partai Bulan Bintang, or the Moon and Star Party).

PBB is the only significant party which can be said to be sectarian or hold to Islamist views, and fortunately for Indonesia it continues to attract the support of only a small percentage of voters. Both PAN and PKB, despite their firm bases with Modernist and traditionalist Muslims generally, remain inherently moderate parties committed to an open and non-sectarian platform.

Avoiding any hint of sectarianism is vitally important to the success of future Indonesian governments for at least four reasons. First, the primary challenge faced by Indonesia is rebuilding its economy and it can ill afford to lose credibility in the international arena on account of sectarianism in government. Second, Indonesia needs to regain the confidence of Chinese Indonesians, both as investors and as citizens, and for understandable reasons the Chinese have an acute sensitivity to sectarian Islamism. Third, one of the major challenges facing post-Soeharto Indonesia is to build confidence amongst outer island ethnic groups, many of whom are Christian and consequently extremely sensitive to the outlook of the government in Jakarta.

The new Abdurrahman Wahid government

As has already been noted, the parliamentary election of Abdurrahman Wahid as Indonesia's new President, followed by Megawati Soekarnoputri's election to the vice-presidency, caught all but Abdurrahman himself by surprise. Recovering from their shock, most observers, both domestic and international, acclaimed the new leadership as the best possible for the current circumstances. But whilst the new cabinet, dubbed a 'National Unity' cabinet, was praised for its stability-ensuring inclusive nature and for the credibility of most of the new ministers, one obvious problem remained. Indonesia now had a surprisingly good government but one without any natural political opposition. Abdurrahman and Megawati came to power, collectively, with the support of all political parties, an ideal outcome at time of crisis – the result suggesting a Churchillian war-time cabinet – but fundamentally problematic nevertheless.

Clearly, the creation of a 'loyal opposition' at the national level is required as quickly as possible. Even so, it may well be that as Indonesia's political system, previously ill-suited to democratic governance, is re-invented one of the main channels of healthy political opposition will come through locally elected, largely autonomous, provincial governments. The new president has repeatedly stated his conviction that Indonesia needs to shift towards a federal system, even though 'federation' remains a deeply unpopular term in Indonesian society, tainted as it is by Dutch colonial attempts to recapture post-war Indonesia. Certainly, is difficult to see of any other way for the new government to make a meaningful and enduring response to Indonesia's persistent regional unrest. Indeed, done well, such a change would very likely bring economic as well as political benefits. A shift to a 'federation' of reasonably autonomous provinces could lead to significant direct investment flows, particularly to Eastern Indonesian, and unprecedented regional growth and development.

None of this, however, will suffice if the spectre of military violence and terrorising is not laid to rest. In order to respond realistically and meaningfully to past human rights abuses it is likely that Indonesia will attempt a South African style truth and reconciliation commission. This will only be possible, however, in an atmosphere of continuing and profound reform within both the Indonesian armed forces and the newly independent police force – something desperately required in any case if Indonesia is to develop a stable democratic political culture. The appointment of Admiral Widodo as head of the armed forces, together with a clutch of TNI reformists as senior ministers, bodes well for the success of an evolutionary reform process. Similarly, the 'promotion' of armed forces head, Wiranto, to a bureaucratic post suggests that the new President knows what he is about.

Can Indonesia overcome the many challenges it currently faces and develop a mature and robust pluralist democracy? The potential is certainly there and there have been many expressions of political maturity, particularly on the part of the younger generation. Certainly, it may be the world's biggest Muslim nation but that in no way presents an obstacle to the development of full democracy. On the contrary, Islamic intellectuals, not least Abdurrahman Wahid himself have been a the forefront of civil society in Indonesia, and liberal Islamic thought in Indonesia is very well established, widely influential and very much at ease with democratic principles. As the fall of Soeharto in the wake of the economic crises has demonstrated, however, political developments in Indonesia cannot be considered in isolation from international developments. All things being equal, there is good reason for optimism about Indonesia's future. In the face of a global recession or serious regional instability, however, the course could be a very difficult one indeed.

Note

1   Partai Demokrasi Indonesia, one of two permitted opposition parties during the Soeharto era and, until Megawati's accession to the leadership in the mid-1990s, no threat to Soeharto.

2   Megawati Soekarnoputri was ousted from the leadership of PDI in 1996, but she formed a new party, Partai Demokrasi Indonesia-Perjuangan, PDI-P, or PDI-Struggle in 1998.

References

Anderson, Benedict R. O'G. (1990) *Language and Power: Exploring Political Cultures in Indonesia*, Ithaca, NY: Cornell University Press.

Aspinall, Edward (1996) 'The broadening base of political opposition in exile', in Garry Rodan (ed.), *Political Oppositions in Industrialising Asia*, London: Routledge: 215–40.

Barton, Greg and Fealy, Greg (eds) (1996) *Nahdlatul Ulama, Traditional Islam and Modernity in Indonesia*, Melbourne: Monash Asia Institute.

Bourchier, David and Legge, John (eds) (1996) *Democracy in Indonesia 1950s and 1990s*, Melbourne: Centre of Southeast Asian Studies, Monash University.

Budiman, Arief (ed.) (1992) *State and Civil Society in Indonesia*, Melbourne: Centre of Southeast Asian Studies, Monash University.

Forester, Geoff and May, R.J. (eds) (1998) *The Fall of Soeharto*, Bathurst: Crawford House Publishing.

Hefner, Robert W. and Horvatcih, Patricia (eds) (1997) *Islam in an Era of Nation-States: Politics and Religious Renewal in Muslim Southeast Asia*, Honolulu: University of Hawaii Press.

Heryanto, Ariel (1996) 'Indonesian middle-class opposition in the 1990s', in Garry Rodan (ed.), *Political Oppositions in Industrialising Asia*, London: Routledge: 215–40.

Hill, Hal (ed.) (1994) *Indonesia's New Order: The Dynamics of Socio-Economic Transformation*, Sydney: Allen & Unwin.

——(1996) *The Indonesian Economy Since 1966*, Cambridge: Cambridge University Press.

Lowry, Robert (1996) *The Armed Forces of Indonesia*, Sydney: Allen & Unwin.

Pabottingi, Mochtar (1995) 'Indonesia: Historicizing the New Order's Legitimacy Dilemma', in Muthiah Alagappa (ed.), *Political Legitimacy in Southeast Asia*, Stanford, CA: Stanford University Press: 224–56.

Ramage, Douglas (1995) *Politics in Indonesia: Democracy, Islam and the Ideology of Tolerance*, London: Routledge.

Ricklefs, M.C. (1993) *A History of Modern Indonesia Since c. 1300*, London: Macmillan.

Robison, Richard (1986) *Indonesia: The Rise of Capital*, Sydney: ASAA.

——(1996) 'The Middle class and the bourgeoisie in Indonesia', in Richard Robison and David S.G. Goodman (eds), *The New Rich in Asia: Mobil-Phones, McDonald's and Middle-Class Revolution*, London: Routledge: 79–101.

Santoso, Amir (1997) 'Democratization: The Case of Indonesia's New Order', in Anek Laothamatas (ed.), *Democratizaiton in Southeast and East Asia*, Singapore: ISEAS: 21–45.

Schwarz, Adam (1994) *A Nation in Waiting: Indonesia in the 1990s*, Sydney: Allen & Unwin.

Wahid, Abdurrahman (1994) 'Religious Tolerance in a Plural Society: The Case of Islam in Indonesia', in Damien Kingsbury and Greg Barton (eds), *Difference and Tolerance: Human Rights Issues in Southeast Asia*, Geelong, Vic., Deakin University Press: 38–42.

Woodward, Mark R. (ed.) (1996) *Toward a New Paradigm: Recent Developments in Indonesian Islamic Thought*, Tempe: Arizona State University.

PART III
BEYOND THE NATION-STATE

18 DEMOCRACY AND WORLD ORDER

Scott Burchill

With the collapse of communism in the Soviet Union, the long dis-credited school of optimistic liberalism in international relations theory enjoyed a renewal of its 'inside-out' view of links between domestic and international politics. In this chapter, Burchill argues that developments in East and South–East Asia reveal grounds for critical analysis of liberal optimism about a New World Order. It is doubtful whether countries in this region are following the Western path to liberal democracy and capitalism. The suppression of trade unions and the flourishing of child labour reveal that free trade has little if any connection to basic social and human rights, and that capitalism sits uneasily with democracy. Several decades of rapid development revealed little evidence of links between an emerging middle class and trends towards democracy. Finally, the recent economic turmoil in South Asia amply demonstrates that global financial capital holds much greater sway over democracy within unstable or weak nation-states than it does in the West.

The end of the Cold War, in particular the collapse of the Soviet Union in 1990, was celebrated in the West as triumph for both capitalism as a mode of economic organisation, and liberal democracy as a system of government. In this chapter the prospects for the spread of democracy in the post-Cold War period are examined in two parts. First, the debate between optimists (liberals) and pessimists (neo-realists) is critically evaluated. This cleavage is at the centre of theoretical debates in the discipline of International Relations. Second, a number of further questions about the spread of liberal democracy in the post-Cold War period are discussed and, in particular, the challenges posed by the emergence of a number of increasingly self-confident East Asian societies are assessed.

The demise of Soviet communism has revived the reputation of liberal internationalism within the academy, a theoretical approach long thought to have been discredited by perspectives which emphasise the recurrent features of international relations. In a confident reassertion of the teleology of liberalism, Fukuyama has claimed that the collapse of the Soviet Union proves that liberal democracy has no serious ideological competitor: it is 'the end point of mankind's ideological evolution' and the 'final form of human government'. Furthermore, the end of the Cold War represents the triumph of the 'ideal state' and a particular form of political economy, 'liberal capitalism', which 'cannot be improved upon'. There can be 'no further progress in the development of underlying principles and institutions'. For Fukuyama, the end of the East–West conflict confirms that liberal capitalism is now unchallenged as a model of, and endpoint for, humankind's political and economic development. Like most liberals he sees history as progressive, linear and 'directional', and is convinced that 'there is a fundamental process at work that dictates a common evolutionary pattern for *all* human societies – in short, something like a Universal History of mankind in the direction of liberal democracy' (Fukuyama 1992: xi–xii, 48).

Fukuyama's belief that Western forms of government, political economy and political community are the ultimate destination for the entire human race poses a number of challenges for students of international relations. First, his claim that political and economic development always terminates at liberal-capitalist democracy assumes that the non-Western world is striving to imitate the Western route to modernisation; put another way, the Western path to modernity will eventually command universal consent. Second, Fukuyama's approach assumes that the West is the keeper of moral truths which 'progress' will oblige all societies to observe, regardless of national and cultural distinction. Third, he implies that 'capitalism' and 'liberal democracy' are closely linked together, and that they are in some way co-terminous.

Fourth, Fukuyama believes that progress in human history can be measured by the elimination of global conflict and the international adoption of principles of legitimacy which have evolved over time in certain domestic political orders. This constitutes an 'inside-out' approach to international relations, where the international behaviour of states can be explained by examining their endogenous political and economic character. It also leads to Doyle's claim that 'liberal democracies are uniquely willing to eschew the use of force in their relations with one another', a view which refutes the realist contention that the anarchical nature of the international system means states are trapped in a struggle for power and security. (Linklater 1993: 29).

The next section examines whether the optimism of liberals such as Fukuyama and Doyle is justified. It also assesses the relationship between economic and political liberalism, particularly the claim that the latter always follows the former.

Democracy after the Cold War: the optimists

Fukuyama revives a long held view amongst liberals that the spread of legitimate political orders will eventually bring an end to international conflict. This neo-Kantian position assumes that particular states, with liberal democratic credentials, constitute an ideal or model that the rest of the world will emulate. Fukuyama is struck by the extent to which liberal democracies have transcended their violent instincts and institutionalised norms in order to pacify relations between each other. He is particularly impressed with the emergence of shared principles of legitimacy amongst the great powers, a trend that can be expected to continue now that the ideological contest of the Cold War is over. The progressive translation of liberal-democratic principles to the international realm is said to provide the best prospect for a peaceful world order because 'a world made up of liberal democracies . . . should have much less incentive for war, since all nations would reciprocally recognise one another's legitimacy' (Fukuyama 1992: ix–xx).

Doyle has explored the dual themes of domestic legitimacy and restrained and peaceful intentions in liberal-democratic states' foreign policy. In a restatement of Kant's argument that a 'pacific federation', *foedus pacificum*, can be built by expanding the number of states with democratic constitutions, Doyle claims that liberal democracies are unique in their ability and willingness to establish peaceful relations between themselves. This pacification of foreign relations among liberal states is said to be a direct product of their shared legitimate political orders based on democratic principles and institutions. The reciprocal recognition of these common principles – a commitment to the rule of law, individual rights, to equality before the law, and to representative government based on popular consent – means that liberal democracies evince little interest in conflict with each other and have no grounds on which to contest each other's legitimacy; they have constructed a 'separate peace' (Doyle 1986: 1161). This does not mean that they are less inclined to make war with non-democratic states, and Doyle is correct to point out that democracies maintain a healthy appetite for conflicts with authoritarian states; but it does suggest that the best prospect for bringing an end to war between states lies with the spread of liberal-democratic governments across the globe.

The long peace between states of the industrialised world is a cause for profound optimism for liberals such as Mueller and Fukuyama, who are confident that we have already entered a period in which war as an instrument of international diplomacy is becoming obsolete. But if war has been an important factor in nation-building, as Giddens, Mann and Tilly have argued, the fact that states are learning to curb their propensity for violence will also have important consequences for the forms of political community that are likely to emerge in the industrial centres of the world. The end of war between the great powers may have the ironic effect of weakening the rigidity of their political boundaries and inspiring a wave of sub-national revolts. If war has been a binding as well as destructive force in international relations, the problem of maintaining cohesive communities will be a major challenge for metropolitan centres (see Linklater 1997).

Nevertheless, the expansion of the zone of peace from the core to the periphery is the basis of Fukuyama's optimism about the post-communist era (Doyle 1986, 1995: 83–106). Not surprisingly, Fukuyama is profoundly pleased by the collapse of the Soviet Union because one of its most important consequences is a reduction in the number of non-democratic regimes in the world and a commensurate increase in the number of liberal democracies, or at least societies in transition towards a democratic model. As the number of liberal democracies increases, the permutations and combinations of possible conflicts (between democracies and non-democracies) diminishes, making the incidence of war less likely.

Democracy after the Cold War: the pessimists

This 'optimistic' approach is rejected by neo-realists such as Waltz who claim that the moral aspirations of states are thwarted by the absence of an over-arching authority which regulates their behaviour towards each other. The anarchical nature of the international system homogenises foreign policy behaviour by socialising states into the system of power politics. The requirements of strategic power for survival are paramount in an insecure world, and they soon over-ride the ethical ambitions of states, regardless of their domestic political complexions. Waltz highlights the similarity of foreign policy behaviour amongst states with diverse political orders, and argues that if any state were to become a model for the rest of the world, one would have to conclude that 'most of the impetus behind foreign policy is internally generated'.

Waltz frequently cites the example of superpower behaviour during the Cold War to refute the argument that it is possible to infer the condition of international politics from the internal composition of states. The Soviet Union and the USA comprised quite different, if not antithetical, political and social orders. And yet, as Waltz points out, their behaviour during the period of East–West tension is remarkably similar. Their pursuit of military power and influence, their competition for strategic advantage and the exploitation of their respective spheres of influence were strikingly parallel. The explanation, according to Waltz, can be found in the systemic constraints on each state rather than their internal composition. These systemic forces homogenise foreign policy behaviour by interposing themselves between states and their diplomatic conduct (Waltz 1991: 667; see also Linklater 1993: 29–31).

By stressing the importance of legitimate domestic orders in explaining foreign policy behaviour, Waltz believes that liberals such as Fukuyama and Doyle are guilty of reductionism when they should be highlighting the systemic features of international relations. This conflict between 'inside-out' and 'outside-in' approaches to international relations has become an important line of demarcation in international theory. The extent to which the neo-realist critique of liberal internationalism can be sustained in the post-Cold War era will be a major debate within the discipline (see Doyle 1986: 1151–69).

Far from sharing the optimism of the liberals, neo-realists such as Waltz and Mearsheimer are profoundly disturbed by the collapse of

Soviet strategic power. If mutual nuclear deterrence between the USA and the Soviet Union accounted for the high level of international stability in the post-war period, the end of bipolarity casts an ominous shadow over the future world order. Because there is no obvious replacement for the Soviet Union that can restore the balance of strategic power, the world is entering a new and dangerous phase of uncertainty and instability. As Waltz concedes, 'in international politics, unbalanced power constitutes a danger even when it is American power that is out of balance' (Waltz 1991: 670).

Waltz and Mearsheimer continue to stress the importance of strategic interaction in shaping the contours of international relations. For them, the distribution and character of military power remain the root causes of war and peace (Mearsheimer 1990: 6). Instead of highlighting the spread of liberal-democracy and a concomitant zone of peace, they regard the rapid demise of bipolarity as the single most dramatic change in contemporary world politics. The pacification of the core, while desirable and perhaps even encouraging, is merely a transient stage which needs to be superseded by a restoration of the strategic balance between the great powers. Echoing E. H. Carr's critique of liberal utopianism on the eve of the Second World War, Waltz believes that the 'peace and justice' which liberals claim is spreading beyond the central core 'will be defined to the liking of the powerful' (Waltz 1991: 669).

According to Waltz and Mearsheimer, the recurrent features of international relations, most notably the struggle for power and security, will eventually reassert themselves: 'in international politics, overwhelming power repels and leads others to try to balance against it' (Waltz 1991: 669). However, the immediate absence of a likely countervailing power to the USA means there are few clues about the period we have entered. According to Mearsheimer, the long peace of the Cold War was a result of three factors: the bipolar distribution of military power in continental Europe, the rough equality of military power between the USA and the Soviet Union, and the pacifying effect of the presence of nuclear weapons (Mearsheimer 1990: 6–7). The collapse of the Soviet Union removes the central pillar upon which the bipolar stability was built. Multipolar systems, on the other hand, are notoriously less stable than bipolar systems because the number of potential bilateral conflicts is greater, deterrence is more difficult to achieve, and the potential for misunderstandings and miscalculations of power and motive is increased (Mearsheimer 1990:

14–19). Based on the experience of previous multipolar systems, in particular both pre-world war periods, the new era is therefore more a cause for concern than celebration: according to Mearsheimer, the stability of the last 45 years is unlikely to be repeated.

Neo-realists have regarded nuclear weapons, and the rough parity between East and West, as a source of stability and pacification during the Cold War. They provided security to both blocs, generated caution amongst decision-makers, imposed a rough equality, and created a clarity of relative power between both camps (Mearsheimer 1990: 32). The absence of a first strike capability and the destructive potential of a direct conflict forced the USA and the Soviet Union to manage their differences without recourse to violence. In addition, the binding force of having a common enemy – a form of bonding by exclusion – imposed a discipline upon and within each bloc. According to Mearsheimer, if this level of stability is to be reached in the new multipolar environment, the 'carefully managed proliferation' of nuclear weapons in Europe may be required to preserve the peace, or at least keep a check on the strategic primacy of the USA (Mearsheimer 1990: 7–8).

Depending on the persuasive force of each argument, students of global politics will be either profoundly optimistic or pessimistic about the post-Cold War period. The realist critique of liberal internationalism is one that deserves serious engagement. On the question of how liberal states should conduct themselves with non-liberal states, for example, Fukuyama and Doyle are equally and surprisingly silent. Recent conflicts between Western democracies and Iraq and Serbia confirm the inherent volatility of these relationships. It is also clear that the greatest barrier to the expansion of the zone of peace from the core is the perception within the periphery that this constitutes little more than the domination of one culture by another. These suspicions are well founded given that peripheral states have traditionally been the victims of Western intervention.

Fukuyama's argument is not simply a celebration of the fact that liberal democratic capitalism has survived the threat posed by Marxism; it also implies that neo-realism has overlooked the 'the foremost macropolitical trend in contemporary world politics: the expansion of the liberal zone of peace' (Linklater 1993: 29). Challenging the view that the nature of anarchy conditions international behaviour is Doyle's argument that a growing core of pacific states have learnt to resolve their differences without resorting to violence. The likely expansion of this pacific realm is said to be the most significant feature of the post-communist landscape. If this claim is upheld it will constitute a remarkable resuscitation for an international theory widely thought to have been refuted by Carr in his critique of liberal utopianism over 50 years ago. It will also pose a serious challenge to a discipline which until recently has been dominated by assumptions that war is a recurrent and endemic feature of international life.

Democracy after the Cold War: further challenges

If democracy is the wave of the future, as liberals would have us believe, it will need to overcome a number of additional challenges, most notably from the economically dynamic states of East Asia, many of which, prior to Asia's economic crisis in mid-1997, rejected the very foundations of Western-style liberal democracy [as we saw in Chapter 17]. The challenges to the two-party system and the powerful forces of globalisation also pose new questions for liberal optimists. In this section, four of these challenges will be briefly discussed.

First, the suggestion that the Western path to modernity will eventually command universal consent, or that there is even a universally agreed definition of democracy, is problematic. The West has little difficulty in defining democracy in procedural terms where the citizens of a state can meaningfully participate in political decisions which affect their lives. This usually takes the form of representative democracy expressed in institutional form after free and fair elections. Universal suffrage and freedom of conscience, speech, association, religion, assembly and the press are considered the normal ingredients of a democratic political culture. Organised and permanent political opposition is also regarded as both a legitimate and necessary activity in a healthy democracy (Held 1995a, 1995b).

This definition of democracy, however, is now under serious challenge from a number of increasingly self-confident East Asian societies which question the cultural relevance of Western-style liberal democracy. Although frequently cast in terms of 'Asian values' by conservative leaders seeking to deny legitimacy to their domestic political opponents, concerns about human rights and democracy in East Asia should be understood as a rejection of the liberal argument that the Western path to modernity is universally valid or that political development always terminates at liberal democracy. There is therefore some merit to the claim that the West's political and human rights agenda in East Asia is a thinly disguised form of cultural imperialism which attempts to thwart the comparative economic advantages of states in the region.

However, it is also ironic that the basic procedural freedoms and rights which citizens in liberal democracies take for granted, including freedom of association, the right to organise and bargain collectively, the right to work in a safe environment, the prevention of forced labour, and so on, are being eroded and denied in a number of developing East Asian societies by policies of market liberalisation which Western elites are encouraging. Industrial accidents, due to poor or non-existent safety standards, are on the rise in China and Thailand. Trade unionists have been threatened, attacked, arrested and murdered in Indonesia. Workers' rights in Malaysia and Singapore are denied in the interests of 'economic development'. Child labour is exploited in South Korea and China. Recent attempts by US governments to draw attention to these abuses have been condemned by other liberal democracies more enamoured with the ideology of free trade and concerned by any threats to the region's comparative advantage in cheap labour.

The problem with this argument is that the link between workers' rights and free trade is made by the East Asians themselves. When the Suharto government in Indonesia, for example, kept wages in that country artificially low by outlawing freedom of association, banning independent trade unions, arresting, incarcerating and often murdering labour activists, it was explicitly violating free market principles. This policy is really an example of state intervention lowering the price of labour, thus providing a hospitable climate for transnational capital (a sharp departure from the neo-liberal doctrines so favoured by policy elites in the West). Labour markets in East Asia are anything but free.

Nevertheless, the region has demonstrated that the absence of Western-style democracy is certainly no impediment to international competitiveness.

Second, in theory at least, the citizens of liberal-democratic states are able to choose their preferred policy outcomes at parliamentary elections. In recent practice, the choices, particularly in the domain of economic policy, are very limited. Critics argue that the function of the two-party system is to offer voters the illusion of choice while maintaining continuity in the system's administration: that is, support for the existing economic structures and class divisions. In the field of political economy, the electorate is really only deciding on the degree of state intervention it wants within a state capitalist model. The spectrum of available policy options is so narrow that it is really not accurate to speak of a real choice at all.

While political parties in liberal-capitalist states compete for office through democratic political processes, the policy options they can present to the electorate are severely limited by the knowledge that the state is heavily dependent on resources largely generated by private capital accumulation. Only by taxing profitable production can the state raise sufficient revenue for its needs. In the modern period, the state therefore has a vested interest in facilitating capital accumulation: what Offe has called an 'institutional self-interest'. Though the state is largely excluded from directly controlling private decisions of production and investment, it must make policy decisions that are broadly compatible with business-capitalist interests, sustaining a climate of confidence while promoting conditions for accumulation and profitability. Although the state is both excluded from and dependent upon the accumulation process, its intervention is crucial to the maintenance of the process. This requirement severely constrains the proper functioning of the democratic process as the relationship between the state and the private economy narrows the range of actual policy choices. [As we have seen in Chapter 12, the relationship between parties, democratic order, and capitalist prosperity is indeed problematic.]

Third, despite the claim of conservatives that the new middle classes of the developing world will demand commensurate political influence in the affairs of state, there is little evidence of a link between economic and political liberalisation. China, Malaysia, Singapore and Indonesia, to name only four Asian examples, have shown that rapid economic development can be achieved with few if any concessions to the democratic freedoms familiar in the West, although recent democratic transitions in Taiwan, Thailand, the Philippines and South Korea may challenge this argument. In fact they openly suggest that social justice and democracy are actually incompatible with economic growth and international competitiveness. In this claim they are supported by neo-liberal economists in the West who seem more concerned with the adoption of free trade and the de-regulation of the finance sector than they are with the spread of democracy. In some quarters democracy is considered dysfunctional and 'inefficient', and must therefore be restricted in 'the national interest', usually defined in elite terms.

A related argument, that 'rice must come before rights' – that economic, social and cultural rights should precede civil and political rights – is made by a number of East Asian governments.[1] It implies that poverty alleviation and economic development in these societies depends on the denial of political freedoms and human rights to their citizens. However, the claim that rights can be prioritised in this way or that procedural and substantive freedoms are incompatible is highly problematic and widely seen, with justification, as a rationalisation by governments for non-democratic political cultures. The exclusivist argument privileges economic, social and cultural rights and is a direct challenge to the idea that human rights are indivisible and universal.

An increasing number of conservative political leaders in East Asia have also argued that there is a superior Asian model of political and social organisation comprising the principles of harmony, hierarchy and consensus (Confucianism) in contrast to what they regard as the confrontation, individualism and moral decay which characterises Western liberalism. Regardless of how self-serving this argument is – and it is never offered by democratically elected rulers – it poses a fundamental challenge to Fukuyama's suggestion that in the post-Cold War period liberal democracy has no serious ideological competitors. It is clear that these states are not striving to imitate the Western route to political modernisation (Robison 1996).[2]

Fourth, globalisation poses a number of challenges for Western concepts of democracy. Globalisation is a description of economic, technological and cultural processes of global change which have escaped the sovereign control of nation-states. These processes have advanced across national boundaries with astonishing speed and remarkable ease since the 1970s. They include communications technology and media coverage, integrated and de-regulated capital markets, the international division of labour and unprecedented levels of economic interdependence, modern instruments of intelligence and surveillance and the worldwide transmission of ideas and images (Macmillan and Linklater 1995: 4).

Private business can now shift capital, technology, production and (to a lesser extent) labour around the world to wherever profit is maximised. The globalisation of production means that manufactur-

ing centres can be moved to wherever the most advantageous combination of factors exist: in other words, to where the cost of land and
labour is cheapest, taxation rates are lowest, interest rates are highest,
exchange rates are most favourable and environmental and health
regulations are least intrusive. This is possible because the obstacles
to the free movement of money and goods around the world (financial de-regulation and trade liberalisation) have been increasingly
removed since the early 1970s.

Globalisation has made it increasingly difficult for individual governments to set their own economic policies independently of these
extraordinary changes to the nature of the world economy. National
economic sovereignty, or the capacity of governments to set their own
economic goals and priorities, has been steadily eroding since the
early 1970s. Economic self-reliance and self-sufficiency are now
anachronistic concepts. The 'disciplines' of world markets impose
themselves as irresistible forces on the minds of policy elites, who
increasingly recognise the expectations of global markets as the fundamental constraints upon policy-making (see Held, McGrew, Goldblatt and Perrator 1999). [As we have seen, in Chapter 14, South
Africa shows that the constraints imposed by global capitalism are
especially harsh when the democratic demands for social and economic justice are great.]

One consequence of these forces has been a substantial challenge
to the idea of democratic rule within delimited territories. A new class
of decision-makers who are not democratically accountable within
any one particular jurisdiction has emerged to rival the authority of
elected governments. The foreign investment community – comprising fund managers, financial speculators, stockbrokers, insurance companies, banks, transnational corporations, and so forth – now exerts
enormous influence over the policy settings within most countries.
This community has no particular national loyalties. It is uncon-
strained by territorial boundaries and supported by the economic
orthodoxy of neo-liberalism because it represents elite economic
interests. Most importantly, the international financial community has
thrived on the interdependency of the world's economies, which are
now judged by their comparative 'hospitality' to foreign capital. These
transnational elites determine which states will be infused with much-
needed capital but, in the process, extract policy concessions that
maximise the profit returns for themselves and their clients. Their
capacity to add conditions to capital loans to the developing world

induces policy changes with threats of a capital strike, a reduction in a nation's credit rating, or a run on the value of a national currency. This gives them extraordinary power and influence, and yet they are not democratically accountable for their behaviour (see Lasch 1995; Saul 1995; Chomsky 1996).

Regardless of the longevity of the nation-state or whether new forms of political community are evolving, globalisation has further removed the prospect that individuals will soon have democratic control over their economic lives. This is a serious dilemma for liberals who for 200 years have encouraged the removal of barriers to international commerce but simultaneously championed the spread of liberal democracy.

Notes

1   Bangkok Declaration from the Asia-Pacific Conference on Human Rights in March/April 1993.
2   See also Chapters 2 and 5 in the same volume.

References

Chomsky, N (1996) *Power and Prospects*, Sydney: Allen & Unwin.
Doyle, M (1986) 'Liberalism and World Politics', *American Political Science Review*, Vol. 80, No. 4: 1151–69.
——(1995) 'Liberalism and World Politics Revisited', in C.W. Kegley Jr (ed.), *Controversies in International Relations Theory*, New York: St. Martin's Press.
Fukuyama, Francies (1992) *The End of History and the Last Man*, Harmondsworth: Penguin.
Held, D. (1995a) *Democracy and the Global Order*, Cambridge: Polity Press.
——(1995b) 'Democracy and the New International Order', in D. Archibugi and D. Held (eds), *Cosmopolitan Democracy*, Cambridge: Polity Press.
Held, D., McGrew, A., Goldblatt, D. and Perraton, J. (1999) *Global Transformations*, Cambridge: Polity Press.
Lasch, C. (1995) *The Revolt of the Elites and the Betrayal of Democracy*, New York: W. W. Nortor.
Linklater, A. (1993) 'Liberal Democracy, Constitutionalism and the New World Order', in R. Leaver and J. Richardson (eds), *The Post-Cold War Order: Diagnoses and Prognoses*, Sydney, Allen & Unwin.
——(1998) *The Transformation of Political Community*, Cambridge: Polity Press.
Macmillan, J. and Linklater, A. (eds) (1995) *Boundaries in Question*, London: Pinter.

Mearsheimer, J.L. (1990) ' "Back to the Future": Instability in Europe After the Cold War', *International Security*, vol. 15, no.1 (Summer): 5–56.

Robison, R. (1996) 'Looking north: myths and strategies', in R. Robison, *Pathways to Asia*, Sydney: Allen & Unwin.

Saul, J.R.(1995) *The Unconscious Civilization*, Harmondsworth: Penguin.

Waltz, K. (1991) 'America as a Model for the World?', *Political Science and Politics*, vol. 24, no. 4: 667–70.

19 CYBERCITIZENSHIP AND DIGITAL DEMOCRACY*

Andrew Vandenberg

This chapter draws on themes raised by Turner, Hindess and Davidson in their chapters and returns to the theme of essentially contested concepts in Chapter 1. Despite high-flown rhetoric about a new era and the premium of education in the dawning information society or economy, there is reason to think closely about the possibilities that many-to-many communication may offer citizenship and democracy in the next few decades. On the one hand, the cybercitizens of virtual communities can establish forms of interaction and self-government that are more meaningful to the participants than citizenship is in either ethnically or territorially bounded nation-states. On the other hand, the exclusivity of cybercitizenship (among the mostly male, well educated and well-to-do in rich countries) has little connection with either traditional 'analogue' democracy or more recent trends towards the digitalisation of democracy. The rise of multimedia capitalism has accompanied the rise of ever more sophisticated opinion polling, talk-back radio, dedicated telephone numbers for television viewers to express yes or no to a controversial proposition, and the degradation of conventional election campaigns. At the same time, there is a slight hope that the sober rationality made possible by the anonymity of cybercitizenship can

* Some aspects of this chapter were presented to the *Culture and Citizenship Conference*, Brisbane 30 September–2 October 1996. Other aspects have been published in Vandenberg (1997a: 26–32; 1997b). The chapter has also benefited from discussion with students (Graham 1996).

combine with digitalisation of traditional processes of democracy. The prospects of citizenship combining with democracy via computer-mediated communications are therefore bleak but there is some hope that worthwhile developments may also eventuate.

The rapid development in computers and various allied services since the early 1970s, and then convergence of digitalised newspapers, telephone, radio and video into 'multimedia' since the early 1990s, has. prompted wide discussion about computers and how people are using them. This discussion has largely focused on a contrast between ideas, dreams or nightmares and material or commercial realities (Roszak 1986; Winner 1986; Dunlop and Kling 1991; Taylor and Saarinen 1994; Brook and Boal 1995; Stallabrass 1995; Whittle 1997). The turn to a classical contrast between ideas and realities, or the ideal and the material, whether optimistic or pessimistic, utopian or dystopian, is obviously an attempt to foresee the political and social consequences of extraordinarily rapid developments that are perhaps historically important. However understandable this turn to a contrast between ideas and realities, it tends to maintain some unhelpful assumptions about the social and political boundaries of nation-states and the social and political constitution of people as citizens of such states (Kling and Iacono 1991; Poster 1995; Baddeley 1997). The ethereality of cyberspace and the fluid identity of computer users calls long-standing assumptions about political community and individuality into question.

Cyberspace poses some interesting issues for citizenship and democracy both within the familiar processes of nation-state politics and within what Howard Rheingold (1995) calls 'virtual communities'.[1] But 'cyberspace' is a vague term for a concept that is a little difficult to pin down. It describes the place that people take themselves off to when they (we) talk on the telephone, play video games, correspond by e-mail, bulletin boards or Usenet groups, look at World Wide Web pages, or more generally become 'wrapped in media' (Lyon 1997: 27). Cyberspace involves collective hallucination about a place that differs from 'real' time and space (see Poster 1995: 3–42; Loader 1997: 23–110; Whittle 1997: 3–9). Despite semantic imprecision it has some interesting possibilities, as Michael Benedikt notes:

> Like Shangri-la, like mathematics, like every story ever told or sung, a mental geography of sorts has existed in the living mind of every culture, a collective memory or hallucination, an agreed-upon territory of mythical figures, symbols, rules, and truths, owned and traversable by all who learned its ways, and yet free of the bounds of physical time and space. What is so galvanising today is that technologically advanced cultures, such as those of Japan, Western Europe, and North America, stand at the threshold of making that ancient space both uniquely visible and the object of interactive democracy. (Benedikt 1991: 3)

In this chapter I partly follow the example of critical writers who pose pointed analytical questions about what the sweeping rhetoric on computers and cyberspace might mean for students, consumers, citizens, schools, universities and present political processes (Roszak 1986; Winner 1986; Noble 1997). But I depart from their dystopian conclusions in favour of considering how computer-keyboard mediated communication can focus people's attention on the content of interaction, making the identity of the correspondents less important. Cybercitizens have instigated invigorating processes of direct democracy among themselves and as a group they are more actively involved in debates and decision-making amongst themselves than are the twentieth-century citizens of liberal democratic nation states (see Poster 1995; Baddeley 1997; Lyons 1997). But I argue against the utopian rhetoric about virtual community and Netizens that is widely deployed on the Internet (see Hauben, no date). It is misleading or at least naive to assume that cybercitizens will transform conventional democracy within nation-states as computers come to allow more interactive processes of communication (see Hindess 1991, 1993).

Opportunities and worries

Those who are enthusiastic about the political possibilities of computer-mediated communication commonly raise three arguments. The first is about an epoch-forming and revolutionary transition to a new society or era. The second entails observations on the effects of the accelerated rapidity of change. The third is about the effects of new patterns and relations of communication on the formation of political communities. I look at the first two below and in the rest of the chapter I look at the third argument in more detail.

Those who advance arguments about the historic beginning of a new epoch in human history often assume that previous technological developments have caused or determined accompanying social, economic and political developments. Dale Spender (1995: 1) provides an example of this argument when she asserts:

> The printing press changed the course of human history. It produced an information revolution. . . . in examining some of the changes that took place with the introduction of print, we can also see the parallels with the changes that are taking place with the current information revolution: it too is altering the course of human history.

Against such an assertion, Winner (1986: 99–102) poses an acerbic question: if recent developments in computer technology do amount to a 'revolution', is it one led by corporate interests and comparable to a Third World *coup d'état*, which we therefore should resist? Or is it a revolution of ordinary people rebelling against tyranny, which ought to be supported? Winner concludes his chapter with an ironic observation on the shallowness of hopeful speculation about artificial intelligence and electronic butlers that browse the World Wide Web gathering information from sites (news, weather, stock reports, and so forth) that a user has visited before. Such speculation is shaped not by artificial intelligence but a familiar foible: the absent mind. All too often talk of an information or computer revolution remains entirely unspecified about how 'revolution' describes recent developments in computer technology or in its social, political or economic reception.

On the other hand, Peter Drucker (1993: 24; 1999) provides an example of enthusiastic argument about the possibilities posed by computers that is tempered by an appreciation that the unfolding of history always involves multiple causes or explanations, of which technology and its reception can only ever be but one. I agree with Drucker (and Poster 1995) that it is reasonable to speculate that major historic changes are afoot, but unreasonable to assume that technology *per se* is driving or determining those changes, or that previous historic changes associated with previous technological developments will be repeated on a comparable scale. How can anyone know that computer-mediated communication will be as historically important as the invention of the printing press, the telephone, broadcast radio, and television? Perhaps it will be no more significant for politics and social relations than citizen band radio, video recorders, or compact disc players.

Simon Baddeley (1997: 74–5) goes considerably further than Drucker when he rejects usage of the pronoun 'we', either in the utopian sense of 'in the future we will all work from home and telecommute' or in Winner's dystopian sense of a top-down revolution 'we' should oppose. Baddeley draws heavily on Foucault's far-reaching analysis of liberal individuation and suggests that cyberspace has heralded the emergence of new forms of self and community. I return to this argument in the third section of the chapter. For the moment we can note that Winner's critical questions about a computer revolution are based on assumptions about the commensurability of a people, a nation and a political community, but computer-mediated communication has begun to undermine such assumptions.

The accelerating pace of rapid change in computer technology supports a second argument that education and know-how will become more important both for particular people and for whole societies. Obviously, education is a good means of coping with new challenges and greater uncertainties. It helps people cope with what Alvin Toffler (1970) termed 'future shock', in which people suppress appreciation of, or even consciously attempt to ignore, the changes that are happening too quickly on too great a scale. Here sceptics point out that computers are very good at compiling and organising information in databases, indexes and more recently also on web pages but that this most impressive and useful capacity does not lead directly to education or understanding, let alone empowerment (Roszak 1986; Winner 1986). However necessary it has become to understand more about the world, computer users still face problems overviewing or appreciating the worth of the vast amounts of information that they now can access.

The current hype about computers and an information society derives in part from a shift in the meaning of 'information' (Roszak 1986: 3–21; 172–6). Once it simply meant useful data. If, for example, a caller wanted a telephone receptionist to connect him or her to a telephone number finding service the caller would ask for 'information, please'. Now information has come to denote something that is supposed to be an essential aspect of life in a modern society.[2] This shift to a much more general meaning of information corresponds to the dispersion of Benthamite utilitarian epistemology and related methodologies of individuation and social control, but it was prompted by applied mathematicians' success with code-cracking during the Second World War and then the discovery of DNA in 1951. These developments saw Norbert Weiner's theory of cybernetics attract wide interest after it was published in 1948. Weiner combined applied mathematics and control theory to expound on the way electronic feedback allowed information-processing machines to learn about their environment. Subsequently, early research into cybernetics, artificial intelligence and chess-playing computers spawned a tradition of anthropomorphising the computer (talk of 'viruses' and 'memory', for example) and making fantastic predictions about future developments. Since the mid-1960s, Marshall McLuhan (1994 [1964]), Alvin Toffler (1970), Daniel Bell (1973) and many others (Sculley 1991, for example) have amplified the rhetorical tradition of cybernetics, artificial intelligence, a global village, futurology, and the post-industrial information society or economy.

Roszak (1986: 172–6) concludes that if all the hype about information technology were indeed a matter of mass education and democratic empowerment, then surely the primary focus of attention would be a major expansion of public libraries. Libraries have become important places for people to access the World Wide Web and cataloguing information services, but Roszak has a strong point when he concludes that a so-called information society is basically a matter of selling sophisticated machines and services to corporations, large organisations and affluent young men. Special deals for students and educational institutions have been a matter of seeding future sales. The female workplace that is a library has become a 'missing link' in the argument that individuals using their own desktop computers will undermine the power of central governments and large corporations.

The third argument commonly raised by enthusiasts is that the new technology will undermine the authoritarian, top-down, one-way and one-to-many communication that characterises interaction between the authors and mass readers of books, pamphlets and newspapers, between playwrights and theatre goers, and between electronic broadcasters and radio listeners or television viewers. A democratic, bottom-up, two-way, many-to-many form of broadcasting (or 'netcasting') via e-mail, Usenet and the World Wide Web will complement if not supplant traditional relations of communication. In the next section, I look at the more straightforward aspects of this argument. In the third section of the chapter, I take up the post-structuralist aspects of what many-to-many communication can mean for the constitution of citizenship.

Digital democracy

In the USA, the way development of cheap and accessible networked desktop computers outflanked the old mainframe computers during the 1980s has often been considered symptomatic of the advantages of decentralised market or democratic power over centralised and concentrated corporate or dictatorial power. Numerous illustrations of the democratic empowerment and decentralisation argument can be found among movements of dissent against dictatorial regimes. Access to the international news media via e-mail, Usenet and the Internet was important to the student protesters in Tiananmen Square, Beijing, and to protesters against the Soeharto regime in Indonesia. More generally, the fall of communist regimes has commonly been considered an indicator of the decentralising effects of an emerging information society and economy. But the democratic possibilities of networked computers have always had a tendency to descend into populist marketing strategies.

Populism about the empowering possibilities of computers has its roots in the rebelliousness of young researchers in the 1970s. Right from the beginning of the Internet in 1971–2, when US defence research institutions linked up their mainframe computers for the sake of preserving a counterattack command capacity in the event of nuclear attack, irreverent researchers used the network to send each other personal messages.[3] Outside those research institutes, computer enthusiasts launched highly ambitious schemes to bring networked computers out into local communities. They included Community Memory and Resource One at Berkeley in 1973–5 (Roszak 1986) and later the WELL (Whole Earth 'Lectronic Link) which was a computer bulletin board system in the San Francisco telephone district that thrived between 1985 and 1990 or so (Rheingold 1995). However, marketing based on the utopian dreams of these enthusiasts has had a much wider impact than their actual schemes ever had.

In early 1984, Apple Computer played on its roots among the computer hackers of the San Francisco counterculture when it paid a fortune for a one-minute spot towards the end of the final quarter of the American football final that year. The extravagantly expensive advertisement drew powerful images from Orwell's novel, *1984*, presenting the Apple Computer as a means of defying an IBM-like 'Big Brother' to liberate the people (Roszak 1986: 153). Ten years later, the democratic aspirations of Apple Computer and the Californian counterculture had been more or less sidelined but Microsoft used its own extravagant expenditure on an advertising campaign that played on a sense of rebellion. It paid a fortune to use the Rolling Stones song 'Start Me Up' to launch its graphics-based operating system, *Windows 95*. Alongside these marketing strategies, conventional politicians in the USA have also deployed populist themes about the empowering possibilities of computers in their election campaigns during the 1990s (see Grossman 1995; Herman and McChesney 1997; Rash 1997).

In the early 1980s, the Californian Governor Gerry Brown was the first conventional politician to take up the democratic possibilities of networked desktop computers (Roszak 1986: 144–5). Brown conferred often with Stewart Brand, who was a founding editor of *The Whole Earth Catalogue* in 1969, went on to become one of the founders of WELL, and later was a prominent member of the Electronic Frontier Foundation (formed to lobby against electronic censorship and protect privacy on the Internet *http://www.eff.org/*). When Ronald Reagan became the Governor of California the link between high-tech hippies and conventional politicians disappeared.

In the early 1990s, national politicians in the USA became interested in computers and the 'information society'. Ever quicker and more powerful computers were becoming cheaper and the Internet had become much easier to access and use. In 1989–91, the advent of hypertext mark-up language (html) programming and search engines that used plain language terms to sift through great numbers of pages on the World Wide Web (*Alta Vista* from Digital Equipment and *HotBot* from *HotWired* magazine) made 'surfing the Internet' intuitive. Microsoft's Windows operating system launched in 1995 supplanted the old command-based DOS programmes in favour of a comprehensively graphics-based and user friendly environment that was comparable to the Macintosh platform but ran computers that were considerably cheaper. The precise command strings used in telnet, bulletin boards, the DOS programmes and the old Internet had been comprehensively replaced by graphics and clicking mouses. At the same time, the ongoing switch from analogue to digital processes in telephone exchanges and cabling and in the production processes of newspapers, radio, video, and television has prompted many predictions about the convergence of multimedia and older broadcasting communication patterns. During the 1990s, therefore, talk of the information society and the political possibilities of computer-mediated communication became more common.

Before Bill Clinton chose Senator Al Gore as his candidate for Vice President, Gore argued that the Federal Government should finance the laying of fibre cabling and outlays on other infrastructure necessary for networked computers to be established in every school and town across the USA (Gore 1991). Construction of what he called 'the information superhighway' would be comparable to construction during the 1950s of a network of interstate highways, in which his father, also a US senator, had been closely involved. Gore mentioned the popular empowerment and political decentralisation arguments in favour of networked computers but his primary justification for public expenditure on an information superhighway was economic rather than political. Just as the interstate highways had promoted national economic integration and development, the information superhighway would keep American industry at the international forefront of high technology developments. However, the president of Microsoft, Bill Gates (1995: 5–6) argued in his book *The Road Ahead* that everything would be best left in the hands of private enterprise. Gates's view has prevailed over Gore's somewhat neo-Keynesian view. Either way, the interest of first Gore and later Perot, Clinton and Gingrich in networked computers had nothing to do with the counterculture of California. Their interest had everything to do with protecting the USA's strategic industrial advantage over Japan in armaments and high technology (Poster 1995: 27). However, no matter what populist initiatives corporate and political leaders in the USA undertake and however they finance expansion of the information superhighway, the prospect of many-to-many communication raises at least the prospect of subverting the processes of representation and misrepresentation.

An experiment in Minnesota, a north mid-western state of the USA, provides some pointers to how digital democracy can develop. Since 1994, candidates for gubernatorial elections have presented themselves on moderated e-mail discussion lists, which are open to subscribers anywhere in the world. The first of these lists, MN-FORUM, is read-only. In February 1998 it had 300 subscribers. The moderator limits the number of messages delivered to a subscriber's mailbox but, for an outsider, they are still quite numerous. During the election campaign, subscribers receive messages containing the 12 candidates' responses to six questions, their rebuttals of aspersions or criticisms, and weekly comments from an 'E-Democracy Media Panel'. These postings are all issue-oriented and brief but specific. Then subscribers can contribute to two lists. They are MN-FORUM-DISCUSS and MN-POLITICS. The first covers election issues and the latter covers Minnesota politics more generally. According to the moderators, MN Forum-Discuss generates 5–20 messages a day and MN Politics averages 10–15 messages a day. In each of these lists, all contributors must sign messages with their real name. No one may post any more than twice a day and everyone must discuss only Minnesota issues. Finally, the following rule clearly contributes to improving the quality of debate: 'One-on-one attacks, arguments, or abusive language are not acceptable. Please focus on the issues and topics generally and avoid personalized phrases like "you are X" "I can't believe you said Y". Over use of the word "you" tends to personalize the discussion away from the issues.'[4]

The moderator promised 5–20 messages a day from the various lists, but when they began to arrive I felt like an outsider looking in on what was happening in Minnesota. Clearly the active participants were also daily watching the candidates on television, listening to them on the radio, and reading about them in the press during an intensely contested election. However specific and to the point, the e-mail exchanges were obviously a secondary supplement to a more important contest in the traditional communications media. It seemed that candidates were attempting to win over journalists, academics, the wealthy and the well educated who use e-mail. These small numbers of people are an insignificant electorate in itself but the candidates seemed to think it was important to win them over, presumably because of an assumption that they influence the traditional news media. It seems to me that in Minnesota digital democracy is very much a secondary supplement to the familiar processes of conventional liberal democracy. But cyberspace surely entails much wider possibilities if – or perhaps when – it comes to encompass large proportions of adult residents in the industrially advanced nation-states.

However influential the democratic empowerment and political decentralisation arguments have been among political and corporate leaders, along with many computer users and enthusiastic commentators, it fails to address a long-standing tension between democracy and capitalism which since the Second World War has been resolved by degrading the importance of citizenship. The prospect of direct democracy among active cybercitizens has revived that tension.

Cybercitizenship

Since the Second World War and the defeat of Nazism, it has become a commonplace to think that democracy and capitalism go hand in hand. But for about 150 years before that, it was common to think that democracy was bad for business and civilisation [I argued this point in Chapter 1]. It was a commonplace that the social and political levelling necessary to institute democracy would undermine the inequality required for a capitalist economy to prosper and for a civilised culture to flourish (Hodgson 1984). Between the First and Second World Wars, political parties became the means of reconciling economic inequality and capitalist prosperity with the political equality and social levelling required by democracy. Parties produced leaders who could *both* establish enough distance from citizens to deliver the policies required for capitalist prosperity (and healthy donations to the party) *and at the same time* marshal sufficient charisma to remain electable and to form viable governments (Macpherson 1977: 69). In 1943, Joseph Schumpeter (1976) was one of the first to recognise the emergent importance of parties and their leaders when he posed a market model of democracy [as we saw in Chapter 3]. This model maintains a central position as conventional wisdom. It rests on a reduced concept of citizenship as nothing more than voting for one party of government rather than another. The model is constructed around parallels between political leaders and entrepreneurs, voters and consumers, and political persuasion and product advertising. The conventional wisdom about politics as a market place in ideas has subsequently witnessed a large and widely dispersed increase in both leaders' cynicism about voters and voters' disillusionment with politics, politicians, parties and journalists.

From this historical and international perspective, active cybercitizens who consult directly with each other and sidestep elected representatives, parties and party leaders constitute a threat to longstanding practices of party politics and entrenched concepts of reduced citizenship. However, the mainstream custodians of post-war developments in liberal democracy and citizenship see that threat as stemming from new populist politicians, such as Ross Perot in the USA or Silvio Berlusconi in Italy (Grossman 1995: 17–21). In the 1992 US Presidential elections, Perot mobilised a surprisingly strong following in the early stages of his campaign when he appeared on many talk shows fielding phone calls directly from viewers and listeners, and chalked up popularity ratings of 90 per cent. He gave no press conferences, avoiding both the mainstream parties and the mainstream media that had so disillusioned voters. He canvassed ideas about national plebiscites, televised town meetings, and public feedback. He promised to hold referenda on any new Federal taxes and to resign from the Presidency if enough people phoned or faxed him saying that he should resign. In all this, Perot's campaign methods were new but his populist appeals were old (Grossman 1995: 18). Many politicians before him have promised to sidestep party professionals and elites and go directly to the people. Perot's campaign petered out under the sustained criticism of mainstream journalists who persistently pressed him for more detail, which he failed to provide. The cybercitizenship that Perot's various proposals invoked was no different from the citizenship invoked by traditional populist criticisms of the plutocrats and government mandarins.

Many newspaper editors and commentators worry that sidestepping representatives and the processes of lengthy deliberation that are commented upon in the news media would see digital direct democracy degenerate into what liberals and conservative observers alike before the Second World War termed mob rule. Grossman sums up the dystopian threat to representative democracy, the party system and mainstream news media posed by populist digital democracy with a plausible image of impoverished cybercitizens as:

> alienated, silent voters, sitting alone in an electronic cocoon . . . these modern-day robotic voters absorb virtually all their information about the outside world electronically – through CNN-style live coverage, tabloid-news shows, and sensational news magazines: and, increasingly, at programmed computer terminals. The wired public then feeds back its ill-formed, unsophisticated, unmediated opinion instantaneously, without deliberation, following on-screen instructions to press Y for yes, or N for no. (Grossman 1995: 17)

However, where for instance Robert Putnam (1996) blames the socially isolating effects of television *per se* for the decline in group membership totals and social or political activism, Grossman (1995: 93–142) offers more nuances. He blames the ongoing commodification and 'dumbing down' of news on several factors, including owners' sharper insistence on strong and immediate profits, the increasing expense and effectiveness of personalised and negative political advertising, and politicians' increasing reliance on ever more finely detailed opinion polls.

A shortcoming in these various historically informed arguments about tension between active citizenship and the capitalism of the multimedia corporations is that they fail to consider issues of fluid identity and community in cyberspace. Both mainstream critiques of digital democratic populism and other critiques of the power of the multimedia corporations and public authorities rest on the rational and modernist assumptions of what Poster (1995) calls the age of broadcast communication. Modernist assumptions about public control and individual liberty, or systemic exploitation and people's liberation, rest on a series of dichotomies between ruler and ruled, producer and consumer, author and reader, sender and receiver [In Chapter 2, Hindess similarly questions the usefulness of such dichotomies]. Poster (1995: 3–23, 36–8, 43–56) argues that the tradition of critical theory, from Adorno and Horkheimer to Habermas, focuses on any potential for an emancipation of individual subjects from systems of exploitation while various post-modernist analyses, including Foucault, Derrida, Baudrillard and Lyotard, offer better means of appreciating the 'post-modern subject' in 'the second media age' (Poster 1995: 18–22, 31–6). Critical theory contributes important insights (for example, Gore 1991 was primarily concerned about supporting the American information technology industry against Japanese competition) which Poster keeps in mind, but at the same time he also takes up considerations of cyberspace's constitution of fluid identities and communities. In the 'new media age' of two-way communication between people who are writers, readers and publishers all at once, it is important to recognise that all community among people is imaginary and based on language (Poster 1995: 35–6, 43–56).

On this analysis, assumptions about the rationality and autonomy of a human subject support the themes of individual privacy in, for example, the Electronic Frontier Foundation's (http://www.eff.org) successful campaign against the Clinton administration's Communications Indecency Act, 1996. But such assumptions and campaigns are misleading because computer-mediated communicators differ fundamentally from the readers and writers of traditional text, or the broadcasters and listeners or watchers of electronic news media. Similarly, Rheingold's (1995) argument about 'virtual community' is misleading because the contrast between 'virtual' and 'real' community rests on a classic sociological theme that modern people yearn to revive a lost sense of community. Rheingold believes that virtual community among the participants of the WELL derives from suburbanites' attempts to create a sense of community that is otherwise insufficient in their lives. Poster's point is that in cyberspace the distinction between taped and 'real' time broadcasts, virtual reality simulations and 'real' reality, virtual community and face-to-face community maintains the analytical categories of modern sociology but cannot appreciate the fluidity of either identity or community in cyberspace (see also Lyons 1997: 32).

Any group of people who aspire to political community must work as a self-governing body of autonomous citizens and be capable of dealing with the internal consequences of unpredictable and uncontrollable external developments [Davidson also discusses this point in Chapter 7]. Hindess's (1991, 1993; and Chapter 3, above) argument against so-called realist theories of democracy and against the Whig view of history in Marshall's theory of social citizenship offers a useful analysis. The internationalisation of financial markets and the rising problem of refugees are obvious examples of difficult and uncontrollable external problems for nation-states. Various governments' attempts to impose some degree of censorship on the Internet provide another example.

In cyberspace, therefore, if a Usenet group, e-mail discussion list or a multiple-user dungeon aspires to call itself a self-governing community then it must develop some means of coping with external developments. The control that nation-states and multimedia corporations exercise over the use and cost of accessing telephone networks would arguably surpass the capacity for self-government among, say, a group of terrorists or paedophile pornographers. Obviously Islamic nation-states have a greater capacity to govern themselves and defy US pronouncements of 'state terrorism' than do any virtual community of terrorists. On the other hand, cybercitizens can regroup, multiply, relocate and rename themselves and their communities far more quickly than any nation, people, state or even any group of guerillas in a remote jungle. But that capacity may well diminish as many more people gain access to cyberspace. Virtual community and cybercitizenship will have little or no independent future beyond the realm of existing nation-states. That future is, however, far from negliglible.

Within well-ordered and stable states governing large populations, there must be voluntary associations, private publishers, and news media that are independent of the state and uphold the democratic order. However, defending freedoms of association and speech is not their only purpose and neither are they the only organisations necessary in large democratic states. Besides lobbyists, activists, independent writers and professional journalists who all contribute to maintaining the accountability of government, there are organisations such as established political parties, churches and private corporations which outwardly uphold freedoms of speech. At the same time, these large organisations have an interest in maintaining some secrecy around the winning and operation of governmental office. Thus the large political parties listen to their members and transmit the views of wide sections of the population, but they also need to attract financial and political support from private corporations, trade unions and churches which thereby become important political actors in their own right. This leads to the dark conclusion that: 'Considered as communities of citizens, modern Western societies are not self-governing. Considered as self-governing communities, they are not communities of citizens' (Hindess 1991: 190). Communities with large populations and industrially advanced economies cannot both govern themselves and be communities of citizens. The extent to which communities cope with external circumstances is also the extent to which powerful organisations usurp citizens' control over what is included on and what is excluded from the agenda of democratic government. Large and industrially advanced communities cannot therefore combine democracy and citizenship.

In cyberspace, a similar conclusion holds. On the one hand, to the extent that groups of Usenet members, e-mail discussion list participants, and so forth can aspire to cybercitizenship they must be exclusive clubs. It would have to be at least as difficult to join a group that engages in activities deemed illegal by nation-states as it is to immigrate into an industrially advanced country. On the other hand, to the extent that cybercitizenship is open to large numbers of people their deliberations must be prone to manipulation by powerful organisations and their decisions prone to degrade into populist mob-rule.

Conclusions

The degree to which citizenship, democracy, political discussion and language in the present nation-states is improved or degraded by a shift towards computer-mediated communication is hard to predict. But my analysis above would suggest that digital democacy may well become a matter of voters' ill-formed direct reaction to prompts from television talk-shows, while cybercitizens *at the same time* develop protocols for meaningful and stimulating interaction amongst themselves. On this scenario, it seems unlikely that groups outside the mainstream of nation-state politics will gain a greater voice or presence in national politics. Cybercitizens are not likely to establish self-governing alternatives outside of nation-states. It seems likely that 'rule by applause meter' will develop apace with the technological convergence of polling, television channel popularity rating meters, the World Wide Web, and cheaper, easier-to-use computers, but it also seems likely that some computer-mediated communication will develop alternatives to superficial and commodified news stories. Cybercitizens may well improve the quality and accessibility of debate among themselves and perhaps within the wider public debate of nation-states, but these positive possibilities of cybercitizenship are unlikely to outflank the worrying trends in digital democracy and multimedia capitalism.

Notes

1   When his widely influential book went out of print, Rheingold published it on his own web page *http://www.rheingold.com/*.
2   Martin Amis gently mocks this supposition with entertaining irony about the fate of modern authors in his novel *The Information* (London: Flamingo, 1995).
3   Baddeley (1997: 71) quotes an evocative image of the way development of the Internet has contradicted its origins. It is as if a 'grim nuclear fall-out shelter had burst open and a full scale Mardi Gras parade had come out'.
4   From: 'E-Democracy', *clift@publicus.net*; Organization: Democracies Online; To: mn-forum@mr.net; Date: Wed, 11 Feb. 1998 11:13:56 +0000; Subject: MF: Host M4 – Interaction! and Notes.

References

Baddeley, Simon (1997) 'Governmentality', in Brian Loader (ed.), *The Governance of Cyberspace*, London, New York: Routledge.

Bell, Daniel (1973) *The Coming of Post-industrial Society: A Venture in Social Forecasting*, New York: Basic Books.

Benedikt, Michael (1991) *Cyberspace: First Steps*, Cambridge, MA/London: MIT Press.

Bollier, David and Firestone, Charles (1995) *The Future of Community and Personal Identity in the Coming Electronic Culture*, Washington, DC: The Aspen Institute.

Brook, James and Boal, Iain (eds) (1995) *Resisting the Virtual Life: The Culture and Politics of Information*, San Francisco: City Lights Books.

Drucker, Peter (1993) *Post-Capitalist Society*, New York: HarperCollins.

——(1999) 'Beyond the Information Revolution', *The Atlantic Monthly*, vol. 284, no. 4 http://www.theatlantic.com/issues/99oct/index.htm.

Dunlop, Charles and Kling, Robert (1991) *Computerisation and Controversy: Value Conflicts and Social Choices*, San Diego, London: Academic Press.

Dunn, John (ed.) (1994) *Democracy: The Unfinished Journey: 508 BC to AD 1993* Oxford: Oxford University Press: 91–106.

Fisher, Bonnie, Margolis, Michael and Resnick, David (1994) 'A New Way of Talking Politics: Democracy on the Internet', paper presented at the Annual Meeting of the American Political Science Association in New York City, 1–4 September http://www.eff.org/pub/Activism/E-voting/net_civics.survey.

Gates, Bill (with Nathan Myhrvold and Peter Rinearson) (1995) *The Road Ahead*, New York: Viking.

Graham, Calvin (1996) 'Cybercitizenship' http://arts.deakin.edu.au/sais/courses/Postgrad_units/Aip 605/cyber.htm.

Gore, Al (1991) 'Infrastructure for the Global Village', *Scientific American*, September: 108–11.

Grossman, Lawrence (1995) *The Electronic Republic: Reshaping Democracy in the Information Age*, New York: Viking.

Hauben, Michael (no date, circa 1993) 'The Net and Netizens: the Impact of the Net on People's Lives' http://www.eff.org/pub/Net_culture/netizen.paper.

Herman, Edward and Robert McChesney (1997) *The Global Media – The New Missionaries of Corporate Capitalism*, London: Cassell.

Hindess, Barry (1991) 'The imaginary presuppositions of democracy', *Economy and Society*, vol. 20, no. 2: 173–95.

——(1993) 'Citizenship in the Modern West', in Bryan Turner (ed.), *Citizenship and Social Theory*, London: Sage.

Hodgson, Geoffrey (1984) *The Democratic Economy*, Harmondsworth: Penguin.

Katz, Jon (1995) 'The Age of Paine', *Wired*, vol. 3. no. 5 (May): *http://www.hotwired.com/wired/toc.html*.

Kling, Rob and Suzanne, Iacono (1991) 'Making a "computer revolution"', in Dunlop and Kling (1991): 63–75.

Loader, Brian (1997) 'The governance of cyberspace: politics, technology and global restructuring', in B. Loader (ed.), *The Governance of Cyberspace*, London, New York: Routledge.

Lyon, David (1997) 'Cyberspace sociality: controversies over computer-mediated relationships', in Brian Loader (ed.), *The Governance of Cyberspace*, London, New York: Routledge.

McLuhan, Marshall (1994 [1964]) *Understanding Media: the Extensions of Man*, Cambridge MA/London: MIT Press.

Macpherson, C.B. (1977) *The Life and Times of Liberal Democracy*, Oxford: Oxford University Press.

Mitchell, William (1995) *City of Bits: Space, Place, and the Infobahn*, Cambridge MA/London: MIT Press.

Negroponte, Nicholas (1995) *Being Digital*, New York: Alfred Knopf.

Noble, David (1997) 'Digital Diploma Mills: The Automation of Higher Education', October 1997, *marxism-international@lists.village.virginia.edu*, reposted extensively during December 1997 by editors of e-mail lists administered by the American Political Science Association.

Poster, Mark (1995) *The Second Media Age*, Cambridge: Polity Press.

Putnam, Robert D. (1996) 'The Strange Disappearance of Civic America', *The American Prospect*, no. 24 (Winter) http://epn.org/prospect/24/24putn.html.

Rash, Wayne (1997) *Politics on the Nets*, New York: W.H. Freeman.

Rheingold, Howard (1995) *The Virtual Community*, London: Secker and Warburg.

Robins, Kevin and Frank Webster (1987) 'Athens without Slaves . . . or Slaves without Athens? The Neurosis of Technology', *Science as Culture*, vol. 1.

Roszak, Theodore (1986) *The Cult of Information: The Folklore of Computers and the True Art of Thinking*, Cambridge: Lutterworth Press.

Sandell, Michael (1996) *Democracy's Discontent, America in Search of a Public Philosophy*, Cambridge, MA: Harvard University Press.

Schumpeter, Joseph (1976) *Capitalism, Socialism and Democracy*, London: Allen and Unwin.

Sculley, John (1991) 'The Relationship Between Business and Higher Education: A Perspective on the 21st Century', in Dunlop and Kling (1991).

Spender, Dale (1995) *Nattering on the Net, Women, Power and Cyberspace*, Melbourne: Spinifex Press.

Stallabrass, Julian (1995) 'Empowering Technology: The Exploration of Cyberspace' *New Left Review*, no. 211 (May–June): 3–32.

Stoll, Clifford (1996) *Silicon Snake Oil, Second Thoughts on the Information Highway*, London: Pan Books.

Taylor, Mark and Esa Saarinen (1994) *Imagologies*, London/New York: Routledge.

Toffler, Alvin (1970) *Future Shock*, London: Pan Books.

Vandenberg, A. (1997a) 'Cyber-citizenship', in A. Vandenberg, *Democracy and Citizenship, Study Guide*, Geelong: Deakin University.

——(1997b) 'Cyber-citizenship and digital democracy' *Forum*, no. 10: 4–5 http://arts.deakin.edu.au/cchr/.

Whittle, David (1997) *Cyberspace: The Human Dimension*, New York: W.H. Freeman.

Winner, Langdon (1986) *The Whale and the Reactor: A Search for Limits in an Age of High Technology*, Chicago: University of Chicago Press.

INDEX